INCREASING STUDENT ENGAGEMENT AND RETENTION USING MOBILE APPLICATIONS: SMARTPHONES, SKYPE AND TEXTING TECHNOLOGIES

CUTTING-EDGE TECHNOLOGIES IN HIGHER EDUCATION

Series Editor: Charles Wankel

Recent Volumes:

CUTTING-EDGE TECHNOLOGIES IN HIGHER
EDUCATION   VOLUME 6D

INCREASING STUDENT ENGAGEMENT AND RETENTION USING MOBILE APPLICATIONS: SMARTPHONES, SKYPE AND TEXTING TECHNOLOGIES

EDITED BY

LAURA A. WANKEL
Northeastern University, Massachusetts, USA

PATRICK BLESSINGER
St. John's University, New York, USA

IN COLLABORATION WITH

JURATE STANAITYTE
NEIL WASHINGTON

Created in partnership with the Higher Education
Teaching and Learning Association

http://hetl.org/

United Kingdom – North America – Japan
India – Malaysia – China

Emerald Group Publishing Limited
Howard House, Wagon Lane, Bingley BD16 1WA, UK

First edition 2013

British Library Cataloguing in Publication Data
A catalogue record for this book is available from the British Library

ISBN: 978-1-78190-509-8
ISSN: 2044-9968 (Series)

ISOQAR certified
Management System,
awarded to Emerald
for adherence to
Environmental
standard
ISO 14001:2004.

Certificate Number 1985
ISO 14001

INVESTOR IN PEOPLE

CONTENTS

**PART II: APPLICATION OF MOBILE APPLICATIONS:
SMARTPHONES, SKYPE AND TEXTING APPLICATIONS**

LIST OF CONTRIBUTORS

Lars Birch Andreasen	Aalborg University, Denmark
Patrick Blessinger	St. John's University, Queens, NY, USA
Paul Burt	University College London, UK
Wilma Clark	Goldsmiths College, University of London, UK
Mary C. Embry	Indiana University, Bloomington, IN, USA
Jorge Brantes Ferreira	Pontifical Catholic University of Rio de Janeiro, Brazil
Angilberto Freitas	University of Grande Rio, Brazil
Vicki Holmes	University of Reading, UK
Jennifer Little Kegler	The College at Brockport, State University of New York, USA
Amarolinda Zanela Klein	University of Vale do Rio dos Sinos (UNISINOS), Brazil
Skyler Lauderdale	University of South Florida, Tampa, FL, USA
Audeliz Matias	SUNY-Empire State College, NY, USA
Patricia E. Maxwell	The College at Brockport, State University of New York, USA
Andrew Middleton	Sheffield Hallam University, UK
Jørgen Lerche Nielsen	Roskilde University, Denmark
Anne Nortcliffe	Sheffield Hallam University, UK
Christina M. Partin	University of South Florida, Tampa, FL, USA

Bart Rienties   University of Surrey, UK

Eliane Schlemmer   University of Vale do Rio dos Sinos
                               (UNISINOS), Brazil

Susan Stites-Doe   The College at Brockport, State
                               University of New York, USA

Anja Overgaard   Aalborg University, Denmark
Thomassen

Laura A. Wankel   Northeastern University, Boston,
                               MA, USA

Therèsa M. Winge   Michigan State University, Lansing,
                               MI, USA

David F. Wolf II   SUNY-Empire State College, NY, USA

PART I
ADOPTION OF MOBILE APPLICATIONS: SMARTPHONES, SKYPE AND TEXTING TECHNOLOGIES

NEW PATHWAYS IN HIGHER EDUCATION: AN INTRODUCTION TO USING MOBILE TECHNOLOGIES

Laura A. Wankel and Patrick Blessinger

INTRODUCTION

The chapters in this book focus on three key areas of innovation in teaching and learning in higher education today: smartphone devices, texting applications, and multipurpose, multimedia mobile communicative applications such as Skype. Today's educators have at their disposal a wide array of digital technologies that enable them to enhance the teaching and learning process. These technologies, coupled with more valid and reliable learning theories, are revolutionizing the way we teach and are altering our notions of what it means to learn and live in a post-industrial, globalized world. Both individually and socially, these new mobile technologies are becoming increasingly popular and useful as educational tools across a wide range of disciplines as a means to engage and retain students. If used appropriately and purposefully, these mobile technologies are well suited for the increasingly interconnected and interdependent world we live in and they provide educators with another set of tools by which to enrich the teaching and learning process and educational outcomes (Kukulska-Hulme, 2012).

Increasing Student Engagement and Retention using Mobile Applications:
Smartphones, Skype and Texting Technologies
Cutting-edge Technologies in Higher Education, Volume 6D, 3–17
ISSN: 2044-9968/doi:10.1108/S2044-9968(2013)000006D003

Peters (2005) notes that as the cost associated with these technologies comes down, they become more widely used in society and this prevalence helps to facilitate social change by creating new ways to interact with each other. These technologies include new hardware devices such as smartphones and new software applications such as Skype. In addition, this mass diffusion of mobile technologies is being driven by a convergence of technologies that increasingly allows these technologies to interconnect and communicate with each other in a more seamless way. As such, the traditional boundaries between phones and computers and the Internet are becoming more and more integrated. For instance, traditional mobile phones now act more like computers, and traditional computers now act more like phones. Voice, data, and video continue to converge across these platforms with the Internet as the common medium of exchange.

However, these mobile technologies do not just allow us to do our jobs more efficiently and more effectively, they also provide educators with many new possibilities and opportunities to enhance and transform how we connect and interact with our students and our colleagues. As such, they provide us with a means to greatly expand our notions of learning and our notions of the purpose of education, providing us with a potentially broader definition and scope of teaching, learning, and education. The challenge then becomes how do we embrace these new opportunities while, at the same time, continue to maintain the ethos of the academy (e.g., academic freedom, pedagogical pluralism) and continue to maintain a high level of academic quality (e.g., academic integrity and rigor, professional development).

Hwang and Tsai (2011) define mobile-learning (m-learning) as the use of mobile technologies that facilitate learning. M-learning is also defined by Winters (2006) as any form of learning that is mediated through mobile devices and defined by Alexander (2004) as any form of learning that is utilized by nomadic learners. As such m-learning can be viewed as a formal and informal set of contextualized and situated learning activities that are mediated by mobile technologies. This broad definition can be a good starting point for drilling down into the specifics of who, what, where, when, why, and how of mobile technologies in an educational context. So, regardless of whether m-learning is seen as an extension of e-learning or as distinct from e-learning, the notion of the facilitation of learning is crucial since it connotes the idea that these technologies are enablers and tools that create new possibilities. This broad definition connotes the idea that better learning (i.e., more enriched, more meaningful, more purposeful, more authentic) is the main outcome of their use. As such, these tools help to create a more open-ended teaching and learning environment that helps to overcome some of the traditional barriers and boundaries of space and time that result from the fixed space and time constraints of physical classrooms and fixed technologies like desktop computers.

So, with this broad definition in mind, this book presents several studies that illustrate how these mobile technologies are being used in a variety of educational settings and applications as active, "just-in-time" learning tools that have the potential to enable greater levels of engagement among students. As such, technology-enriched instruction that uses mobile technologies can support instructors in creating more interactive participation and a wider array of more meaningful learning activities. In addition, m-learning can support more authentic forms of learning where learning is not solely compartmentalized to strict time and space boundaries (Herrington & Herrington, 2007). As such, these technologies have the potential to support more democratic, more flexible, more autonomous, and more ubiquitous forms of learning, as well as supporting both formal and informal types of learning (Vavoula, Pachler, & Kukulska-Hulme, 2009).

M-learning tools are being used together with a larger set of teaching and learning tools and strategies to (1) increase student access and new ways of engaging with educational courses and learning activities, (2) enhance learning by making it more natural, flexible, and dynamic, and (3) support lifelong learning that is better suited to contemporary lifestyles and work-life demands. Thus, a key element of these tools' power resides in their ability to facilitate anytime, anywhere learning that is not restricted to externally imposed space and time constraints. M-learning environments provide both the instructor and student with another means to foster more dynamic and flexible teaching and learning environments. These tools can be utilized in both undergraduate and graduate level courses and in many different course contexts and learning contexts.

However, it should be noted, as with all technologies, that the uniqueness alone of these technologies is not sufficient to engage and retain learners. As with any teaching and learning technology or approach, these technologies must be used in a purposeful and meaningful way and they must be integrated within a relevant theoretical framework that is appropriate to the teaching and learning context (e.g., institutional mission, educational level, type of course, course objectives, learning outcomes). Using valid and reliable pedagogical methods and learning principles and theories is vital since they form the basis for predicting human behavior and expected learning outcomes. Again, as with all technologies, in addition to relevant and established theory, it is also imperative to be cognizant of the epistemological, ontological, and phenomenological basis that are germane to utilizing such technologies.

ADOPTION PRINCIPLES

Two key principles emerge from the findings of the chapters in the adoption section of the book that help to frame the book's contents for mobile technologies:

1. Mobile learning environments should be viewed as global communities in which access to learning is not restricted by externally imposed space and time constraints but rather where flexible learning is valued and practiced by both instructors and students and where learning (both formal and informal) and academic engagement occurs across all space and time boundaries (e.g., political, economic, social, physical).
2. Anytime, anywhere learning environments have the potential to foster a greater sense of immediacy, interactivity, and authenticity due to their built-in flexibility, and learner self-efficacy and learning autonomy can be increased by fostering self-regulated learning (i.e., more control over one's own learning), by promoting situational learning (i.e., time and space conditions that are more suitable to the needs of the learner), by cultivating a diversity of learning contexts (i.e., contexts that are authentic and meaningful to the learner), and by nurturing more dynamic and spontaneous learning opportunities (Kukulska-Hulme, Sharples, Milrad, Arnedillo-Sanchez, & Vavoula 2011; Sharples, 2000; Traxler, 2009; Winters, 2007).

These principles are indicative of the growing need to seamlessly interact with others in a post-industrial, globalized, networked world that is characterized by interdependence and interconnectivity. Educational institutions and faculty should take the lead in preparing students for life in this rapidly evolving world. Thus, these technologies provide the potential to open up access to learning for a larger number of students who may not be able to overcome the constraints and boundaries imposed by traditional classroom settings, including fixed e-learning environments. In this sense, m-learning environments can be used to mirror the real-life demands of students without sacrificing academic quality. All else being equal, m-learning has the potential to increase educational access and engage students in more flexible and self-regulated ways. The use of Skype and other mobile technologies can provide a useful way to enhance learning (Davis, Germonprez, Petter, Drum, & Kolstad, 2009).

If the course is designed properly using appropriate design principles and facilitated using appropriate mobile technologies that are used in a purposeful manner, these types of mobile technologies can create learning environments that use both synchronous and asynchronous modalities. In other words, the question is not whether the synchronous modality is better than the asynchronous modality but how can both modalities be used in an integrated and purposeful way to enhance the overall learning process. Ferratt and Hall (2009) suggest that using both modalities can enhance teaching and learning. The flexibility of m-learning can therefore provide an effective way to foster individual engagement and group collaboration across traditional boundaries and barriers. Using these technologies can also better prepare students to work more effectively in an increasingly interdependent and interconnected mobile world.

In short, m-learning provides another opportunity to increase teaching and learning effectiveness. It helps to untether teaching and learning from the confines of the physical limits of space and time such as the notion that meeting at a specific time and place each week is the only way and the best way to teach and learn and that one type of learning, such as listening to a lecture, is the only or best way to learn. In fact, there are many ways to teach and learn (both formally and informally) depending on the context and situation. So, with these types of technologies, the focus shifts from traditional space and time considerations which may (and often do) impose unnecessary constraints on learning to more authentic and experiential forms of learning where the focus is on the learning needs of the students. Thus, if designed properly and integrated into the course in a purposeful manner, mobile technologies can provide today's learners with a more sustainable and practical means to augment their learning experience, especially since today's learners are increasingly accustomed to using mobile technologies as a normal part of their lives. As such, higher education institutions should continue to adapt to this digital world in ways that better suit the contemporary lives of learners.

APPLICATION BENEFITS

As illustrated in the book chapters of the application section, these types of learner-centered m-learning environments support

1. contextual and situational learning where learning naturally occurs across home, work, and school domains in a multiplicity of complex

situations and contexts, and where context is constructed by the complex interplay of situated interactions;

2. open-ended and flexible learning, in both formal and informal ways, where learning is flexible and more naturally distributed to suit the context and the needs of the learner;

3. distributed and ubiquitous learning where the responsibility for learning and the locus of control of learning is distributed across learners, instructors, mediating technologies, and knowledge resources;

4. sustainable and self-regulated learning that fits better and more naturally with learning that occurs across the varied life stages of learners, where learning is a natural life-long activity; and

5. personalized and authentic learning that is personally meaningful to each learner and more conducive to how today's learners engage with their life-world environments.

In other words, learning tends to be more effective when learning is more meaningful and relevant to the ways students (and faculty) live their lives (personally and professionally). In short, the question becomes: How do we construct more effective learning spaces such that given that a large part of learning takes place outside the formal classroom setting? Most learners today are continuously mobile, highly networked, and make use of mediated communication technologies. This contemporary lifestyle often transcends traditional space and time boundaries, and as such, the mediating technologies we use as a normal part of our contemporary lives are transforming the ways in which we work, live, and learn. Thus, the role of teaching and learning is also shifting from a passive uni-directional instructional paradigm where the locus of control resides exclusively with the instructor to a more active multidirectional networked teaching and learning paradigm where the locus of control is more distributed. In this emerging paradigm, we must reconceptualize the meaning of learning within the context of the post-industrial age. Mobile technologies are playing an increasing role in the evolution of this emerging paradigm.

THEORETICAL FRAMING

By looking at m-learning from different perspectives, the authors of this volume operationalize mobile technologies in the spirit of social constructivism and activity theory, which are supported by the learning theories of Vygotsky, Leontiev and Luria (1968). Constructivism is an educational philosophy that is built upon several learning theories (e.g., Piaget, Vygotsky, Bandura) and is broadly defined as cognitive and social learning wherein the learner constructs new knowledge and meaning based on his/her own experiences (past and present) and motivations. Activity theory is a theoretical framework built on the work of Vygotsky, Leontiev, Rubinstein, and Luria and views learners as culturally embedded actors who learn within a complex, culturally situated milieu of social phenomena. In this theory, learners are not mere information processors or system components.

Thus, constructivism in general and activity theory in particular can provide a plausible framework for designing m-learning contexts that support engaging and retaining learners and creating a more authentic and personally meaningful learning experience for both instructors and learners. Using this framework, m-learning supports a view that recognizes that a large amount of learning occurs outside the physical confines of the traditional classroom and that a large part of learning is informal, non-sequential, collateral, and tacit. Thus, with m-learning, instructors and learners have the potential to enlarge the capacity to teach and learn in a wider variety of spaces and times.

Core constructivist philosophy and core activity theory stress that learning is complex because it occurs within a milieu of socially situated phenomena. Thus, learning is influenced by a multiplicity of factors such as personal motivations, cultural-historical norms, artifacts and symbols, language, etc. In other words, learning occurs within the complexity of one's life-world and real life activities. In this view, learning in a contemporary society recognizes that learners are continuously mobile and that learning occurs across many different spaces and times and through constantly changing and evolving contexts and situations. In other words, it recognizes that the totality of learning cannot be confined to a singular location and time.

Under this theory, learners are viewed as active participants in their environment (actors) where learning is mediated by tools, motivations, and culture (i.e., a holistic activity system). Thus, this theory focuses on a person's life-world and learning that is intentional, meaningful (e.g., values, goals), and communal and recognizes the importance of collateral and tacit knowledge as well as creativity and spontaneity in the learning process. M-learning environments can be structured such that they inhibit or enable this natural tendency for learning. Hence, there is a need for more holistic, personalized learning contexts that recognize that learners engage in continual learning activities in a variety of creative ways in response to their personal and social needs (Sharples, Taylor, & Vavoula, 2007).

TECHNOLOGY

One of the tools we focus on in this volume – Skype – is a good example of a technology that facilitates the building of and provides a platform where students can engage in m-learning. Skype is a hybrid peer-to-peer and client server technology that allows people to connect and communicate using voice (one-to-one or group audio conferencing), video conferencing, and data (e.g., text message, file exchanging, screen sharing). Skype is one of the most ubiquitous m-learning tools with over 700 million users worldwide. In 2011, Microsoft bought Skype for 8.5B USD and presumably plans to integrate it with its vast array of software and hardware products. One can download and run Skype on a variety of hardware platforms such as laptops, tablets, and smartphones. Skype is used in a variety of disciplines and variety of learning activities such as language learning, project collaboration, and research interviews.

M-learning focuses on the needs of mobile learners and instructors. Anytime, anywhere accessibility of academic resources, content, and communication with fellow learners and instructors is the underlying benefit of m-learning. M-learning not only provides access to content but can allow that content (e.g., e-books) to be stored on the device and accessed even if the device in not connected to the Internet. Hosmer, Jeffcoat, Davis, and McGibbon (2011) also describe how m-learning can be used to conduct assessments and evaluations (e.g., quizzes, tests, polls, surveys), capture evidence of learning activities, and notify learners of upcoming due dates of assignments and projects. Future trends in m-learning include location aware learning, sensors in mobile devices for behavioral based learning, serious gaming, simulation and augmented reality on mobile devices, and context aware ubiquitous learning (Mobile Learning Update, 2008).

In summary, using m-learning technologies should be congruent with the learning objectives of the course. Since cost is normally not the issue since many mobile applications such as Skype are, at the present time, free to use, then the main challenge is ensuring that students have access to the hardware devices (e.g., laptops, smartphones). However, relative to the cost of tuition, for instance, costs associated with these types of devices are very inexpensive. Of course, access to the Internet and having enough bandwidth capacity to use such features as video may also provide a challenge in some cases. Nonetheless, these technologies have generally improved to the point where learning within this context should be beneficial for the learner and provide a more flexible and authentic means to increase academic achievement.

CHAPTER OVERVIEWS

In "Mobile Learning: Definition, Uses and Challenges," by Jorge Brantes Ferreira, Amarolinda Saccol, Angilberto Freitas, and Eliane Schlemmer, the authors define and conceptualize mobile learning, its applications and challenges, evaluating current technologies that can be used for m-learning, aspects that contribute to their diffusion and how they can actually be employed in higher-education settings as a learning tool. Pedagogical and epistemological issues are tackled, with an initial proposal being presented about how m-learning practices should fit together with other more traditional teaching approaches, always aiming to provide apprentices with more engaging, efficient, and fulfilling learning experiences. Through the mobility allowed by technology, ways must be found to adapt the learning experience to the subjects' context, enhancing their participation and, consequently, their acceptance of this new educational modality. Digital technologies, by themselves, including mobile, ubiquitous, and wireless technologies, do not change education – the ways users find to utilize and adapt them for learning purposes do. The technological, economic, and social challenges that the employment of m-learning technologies represent for universities and other institutions are also discussed. The benefits and limitations of mobile learning are evaluated, with possible next steps for effective use of this new learning modality being pointed out.

In "Educational Designs Supporting Student Engagement Through Networked Project Studies," by Jørgen Lerche Nielsen and Lars Birch Andreasen, the authors explore approaches of problem-based learning that stress collaboration and student-directed project activities. The chapter presents cases of how networked technologies are utilized by students and discusses advantages as well as challenges for the students involved in project work. The concept of educational design is used to emphasize an understanding of didactics as a dynamic communicative practice that is continually co-constructed by the practices of the involved participants and the instances of technology and other relevant contexts. In problem and project-based learning, teachers also act as supervisors of students' projects. This challenges the traditional teacher role, and the authors argue that it is crucial for a teacher to establish a balance of being an expert, a facilitator, and a mediator. The development of students' information literacy is seen as central and the authors argue that information literacy does not only cover the technical skills of how to search and find information, but also includes the more general ability to reflect on the knowledge acquired. The cases discussed in the chapter involve students using

Skype, not to hold formal meetings but to establish shared informal spaces, as if they were sitting in the same office. For these students, this was a way of creating a fruitful study environment. Other cases examined by the authors deal with educational designs that involve students as co-designers by letting the students decide the specific topics and examples to be dealt with in online discussions. Here theoretical topics were reflected through students' experiences from their own professional practice.

In "Bringing It All Together: Interdisciplinary Perspectives on Incorporating Mobile Technologies in Higher Education," by Christina M. Partin and Skyler Lauderdale, the authors explore and suggest the need for a paradigm shift regarding the use of innovative technologies to engage adult learners. To support this argument, they outline an interdisciplinary model for student-centered classrooms. This model, with accompanying figures, uses the multidisciplinary framework they outline in their literature review to support a rationale for continual instructor innovation and the inclusion of mobile technology in higher education. Further, to give readers the opportunity to apply this model and interdisciplinary theoretical background to practice, they offer several hypothetical scenarios in which readers are confronted with a classroom problem or issue. These scenarios invite readers to brainstorm practical solutions through applications of mobile technologies. This chapter is not intended to provide specific technologies; other chapters in this volume provide such details. Rather, this chapter opens the door for a theoretical and practical discussion about how the integration of mobile technologies into higher education classrooms can increase learner engagement and retention, and ultimately, student success.

In "Engaging Students in Online Courses Through The Use Of Mobile Technology," by Audeliz Matias and David F. Wolf II, the authors believe that advancing a teaching strategy that incorporates mobile technology for online classes does not need to require a large budget. Two adoption strategies are presented in this chapter: the adoption of learning tools that either can be accessed by mobile devices or have free applications that enable their use by learners without posing extra work for faculty and instructional designers, and the augmentation of courses with tools developed specifically for mobile devices. Despite the fact that these are two different options, this chapter shows that there are significant advantages of bringing together mobile-friendly and mobile-specific technology to easily scaffold mobile learning. According to the authors, the most effective way to view the use of mobile technology for online learning is, perhaps, within the context of pedagogical best practices in an activity-based approach. This approach fits nicely into learner-centered and constructivist environments because students are learning through their own active involvement. Thus, mobile tools should be approached not just in terms of "accessing content" but also as a function of the nature of the learning activities they can support. In addition, this chapter catalogs the potential challenges of mobile learning implementation into three main types: institutional, architectural, and pedagogical.

In "Fashion Design Podcast Initiative: Emerging Technologies and Fashion Design Teaching Strategies," by Therèsa M. Winge and Mary C. Embry, the authors explain how students in the Fashion Design Podcast Initiative created podcasts for a series about fashion design exhibitions (i.e., fashion shows, truck shows, flash mobs, and visual displays). The faculty implemented *Lernen durch Lehren* (*LdL*) or "Learning by Teaching" pedagogy and Bloom's revised taxonomy to encourage and support creativity, independence, confidence, and soft skills (i.e., teamwork, communication, decision making, research, problem-solving, exploration, and presentation skills) with a variety of technologies and software programs. Subsequently, students shared in the teaching activities as active learning. By creating educational podcasts students discovered the intricacies to creating specific types of fashion design exhibitions, as well as develop skills in emerging technologies. Students experienced the agency of educating others and gained confidence in their creativity and technology skills. Overall, faculty and students were extremely positive about the future of podcasts, and the benefits of podcasts for the fashion design industry.

In "The Innovative Use of Personal Smart Devices by Students to Support Their Learning," by Anne Nortcliffe and Andrew Middleton, the authors introduce the reader to the field of mobile learning, in particular how students are using their smart devices for ubiquitous learning. The authors, who have research experience in the field of tutor- to student-generated audio learning resources, found that when students are seeded with the learning opportunity the students are innovative m-learners. The smart devices have enabled students to replace multiple mobile devices with one device. This chapter illustrates the results of a small research workshop-based study of how two groups (a three and a pair) of students have used their own smart devices to support their learning. The workshop demonstrated that the smart devices enabled students to be true ubiquitous learners. The smart devices enabled students to personalize their learning at anytime, anyplace, and with anyone. The chapter defines a typology to describe the informal and formal learning behaviors of the student with their personal smart device and associated applications. The workshop study results show that students use their personal smart devices for productivity, communication, multitasking, and organization learning tasks. Also, the workshop research study provided an opportunity for students to share their smart device learning practices and seeded the students to use their devices more creatively and innovatively to develop new smarter learning practices.

In "Engaging Teachers (and Students) with Media Streaming Technology: The Case of Box of Broadcasts," by Vicki Holmes, Wilma Clark, Paul Burt, and Bart Rienties, the authors looked at the affordances, benefits, and drawbacks of a social media streaming facility called Box of Broadcasts (BoB), which provides a YouTube-like streaming service but is only accessible for academic staff and students at University of Surrey. What makes facilities such as YouTube troublesome is also what makes them valuable: In seeking to address an issue, you may also reduce a benefit. Holmes and colleagues describe YouTube as a "wild meadow" and BoB as a "walled garden," recognizing that they offer different levels of richness and diversity but also of quality and flux. Understanding the dichotomous nature and features of the different systems, and choosing which best fits a given context, is key to effective use. Research suggests that learning is most effective when teachers have appropriate awareness of the complex interplay between pedagogy, technology, and discipline knowledge. What is interesting is that while some of the teachers interviewed approached use of streaming media with a clear rationale, others reported that it was only *after* their use of BoB that they generated ideas about its utility as a support for teaching and learning. Therefore, use of these systems can be a stimulus to shift thinking within an individual context, resulting in a rich variety of creative and innovative use rather than merely replicating practice elsewhere.

In "Business Students' Learning Engagement as a Function of Reading Assigned E-Textbooks," by Susan Stites-Doe, Patricia E. Maxwell, and Jennifer Little Kegler, the authors describe how higher education institutions show a renewed interest in e-textbooks due to their lower cost, improved delivery platforms, and increasing student ownership of tablets and other mobile devices. Research indicates a positive, significant relationship between a person's attitude toward and intent to use technology such as e-textbooks based on what they perceive to be its usefulness and ease of use. Students identify e-textbooks as having the potential to improve learning and engagement outcomes. The Internet is an indispensable part of students' lives. An online e-textbook allows students to transition between reading and research using search engines, Wikipedia, and library databases. Multitasking activities such as Facebook, email, text messaging, and playing/listening to music can negatively impact grades. This study explores whether prior coursework predicts students' satisfaction with e-textbooks, investigates the impact of students' concurrent use of other Internet sites while reading, and considers how student satisfaction and positive attitudes with e-textbooks correlate with student engagement. Overall satisfaction and perceptions of the functionality of e-textbooks are both predictive of students' willingness to recommend e-textbooks. These positive attitudes are irrespective of prior coursework, and regardless of any multitasking while reading e-textbooks.

In "Facilitated Work Based Learning: A New Method for Continuing Education?" by Anja Overgaard Thomassen, the author explores the notion of "the third context." The notion is developed on the bases of an empirical Ph.D. study investigating continuing education based on Facilitated Work Based Learning (FWBL). Theoretically FWBL is inspired by John Dewey and especially the way in which Problem Based Learning is applied in teaching at Aalborg University, Denmark. The frame of the chapter is set through a description of Problem Based Learning, Facilitated Work Based Learning and central elements within John Dewey's pragmatic thinking. The intention is to clarify the theoretical perspective on which the chapter is based along with a description of the method for continuing education applied in the investigated cases. Having set the frame, attention is paid to two cases conducted according to FWBL. It is outlined that the company actors are interested in problem-solving as such whereas the university actors are interested in education – hence the objectives are different. Furthermore, it is made clear that the actors' pre-understanding of work and education belonging to two different and not comparable paradigms extensively influences the company actors' obstacles in grasping FWBL and thus answer the recurring question of "how can work and continuing education be integrated?" As the company actors cannot see the possible outcome in participating, engagement and motivation quickly disappear and the FWBL course is placed at the "side line" in the organization. The notion of "the third context" is presented as an alternative to the traditional understanding containing a separation of work and education. Within "the third context," continuing education is perceived as an *activity* unfolding in a context of its own. The notion is highly inspired by John Dewey's pragmatic thinking. "The third context" is an integration of the FWBL way of continuing education and Dewey's understanding of us being active participants in social contexts. It is argued that reflective thinking has a major say in relation to the notion of "the third context" becoming useful, as new understandings of the relation between work and continuing education must be developed.

CONCLUSION

In this collection of chapters, we have presented different perspectives on how to use m-learning and mobile technologies in order to more fully engage learners in learning activities outside the boundaries of the physical classroom and to extend learning into those domains that are personally meaningful to learners. Current research suggests that a key ingredient in m-learning are authentic, personal, and situated learning activities so it follows that course design should focus on creating learning environments that are congruent with how today's students prefer to learn within the context of life-worlds. Although these enabling mobile technologies have the potential to increase engagement and retention, they are only one piece of the learning puzzle.

One of the ultimate goals of education, regardless of the technology used or the instructional methods employed, is to start students down the path of becoming self-regulated and lifelong learners and to make learning (in all its forms) a natural part of their life-worlds. The authentic and contextual nature of the learning activities highlighted in these chapters helps to achieve this end. Even though new technologies will always appear in the future and that some technologies will fall by the wayside, it does not follow that they should be viewed as passing fads. Rather, these tools should be viewed as opportunities to increase our capacity to connect with students and to reconceptualize our notion of what it means to teach and learn in the post-industrial age. Please join us in exploring the pioneering use of these tools in an attempt to better engage students in an increasingly technological and globalized world.

REFERENCES

Alexander, B. (2004). Going nomadic: Mobile learning in higher education. *Educause Review*, *39*(5), 28–35.
Davis, A., Germonprez, M., Petter, S., Drum, D., & Kolstad, J. (2009). A case study of ofshore development across IS courses: Lessons learned from a global student project. *Communications of the Association for Information Systems*, *24*(21), 351–372.

Ferratt, T. W., & Hall, S. R. (2009). Extending the vision of distance education to learning via virtually being there and beyond. *Communication of the Association for Information Systems, 25*(35), 425–436.

Herrington, A., & Herrington, J. (2007). Authentic mobile learning in higher education. In *AARE 2007 International Educational Research Conference*, 28 November 2007, Fremantle, Western Australia.

Hosmer, C., Jeffcoat, C., Davis, M., & McGibbon, T. (2011). Use of mobile technology for information collection and dissemination. *Data & Analysis Center for Software*, Retrieved from http://www.thedacs.com/techs/abstract/518055

Hwang, G., & Tsai, C. (2011). Research trends in mobile and ubiquitous learning: A review of publications in selected journals from 2001 to 2010. *British Journal of Educational Technology, 42*(4), E65–E70.

Kukulska-Hulme, A. (2012, February 28). Mobile learning and the future of learning: An HETL interview with Dr. Agnes Kukulska-Hulme. Interviewers: Krassie Petrova and Patrick Blessinger. *The International HETL Review, 2*, Article 2. Retrieved from http://hetl.org/2012/02/28/mobile-learning-and-the-future-of-learning

Kukulska-Hulme, A., Sharples, M., Milrad, M., Arnedillo-Sanchez, I., & Vavoula, G. (2011). The genesis and development of mobile learning in Europe. In D. Parsons (Ed.), *Combining e-learning and m-learning: New applications of blended educational resources* (pp. 151–177). Hershey, PA: IGI Global.

Leontiev, A. N., & Luria, A. R. (1968). The psychological ideas of L. S. Vygotsky. In B. B. Wolman (Ed.), *Historical roots of contemporary psychology* (pp. 338–367). New York, NY: Harper & Row.

Mobile Learning Update. (2008). *Learning consortium perspectives.* Retrieved from http://masiecontent.s3.amazonaws.com/content/masie/pdf/MobileLearningUpdate.pdf

Peters, K. (2005, November). *Learning on the move: Mobile technologies in business and education.* Canberra: Commonwealth of Australia.

Sharples, M. (2000). The design of personal mobile technologies for lifelong learning. *Computers & Education, 34*, 77–193.

Sharples, M., Taylor, J., & Vavoula, G. (2007). A theory of learning for the mobile age. In R. Andrews & C. Haythornthwaite (Eds.), *The sage handbook of e-learning research.* London: Sage.

Traxler, J. (2009). The evolution of mobile learning. In R. Guy (Ed.), *The evolution of mobile teaching and learning* (pp. 103–118). Santa Rosa: Informing Science Press.

Vavoula, G., Pachler, N., & Kukulska-Hulme, A. (Eds.). (2009). *Researching mobile learning: Frameworks, tools and research designs.* New York, NY: Peter Lang.

Winters, N. (2006). What is mobile learning? In M. Sharples (Ed.), *Big issues in mobile learning: Report of a workshop by the kaleidoscope network of excellence mobile learning initiative.* University of Nottingham.

Winters, N. (2007). What is mobile learning. In M. Sharples (Ed.), *Big issues in mobile learning.* New York, NY: University of Nottingham.

EDUCATIONAL DESIGNS SUPPORTING STUDENT ENGAGEMENT THROUGH NETWORKED PROJECT STUDIES

Jørgen Lerche Nielsen and Lars Birch Andreasen

ABSTRACT

The chapter discusses how student engagement can be facilitated through educational designs that make conscious use of various online communication technologies. The discussions are based on cases from the practice at the Danish Master Programme in Information and Communications Technology (ICT) and Learning (MIL), where students from all over Denmark within a networked learning structure are studying in groups combining on-site seminars with independent and challenging virtually organized project periods. The chapter discusses the involvement of students as co-designers of how courses and learning environments unfold, and deals with the development of students' information literacy. Various teacher roles are addressed, as implementing new educational technology requires teachers who are flexible and aware of the different challenges in the networked environment. The aim of the chapter is to discuss the application of new technological possibilities in educational settings inspired by problem- and project-based learning.

Increasing Student Engagement and Retention using Mobile Applications:
Smartphones, Skype and Texting Technologies
Cutting-edge Technologies in Higher Education, Volume 6D, 19–46
ISSN: 2044-9968/doi:10.1108/S2044-9968(2013)000006D004

INTRODUCTION

It is our aim in this chapter to discuss how educational designs that integrate various uses of digital media may foster the engagement of learners, especially focusing on the implications of organizing the pedagogical practice as networked project studies. By being 'networked' we refer to a double meaning in the sense of collaborating with other students, and in the sense of being connected to the online facilities and possibilities available for the study processes. By 'project' we refer to the traditions of student-directed and project-driven studies and activities.

The chapter begins by presenting our understanding of the concept of educational design and its relation to concepts of didactics and of instructional design. This is followed by a discussion of four areas of research. First, we discuss research on digital technologies for learning, emphasizing that new technologies do not by themselves guarantee an increased quality of learning. Second, we discuss the so-called Scandinavian approach to problem- and project-based learning and the use of information and communication technologies in this approach. The third area to discuss is the need for students to develop information literacy as part of their general study competencies. The fourth and last area to discuss in this part is the new roles of teachers in a problem- and project-based learning environment.

The second part of the chapter discusses cases of students involved in online learning activities in problem- and project-based learning settings. The cases derive from the Danish Master Programme in Information and Communications Technology (ICT) and Learning (MIL).

THE CONCEPT OF EDUCATIONAL DESIGN

The chapter will explore the development of educational designs that may engage students in taking responsibility for their learning process, and thus create productive learning environments.

By the concept of 'educational design', we refer to the combined process of planning, motivating, carrying out, and evaluating processes of teaching and learning. This follows from the continental tradition of theoretical didactics, where reflections of the conditions for educational activities are seen as integrated with reflections of specific goals and content choices.

The word *didactics* itself may cause misunderstandings, because the continental (German and Scandinavian) approach to didactics addresses the entire context of an educational situation, while the Anglo-Saxon approach is more likely to regard didactics from a methodical point of view (Buhl & Flensborg, 2011; Hopmann & Riquarts, 1995). Furthermore, in English the specific word of being *didactic* often refers to a certain style of teacher-centred instructional lecturing, which is not implied in the theoretical concept of *didactics*.

The origin of 'didactics' comes with Comenius, who in the 1600s stated that the art of teaching is not a God-given ability, but a discipline. The educational philosopher Herbart, who is considered to be the originator of theoretical didactics, introduced in the 1800s the teaching-learning situation as a case of three components: the teacher, the learner and the subject matter – later called the 'didactic triangle'.

The didactic triangle can be criticized for having no place for the context. In a contemporary setting, where the conditions for every social practice must be negotiated and nothing can be taken for granted, this may be seen as a weakness, but might as well be an advantage, since ICT changes the contexts of teaching and learning spaces, in variations of synchronous and asynchronous time and physical and distributed presence. Thus, the didactic triangle changes over time, as the subject matter – the content of the teaching – should not be understood as fixed or given, but as negotiated every time teachers, students and a subject matter interact.

By using the notion of *design* in 'educational design', we are not referring to traditions of 'instructional design'. Instead we build on traditions of integrating ICT in education in terms of 'didactic design' or 'design for learning' that have developed in research groups in Scandinavia (Andreasen, Meyer & Rattleff, 2008; Buhl, 2008; Rostvall & Selander, 2008; Selander & Svärdemo-Åberg, 2009; Sørensen, Audon, & Levinsen, 2010). The concept of design is gaining ground outside its traditional fields of engineering, craftsmanship, fashion and graphics. When didactics – in the broader sense of the continental tradition – is connected with design, it becomes possible to emphasize didactics as *a dynamic* communicative practice. Being as well a noun as a verb, 'design' refers to the interplay of designing seen as a process and design seen as a product.

We aim, in our understanding of educational design, to keep this double perspective, emphasizing that educational design is more than just a fixed design to be rolled out broadly. Instead it is a situated practice that unfolds according to the specific participants involved, the specific instances of technology and other relevant contexts, and the actual ways that the participants make use of the specific contexts. Depending on how people act and what they choose to do and not to do, the specific educational designs will develop differently. It is continually co-constructed through the actions of the teachers and the students engaged in it.

DIGITAL TECHNOLOGIES FOR LEARNING

Globally, there is a focus on the potentials of employing new technologies in education. Digital media have become an integrated part of the everyday life of many citizens, and contemporary students may seem to float untroubled between different forms of media combining what in any given situation is suitable. In their use of media they will often rely more on advice from other peers than from authorities.

During the last couple of years, various kinds of social software with the possibility of users to share, interact, produce and communicate have steadily evolved. Blogs appeared on the scene around the millennium as one of the first examples of social software, giving opportunity for easy creation and editing of personal web pages. Blogs have a dynamic appearance, and many blogs have the option for readers to comment on every posting. Thus, blogs introduced an interactive and reader-involving dimension that made it easy for ordinary people to speak out in public (Andreasen, 2006).

The situation today is that a substantial part of the internet is characterized by not holding institutionally authorized content, but content produced and uploaded by ordinary users. This has also influenced established websites, e.g. when buying at Amazon, you may read other users' reviews or comments on the items you are looking for, alongside the official descriptions and reviews. And when looking at online maps, information and pictures uploaded by other users may pop-up.

This general development has been summarized in the expression 'web 2.0' which indicates that we are dealing with a new version of the Internet that is qualitatively different, implicitly implying that what we previously knew may be described as a kind of 'web 1.0' (O'Reilly, 2005). In web 2.0, it is to a far larger degree the users themselves who are creating content, sharing resources, and interacting with other users about whatever they may have in common. This may however also be seen as a re-focusing on what was one of the original ideas behind the Internet: to be able to share, connect, discuss and develop across existing borders.

According to the Canadian e-learning researchers Terry Anderson and Jon Dron, a main characteristic of web 2.0 facilities are that they provide a looser and more floating way of structuring social interaction (Anderson & Dron, 2007). This may in fact be a challenge when trying to integrate web

2.0 facilities in educational contexts, as education is often organized around fixed groups, teams or classes.

Technologies and Quality of Learning

Common for all new technologies that have been introduced in educational settings throughout history is however that they do not in themselves guarantee an increase in the quality of learning. As summarized in a study by the Organisation for Economic Co-operation and Development's (OECD) Centre for Educational Research and Innovation (CERI): 'ICT has penetrated tertiary education, but has had more impact on administrative services (e.g. admissions, registration, fee payment, purchasing) than on the pedagogic fundamentals of the classroom' (OECD/CERI, 2005, p. 15).

Furthermore, the acquisition of a learning management system or an e-learning platform – which has been the basic ICT-based activity of many higher educational institutions – does not in itself create new and challenging learning activities. As argued by Zemsky and Massy, the rapid introduction of course management tools may actually have the risk of reducing the impact of e-learning on the actual teaching practice, because it is almost too easy to transfer existing standard teaching materials to the web without a conscious remediation (Zemsky & Massy, 2005, p. 248).

A focus on dialogue and collaboration has been central to many developments of e-learning. Addressing the problem that online courses generally suffer from lower retention rates than campus-based courses, Poellhuber and Anderson have studied the readiness of distance students to engage in collaboration with their peer students. Based on findings that 'access to peer work and peer relations improved both the perception of social presence and students' motivation' (Poellhuber & Anderson, 2011, p. 103), their study was composed of more than 3000 students from four Canadian universities.

Regarding the students' previous experiences, it showed that male students and younger students reported a higher degree of experience with social media and a higher level of positive experiences with teamwork than female students and older students, respectively (Poellhuber & Anderson, 2011, p. 118). Regarding students' interest in using social media to collaborate with peers in a distance course, however, this interest was found to increase with the age of the students: 'While being less experienced than their younger colleagues, older students show more interest in learning with social software' (Poellhuber & Anderson, 2011, p. 120).

Poellhuber and Anderson point out the dilemma that students often choose online or distance education in order to obtain flexibility and individual freedom in planning their studies, but that this might be compromised by the integration of collaborative tasks through social media, because this increases the need of time scheduling and synchronizing pace with their peers.

These communicative and collaborative aspects are especially in focus in the dialogically inspired traditions of, e.g., computer-supported collaborative learning (CSCL), where net-based discussions and student collaboration on shared projects are used as key elements in a student-centred learning approach (Dillenbourg, Järvelä & Fischer, 2009; O'Malley, 1995; Rambe, 2012; Sundararajan, 2010). The MIL programme discussed in this chapter is located in this tradition.

PROBLEM AND PROJECT-BASED LEARNING

New pedagogical approaches emphasizing collaboration or learning in networks have been developed following the introduction of new technologies, especially the spread of social media (e.g. Anderson, 2008; Siemens, 2005). We find that these approaches of building on networked student learning can be understood in relation to approaches of problem- and project-based learning developed at the Danish universities of Roskilde and Aalborg, stressing the importance of collaboration and student-directed project work (Dirckinck-Holmfeld, 2002; Kolmos, Fink, & Krogh, 2004; Olesen & Jensen, 1999; Olsen & Pedersen, 2005). These approaches share certain characteristics with *problem-based learning (PBL)*, but also differ from it.

Problem-based learning dates back to the early 1970s, developed primarily in the United States and Canada, but also in Maastricht, the Netherlands, and Linköping, Sweden. In PBL, students learn through working with a case or a problem. According to Barrett and Moore, 'a key characteristic of PBL is that problems are presented to students at the start of the learning process rather than after a range of curriculum inputs. The PBL problem can be a scenario, a case, a challenge, a visual prompt, a dilemma, a design brief, a puzzling phenomenon or some other trigger to mobilise learning' (Barrett & Moore, 2011, p. 4). Put briefly, in PBL it is the responsibility of the teacher as an expert to present the problems to be dealt with and demonstrate how students in a constructive way can relate curriculum and theories to praxis. Barrett and Moore thus explains: 'It is important for us, as PBL practitioners, to continually find new ideas for selecting and designing relevant, motivating, challenging, interesting, multi-faceted and up-to-date problems for our students' (Barrett & Moore, 2011, p. 5). Within this framework students are offered the opportunity to deal with the presented problems.

In *problem- and project-based learning*, on the other hand, there is a bigger emphasis on the independent work of the student group. The starting point of a project is for the students to choose a topic or problem to investigate that represents a challenge for them, similar to what the cultural anthropologist Michael Wesch underlines as the importance of supporting students' ability to wonder. The process of defining a problem involves questions such as 'What is the meaning and sense of this problem in the first place? Why should I try to solve it? How did it emerge? Who designed it, for what purpose and for whose benefit?' (Engeström, 1987, p. 151). Working with questions like these can be a challenging, but productive process. Furthermore, it is interdisciplinary in that it combines knowledge and ideas from different kinds of academic fields (Olsen & Pedersen, 2005).

Problem- and project-based learning is characterized by collaborative project work in groups; following the development of the research question, the group members embark on a dialogically organized process in which they collect relevant material, data and information; analyse it; and, guided by relevant theories and methods, work to transform this material with the goal of investigating and answering the research question, while continually reflecting on and clarifying this research question. Hereby the students learn how to plan, manage and evaluate projects. Through this process the students are engaged in a dialogue with a teacher as their supervisor. The supervisor's role is to give the students critical constructive feedback and facilitate them in their learning processes.

Frank and Barzilai state that students working in a PBL environment are likely to engage themselves in processes of active learning and gain multidisciplinary knowledge. They note that 'project learning increases motivation to study and helps students to develop long-term learning skills. Students [...] share the responsibility for the learning process' and 'the PBL environment [...] increased students' self-confidence, motivation to learn, creative abilities, and self-esteem' (Frank & Barzilai, 2006, p. 40).

We find it important to acknowledge that problem-based study processes are however also characterized by contradictions and challenges for the persons involved. During study periods the level of frustration can be high. Students participate with different backgrounds, skills and qualifications and the processes of dialogue, discussion and negotiation may be laborious. One aspect of this is elaborated by the Danish learning theorist Knud Illeris:

'The learning process may take the form of coming through a crisis, in which the learner struggles for a certain length of time with a problem which is of urgent subjective importance' (Illeris, 2004, p. 58). Illeris draws parallels to concepts like Engeström's expansive learning, or Mezirow's transformative learning (Illeris, 2004, p. 59), which also deal with processes that are characterized by reflection and meta-learning. It is important to have in mind the contradictions at play for the students involved in such learning processes.

From a dialogic perspective on education, inspired by Bakhtin, differences between students can be seen as having a learning potential (Bakhtin, 1986). The Norwegian psychologist Rommetveit emphasizes that asymmetry between participants in a dialogue can be supportive of discovering new perspectives (Rommetveit, 1996, p. 95). A creative learning environment is thus not necessarily characterized by harmony and consensus, but rather by asymmetry and difference. In reflections on a course helping new teachers taking advantage of technological resources for teaching and learning, Mahiri notes that they were helped in changing their perceptions through the dialogic relationships in the class and their collaborative writing of texts (Mahiri, 2004, p. 230). Wegerif and De Laat argue that designing groupware that focuses specifically on facilitating the collaborative learning processes may help students in developing group dynamics and regulate their discussions (Wegerif & De Laat, 2011, p. 322).

In problem- and project-based learning, the students ideally work with theories and concepts to achieve an understanding that goes beyond the specific project, thus helping them to build and consolidate a broader study competence. This may prove beneficial in the students' future work and activities, as according to Barrett and Moore '[e]mployers regularly highlight the importance of key skills, which include: communications, teamwork, information literacy, critical and creative thinking, and problem solving, together with self-awareness, self-assessment, ethical behaviour, reflection, and responsibility for continuous development' (Barrett & Moore, 2011, p. 7). In the following part, we will discuss information literacy as an integrated part of students' study competence.

DEVELOPING INFORMATION LITERACY

When students are involved in self-directed study practices as discussed above, their reflective processes of searching and selecting information and building new knowledge are central. Information literacy is therefore part of the development of the students' study competence. In the problem- and project-based learning approach, where students are themselves responsible – in continuous dialogue with their supervisor – for identifying which problem to work with, the very act of formulating a problem is a large part of the learning process. To work in a group means that students must learn to work together in order to make decisions, to share and coordinate work, and to handle the large amounts of information that are within reach through libraries, databases and the Internet.

Information literacy requires not only that students are able to locate data and information, but also that they are able to select critically within the huge body of information, to judge and evaluate its use, and to let the information contribute to their construction of knowledge within the group. This understanding builds on the American Library Association's definition of information literacy:

> To be information literate, a person must be able to recognize when information is needed and have the ability to locate, evaluate and use effectively the needed information [...] information literate people are those who have learned how to learn. They know how to learn because they know how knowledge is organized, how to find information, and how to use information in such a way that others can learn from them (American Library Association, 1989).

This definition emphasizes that the concept of information literacy does not only deal with how to search for information and literature, but more generally with learning how to learn. In library contexts, this definition paved new ways through its coupling of information handling and learning. Libraries were able to orient their practice closer to the practice of educational institutions (Egeland, 2004, pp. 37, 38), and to change focus from merely being a provider of information to being actively supporting learning processes. In practice, however, information literacy is often used in a narrow sense of learning to search and find information. Even though this is indeed an important aspect of the learning process, there is – according to the definition above – a crucial step before this: before being able to search for something, you must have reached the understanding that there is something you need to know.

Only when you are aware what kind of non-knowledge you have, you may start acquiring knowledge on how this can be met. The development of information literacy is, therefore, according to our view, a way to handle finding out what it is that you do not yet understand. This has implications for the specific ways of searching that you engage in.

We see information literacy in relation to the modern, complex society, which demands as a fundamental quality being able to reflect on your knowledge in relation to new developments and challenges. For students, the development of information literacy can be seen as closely related to their broader study competence, for example when students are developing their project work, defining a specific field of study and formulating the research questions to investigate further through the project.

A Study on Information Literacy

As part of a project exploring the relations between educational institutions and educational libraries, we conducted in 2006 a study on information literacy in students' project work (Nielsen, Andreasen, & Jørgensen, 2006). In the study we carried out a small survey of the experiences and search practices of 21 students from Roskilde and Aalborg universities enrolled in classes that were involved in the project. The study showed that the students had limited knowledge of some of the central library services that were available; for instance only half of the students knew at the time of the study that they had online access to the electronic resources of the library from their homes, and only 10% had heard of an online 'ask-a-librarian-service' that were available through e-mail or chat. The study also showed that some of the students' problems on finding relevant information dealt with not knowing where to search, and with difficulties in phrasing search terms that would bring useful search results (Nielsen et al., 2006, pp. 16, 17).

The study indicated a need for developing ways of improving students' knowledge of finding relevant information. One way of learning how to search effectively would be to develop the traditionally technical and abstract library courses (Skov, 2004) in a way that would make them more relevant to the students' project work. Instead of introducing to the general principles of search queries and how databases work, the students need time during a library course to explore what would be relevant search terms and databases in relation to the research questions they are currently working on. It might be a challenge for the students to be specific in phrasing relevant keywords, and it might be a challenge for the librarians to target the specific groups of students and their questions, but such library courses would be more closely related and productive in relation to the students' study processes.

Breen and Fallon argue accordingly that the acquiring of information literacy should be connected to the students' actual study level, and should be integrated 'within the context of course curricula, and not separated from it' (Breen & Fallon, 2005, p. 182). Information literacy is hereby tied to a reflecting and critical attitude towards the information one is seeking.

TEACHER'S ROLES: LECTURER, FACILITATOR AND MEDIATOR

When students are involved in their self-directed study processes, they are continually in contact with a teacher, who acts as a supervisor in relation to their project. Within the framework of project studies the role of the supervisor is different from the role of the traditional teacher.

A teacher acting as a supervisor have to be facilitating, dialogically minded, capable of assisting the students in their work and receptive to the needs of the students. At the same time a teacher should be able to act as a coach, mentor, discussion partner, who supports *and* challenges the students in their project work. A productive supervisor can be understood as functioning as a catalyst that initiates processes. He or she takes the background and experience of the students seriously, and has a readiness to engage in new technologies or applications that are suggested or introduced by the students. This may not be an easy task for professional academics who have in mind a traditional expert role.

Donald Schön outlines this traditional expert role in contrast to that of a democratically oriented, reflective practitioner in his discussion of two different notions or contracts between the professional and the 'client'. In our context, these two types of attitudes can shed light on the teacher-student relationship. According to Schön, the professional person taking on a traditional *expert role* has the conviction that 'I am presumed to know, and must claim to do so, regardless of my own uncertainty'. Furthermore, he or she deliberately maintains a distance from the client and holds onto the expert's role, looking for deference and status in the client's response to his or her professional persona (Schön, 1983, p. 300). A contrasting approach can be seen with the *reflective practitioner*, who finds that 'I am presumed to know, but I am not the only one in the situation to have relevant and important knowledge. My uncertainties may be a source of learning for me and for them'. This kind of supervisor will allow the student's respect for the supervisor's knowledge to emerge from the student's discovery of it in the situation (Schön, 1983, p. 300).

As a supervisor facilitating the students' project work, the teacher should at the same time be capable of showing and demonstrating for the students possible ways to go, and being initiating without taking too much responsibility in relation to the students' projects. The reciprocity in the teacher-learner relationship is of great importance, as is also pointed out later by students in one of the cases discussed. In general, we can outline three different positions of a supervisor: being instructive, methodological and social mediator.

The first position is *lecturing,* giving professional advice as an expert, stressing the importance of the students' report being coherent and an expression of sound academic work with the 'right' answers to the research question at stake. This instructive teacher position primarily focuses on the students' final project (Nielsen & Danielsen, 2012, p. 263).

A second position is *facilitating,* and more related to methodological aspects and the continuing evaluation of the process. As a supervisor, the teacher will aim to guide the group towards the final project through stimulating discussions, supporting the students' effort to reach a fruitful integration of the empirical data and relevant theoretical positions. Important in this type of supervision is the students' heightened awareness of their study and work styles. Stressing this dimension of the supervisor role, the teacher should support students in being able to constantly reflect on their way of acting and working with the material, what kind of choices they make and what they are writing (Nielsen & Danielsen, 2012, p. 264).

A third position is more related to the difficult and challenging elements of collaborative group work. When members of a group can talk at cross-purposes or even patronizing one another, the supervisor as a *social mediator* can intervene, for example, if students have difficulties making decisions or embarking on constructive dialogical processes. A mediating supervisor will mainly be enquiring and questioning in order to facilitate student engagement in explorative dialogues (Nielsen & Danielsen, 2012, p. 265).

In practice a good teacher acting as a supervisor should be able to take on all three kinds of positions depending on the phases of the project work and the situation of the students.

Teacher Acting Within an Online Learning Environment

When dealing with online learning activities, new roles and tasks for the teacher appear compared to the well-known practice of classroom teaching. Kahiigi et al. point to this change: 'The paradigm shift from teacher-centeredness to student-centeredness has greatly influenced the higher education learning process. In this case, the teacher takes on a facilitator role while the students take ownership of their learning and personal development' (Kahiigi, Ekenberg, Hansson, Tusubira, & Danielson, 2008, p. 82). The topic of teacher roles was the focus of a seminar for teachers at the MIL programme in April 2012, from which the following points are inspired.

Teaching online creates a need for technological as well as social awareness, where teachers should be visible and accessible through online discussion periods, in other words mobilize tele-presence. At the same time, the teacher should allow adequate space for students to operate and navigate. Especially in online activities it is important to assist the students to stick to their work and hold on to their plans. Another challenge for the teacher is to provide clear criteria and standards to make sure students understand the tasks and activities. When providing written feedback, it is important to write concisely and clearly in order not to be misinterpreted. An online supervisor must be capable of giving constructive feedback, either face-to-face or through synchronous communication programmes such as Skype or Adobe Connect, and sometimes being available at flexible or odd hours.

Earlier a clear distinction was seen regarding online and on-site activities. We often find that the gap between acting online and on-site seems to be not as great as assumed. With the multi-faceted communication modes within reach today, the distinction is to a lesser degree whether people are online or on-site, but may follow other lines, for instance whether one prefers to communicate synchronously or asynchronously.

Within the networked learning environment of the MIL programme there has been a need to create and further develop the role of the teachers involved. We see the team of approximately 20 teachers involved as being part of an evolving community of practice. Kim asserts that 'a community is a group of people with shared interest, purpose or goal, who gets to know each other better over time' (Kim, 2000, p. 28). According to Wenger, communities of practice share a mutual engagement, a joint enterprise or practice, and a shared repertoire that is the 'pool of resources that members not only share but contribute to and therefore renew' (Wenger, 1998, p. 388). From the MIL teachers we have learned how important it is to be part of a supportive and social community, where it is possible to share experiences, challenges, and thus inform our teaching practice. We share ideas, pose questions, and together reflect on the challenges, e.g., related to different kinds of communication technologies. As participants we share our understandings of work, responsibility and knowledge in relation to our mutual practice.

THE MASTER PROGRAMME IN ICT AND LEARNING (MIL)

The cases to be discussed in the following paragraphs derives from the postgraduate MIL, where students with a couple of years of working experience, who wants to qualify themselves further, study within a networked learning structure. The students come from all parts of Denmark, and most of them are employed, full-time or part-time, while studying. We will shortly introduce the programme in order to present the context of the cases.

The MIL programme was established in 2000 as a continuation of a cross-institutional research network and is today a joint programme between four Danish universities. The programme combines on-site seminars (four during a study year) with independent and challenging virtually organized online periods of course activities and project work. The MIL programme is based on a concept of problem- and project-based learning, which is adapted to the virtual study environment. The pedagogical model builds on didactical principles of student engagement in problem formulation, enquiry of exemplary problems and interdisciplinary approaches. The MIL programme can be seen as an example of a dialogue-oriented and discussion-based approach associated with the social constructivist approach of networked learning (Dirckinck-Holmfeld & Jones, 2009, p. 261). The students bring in research problems from their own work practice to study, while using theories, concepts and methods from the academic practice (Fibiger et al., 2004). Half of the modules at MIL are organized as courses, and half are organized as project studies, where students work in small groups around joint research projects (Dirckinck-Holmfeld, 2010, p. 554).

The study programme implements new educational technology, with a virtual learning environment based on the FirstClass system, which holds conferences for asynchronous and synchronous communication, a who-is-online facility, individual mailboxes and profiles. Student groups have their own folders within FirstClass, which they are free to design, and where they can write, share and organize their contributions. Furthermore, they have access to synchronous video meeting facilities (Adobe Connect), peer-to-peer tools and web 2.0 facilities (Skype, Messenger, Google Docs, blogs) and tools to support project and course work (Camtasia for screen recording, Zotero for reference handling).

METHODOLOGICAL CONSIDERATIONS

As teachers and researchers we have been engaged in the MIL programme for 11 years. Thus, we have first-hand experience from the learning environment, and the following cases to be discussed are to be seen as generalized examples from our practice. The first case on a study group's use of synchronous communication have been gathered and described through our observations and feedback as teachers at the programme, here focusing on the work of one project group. The next two cases derives from two courses at the MIL programme; one is a course on ICT and learning in organizations, which takes part in third semester of the four-semester programme, and the other an introductory course on learning theory at the beginning of first semester. The educational design of the two courses are presented and discussed. The second case discusses students' reflections on their project work in the third semester course that took place in September and October 2009 with 19 students participating. The third case analyses students' online discussions in the first semester course in September 2009 with 30 students participating. In the second and third case, data were gathered through collection of log files from the online discussions, employed content analysis of students' postings on the discussion boards and examined the themes and discussion threads, analysed the students' participation, activities and patterns, e.g. how learners responded to each other's contributions. Furthermore, we made use of observations done concurrently during classes and in study groups, and feedback of both qualitative and quantitative art in order to gain understanding of their impression of the activities in the MIL programme. Additionally, in relation to the data from the previously discussed cohort of students from the study on information literacy, we used questionnaires in order to obtain information on the 21 students' habits of searching information and their use of library resources. Responses were gathered through an online survey tool, and the questionnaire contained fixed as well as open-ended questions. In the following part of the chapter, we will present and discuss the three cases.

STUDENTS' INNOVATIVE WAYS WITH TECHNOLOGIES

The first case will deal with how sometimes seemingly simple technologies can be used in innovative pedagogical ways to increase learners' involvement.

From our work as teachers at the MIL programme, we have observed various ways for students to use synchronous audio-based communication to organize their group tasks. As mentioned, the students are collaborating in groups, while being located all over the country. Therefore, Skype meetings are a widely used way of organizing group work processes, usually as an audio-conferencing tool supplemented by the text-based chat facility of Skype. One way of implementing this is to organize virtual meetings in the style of a formally organized physical meeting, with an agenda, a moderator etc. Such a formal Skype meeting can be a way of carrying their task forward, sharing information, keeping up-to-date, discussing key issues, taking decisions and other tasks that are continually due in a group project work.

The student groups usually combine the Skype facilities with shared documents, calendars and other online resources of the groups' own choice. They regularly try out new technologies, and sometimes they develop untraditional ways of using them in their study processes – for instance by summarizing hundreds of contributions from an online discussion through creating a Wordle, which is a kind of tag cloud that highlights the most frequently used words, or for instance as the following example shows by finding new ways of using tools like Skype in their daily studying practice.

Using Skype as a Shared Online Office

A group of five students were living in different parts of the country while they were working together on a student project as part of MIL. During a specific work-intensive period of the group process, the students developed a daily habit of everybody working at the same hours in the morning, and during this period they also developed a special daily routine of using Skype in a special way, not for ordinary meetings.

In this routine, all of the students were working at their desks in their own homes. They started their working day in the morning by opening a Skype audio connection with each other, so everybody could talk to each other, and stayed with the connection open for several hours each day. They all had flat-rate broadband Internet connection, therefore they had no extra costs going online calling each other and staying with the channel open all morning.

During these mornings they sometimes held short online meetings to discuss and plan their activities. Most of the time, however, they would just sit working while their Skype audio connection was turned on, each working on their own tasks as part of their bigger project. In this situation they could hear each other typing their computer, turning pages while reading a book or even pouring coffee – as if they were actually sitting in a shared office. Sometimes one of them would pose a question, which one or more of them would answer or discuss, after which they would return to their working mode. The audio connection was thus used to establish a shared informal space, where the group members could keep connected as if they were sitting physically together working, talking and concentrating.

The students developed this use of Skype as part of their educational practice in the project work. For a first glance such a way of using technology would probably not be considered relevant when discussing how to utilize new technology for educational purposes. From our point of view, however, this was actually exactly what the students were developing. By using Skype to establish a shared virtual room, where they could study, concentrate, and discuss what was needed in a spontaneous way, they found a way of organizing their study work and establishing a study environment that helped them keeping on track and motivated them in their commitment to their shared practice. In this way, they used Skype in new ways to increase learner engagement and learner outcome.

REFLECTIONS ON GROUP PROCESSES AND SUPERVISOR ROLES

The next two cases deal with the design of online learning environments, where students are active contributors and co-designers of the actual educational design. Both of the courses were based on virtual dialogues and collaboration and were designed in a flexible way in that the students could choose, within the overall structure, when it was most convenient for them to make their contributions. The courses had a focus on meta-learning, which means that the students were encouraged to continually reflect on the organization of the courses and their outcome of the virtual dialogues. The following case to be discussed is as mentioned in the third semester course on ICT and learning in organizations as it took place in 2009.

Educational Design of the Course

The course activities started at an on-site seminar where students met for presentations, workshops, discussions and group work. The remaining 2 months of the course were conducted online, structured in four phases:

- *Contemplating and developing questions.* After the seminar, the students had some time to focus on the course literature. Furthermore, they were asked to discuss in groups what specific themes should be reflected during the course, and drawing on their own work practice they prepared the specific questions to be discussed in the following online discussion period.

- *Student-initiated discussions.* For each opening question raised by the students, a discussion board was established. In the following 2 weeks, each student contributed individually with his or her reflections on the raised questions. Hereby the students explored the course topics through online dialogues reflecting on experiences from their own professional practice.
- *Small projects.* Each group of students then conducted an empirical investigation. This small project took place over 4 weeks, and was often carried out in relation to an organization where one of the students had their professional practice. The specific question to investigate was defined by the students. As the students could come from all over the country, some groups organized their work with this task fully online, while others also arranged physical meetings.
- *A final reflective forum.* After the project reports were handed in, a final discussion forum was created for the students to look back on the project they just made, reflect on the methods they used, exchange and evaluate experiences, and build knowledge to be used in their upcoming work on the final thesis. Below, we will discuss the students' use of this final reflective forum.

Discussions During the Final Reflective Forum

The final online discussion period was meant as an opportunity for the students to reflect on the course and their small project work: What insights did they achieve? What did they learn during the process? What would they eventually do otherwise next time in a similar situation?

To have the time for elaborating such reflections in a discussion with other participants of the course was used as a didactic means to have the students go one step further than usually, not just finishing the task and quickly heading on to the next activity. Through this elaboration, the intention was for the students in interaction with each other to learn from their experiences. Such a time for reflection can often be hard to find the time to do, therefore we established it as an integrated part of the course.

During this final reflective discussions among the 2009 group of students, 116 contributions were added by 19 participating students. A review of the contributions shows that especially two themes were raised. The first of these themes dealt with reflections on the students' group processes, and how to handle working together online in a group and to maintain an overview of the work, the deadlines and decisions. The second theme dealt with questions regarding the relation and interaction between students and supervisors online.

Managing Group Processes
In relation to the theme of managing group processes, one of the points discussed was the tension between discussing orally and producing written text. A student, whose group had found it difficult to find a direction for their work, explained that 'we were not good in putting things down in writing, but on the other hand we were really good at talking and talking at our Skype meetings' (Male student, third semester, our translation).

It is an interesting perspective raised here by the student that talking and discussing a number of things can be found easy, as opposed to the hard task of writing down the insights that were reached on the way. Etienne Wenger points out the importance of the interplay between participation and reification, between the momentary process of creating ideas and the longer stretch of forming products and results (Wenger, 1998). Both processes can be seen as necessary parts of productive group collaboration, but some groups face more challenges than others in maintaining and processing in written form the insights from the oral discussions.

Another point discussed by the students concerned the difficulties in establishing and maintaining an overview throughout a complex group process. This might be influenced by the specific technologies used, as can be seen in this reflection: 'Like all other project groups who work 99% through mail or conferences in e.g. FirstClass, we have in our group had difficulties in maintaining overview of our work. I think we have been constrained by not having met face-to-face to clarify deadlines and other questions that needed to be decided' (Student, third semester, our translation). This student points at difficulties arising when working asynchronously through mail or conferences. Interestingly, the student does not suggest supplementing their online communication with synchronous tools that might facilitate their decision-making processes better, but instead wishes for more face-to-face meetings.

A final point in relation to the theme of managing group processes is the meeting of practices and habits that happen when new participants meet, here described by a group member: 'I have experienced it as incredibly relieving and challenging to try this way of collaboration. [...] Ann and I have never before started our Skype meetings by discussing last weekend's matches in the football league, while the boys did not have the habit of ending each meeting by writing a song. In this way we have all been enriched

... I think :-)' (Female student, third semester, our translation). Sometimes group processes mean experiencing new ways of working together.

The Relation Between Supervisor and Students
The other main theme discussed by the students in the final reflective forum dealt with the role of a teacher as supervisor and the relation between students and their supervisors. This was triggered by the question 'What will I do differently next time?' One student indicated that their group had made too little use of supervision. Another student pointed out the pitfalls of turning on the 'automatic pilot' and not reflecting independently when being supervised: 'A supervisor meeting may cause a kind of tunnel vision, because you have a tendency to follow the guidelines from the supervision very strict' (Student, third semester, our translation). There is a delicate balance for a supervisor between being outwardly pushing or patiently waiting, a student writes: 'The ideal supervisor is a person that understands how 'to feed', but also to hold back, in order for the expertise of the group to unfold' (Student, third semester, our translation). This highlights the reciprocity of the teacher-learner relationship discussed earlier.

One of the students reflects on how easy it is to fall into a traditional student role, even though she feels that through her daily work as a teacher and supervisor she 'should know better':

It is just so strange that we often as students at MIL do all the mistakes that we tell our own students not to do! For example, I always want to send the whole pile of papers to our supervisor, 'just to hear that we are on the right track'. Even though I know that it is completely impossible for a supervisor to answer that type of question, and even though I get so tired of it when my own students do it.

Maybe it is because the world just looks different on the two sides of the fence: as a student, you need to know that it is okay, and that you are on the right track; as a supervisor, you are interested in being informed as precisely as possible what the student is writing and what you as supervisor can assist with. Furthermore, as a supervisor you are in contact with many students, and cannot read half-finished drafts all the time, where you almost have to guess what the student thinks; while students have only one dedicated task that makes up a huge part of their life.

In fact it shows that one should problematize the view that knowledge of what is right necessarily should cause the right thing to be done (Female student, third semester, our translation).

She points out here that the two situations of being a student and being a teacher/supervisor are so different, that it is very difficult to transfer knowledge from one situation to the other, even for the same person. This is a meta-reflection on being a student and a teacher at the same time, which also is reflected by Nielsen and Danielsen (Nielsen & Danielsen, 2012, pp. 262–265). What seems logical in one situation may seem very different when situated otherwise. The student's phrasing of this dilemma as part of the final reflective forum may be an important step in the ongoing effort to achieve alignment of expectations between students and supervisors.

ENGAGING NEW STUDENTS IN ONLINE DISCUSSIONS

The last case of the chapter is an example of creating an online learning environment in a short introductory course on learning theory. One of the authors of this chapter was a teacher at the course. The students at the course had just joined the MIL programme.

Educational Design of the Course

When meeting on location for the programme's first seminar, the students had an introductory lecture in support of the main activity of the course, an online dialogue-based discussion that took place over 3 weeks, 10 days before and 10 days after the seminar. The educational design chosen for this discussion period was as follows:

The specific themes to be discussed were defined by the contributions from the students, and not by the teachers. Participants contributed individually, and were not assigned specific roles in the discussion. The participants were encouraged to discuss whatever came to their mind of relevant questions. The course texts were seen as a starter – a trigger for their discussions. Students were encouraged to relate their discussions of the texts to their own practice, and to create at least four contributions during the discussion – among them one initiating a new discussion. Teachers made explicit that students here were given the opportunity to throw themselves in at the deep end, which could provide risks of experiencing a sense of chaos, but also opportunities for improvizations.

The online dialogues at the course took place in September 2009. Thirty students were participating in the discussions. During the 3-week period, 218 student contributions were created in 31 discussion threads with headlines such as 'Dewey and the concept of experience', 'Global knowledge sharing', 'Forget the teacher in the virtual learning environment', 'Constructivism',

'Rethinking learning', 'Documentation of virtual dialogues', 'Use of interactive whiteboards', and 'Reflection and boredom'. In these threads, students reflected on topics from their own daily practice, on specific philosophies of learning or on other empirical questions.

Online Discussions Among the New Students

Only some of these discussions unfolding among the new students can be treated here. In the thread on constructivism, a discussion took place regarding the use of computers in the Danish elementary school. One student stated, 'A traditional curriculum-based pedagogy still prevails even though the teacher uses a computer. [...] There is a focus on transmittance of information and rote learning, and only little room for creativity and communicative work. This form of information processing cannot be seen as an example of constructivist approach cf. Dewey' (Student, first semester, our translation).

This posting led to a sequence of reflections in relation to the understanding of Dewey's concept of experience, where a female student suggests that Dewey's 'concept "Learning by doing" should not be understood as involving a person in concrete physical kind of work activity to be able to learn. Rather learning should be seen as mentally coupling between past and future experiences' (Female student, first semester, our translation).

A third student referred back to this contribution: 'Your contribution inspired me to new thoughts. There is no doubt that he believes that learning is achieved through concrete experiences [...]. But he probably also thinks that education must be based on students' previous experiences, as long as you consider experience as being "flowing, undeveloped, vital"' (Student, first semester, our translation).

This small excerpt of the discussion shows the students' ways of relating to each other's contributions. The topic of the discussion engages them in jointly exploring the meaning of Dewey's concept in relation to their practice. This interchange can be seen as an example of dialogical 'interthinking' where the students relate to and build on each other's thoughts (Mercer, 2000).

Using or Misusing Interactive Whiteboards
Another thread of the discussions dealt with how a tool like the interactive whiteboard has been received in the students' actual practice in their schools. The discussion was opened by a female student, who in her daily

practice was a teacher herself: 'Smartboards have just been installed in most of the classrooms at my workplace. I see it as a great advantage … however Smartboards are greeted with much scepticism among my colleagues. I find that with whiteboards, it is possible to supplement the texts in the books and the spoken word with pictures and animations. [...] Thus it paves the way for an educational design that includes the aesthetic dimensions. [...] The new tools are met with scepticism from teachers [...] many of them feel uneasy and hesitating to the new challenges' (Student, first semester, our translation).

A male student – also a teacher himself – discussed the scepticism of some teachers and invited to further discussion: 'Students are enthusiastic and do not understand teachers' reluctance. [...] Based on the Norwegian learning theorist and philosopher Dale's theories on self-reflection and meta-learning, my approach to motivate the teachers to use these boards has been advocating to develop a strategy around the use of the boards, but often this does not happen and the boards are not being used. [...] How do we change such attitudes – do any of you have fruitful ideas regarding this?' (Male student, first semester, our translation).

A number of participants answered this question. One student reflected that it is a question of using – and getting used to using – the whiteboards: 'My experience is that we as teachers need motivation and confidence and most of all: Daily use. We have a lot of interactive whiteboards and they are only used to present film by and nothing else. The teachers do not feel at ease using these technologies in practice. Daily use would, however, ease this transition process and make it easier for teachers to expand their field of action … and gradually become exploratory teachers' (Male student, first semester, our translation).

A female student found that not only the amount of use, but also the context of the use was important for teachers in need of developing new practices around the interactive whiteboards. She therefore developed the following advice: 'First, let us create an organizational culture which will make it possible for skills and competencies to spread within community of practices (classes, teams and cohorts). Second, KIS "keep it simple" – let us create small catalogues with a few simple and effective advices. Third, let us create a secure workspace with possibilities for legitimate peripheral participation!' (Female student, first semester, our translation). As can be seen, she implicitly referred to Wenger's concept of communities of practice in her suggestions.

Another female participant had not met the amount of sceptical teachers mentioned by others: 'It's fun with your findings – I can't recognize the arguments. I come from a vocational high school where we recently have installed Smartboards in several classrooms and [...] most teachers would like to start using this new tool. [...] Ample time should be reserved to be fully conversant with the new tools' (Female student, first semester, our translation).

A last participant, whose work is to help schools implementing new technologies, pointed to the risk that tools like interactive whiteboards can be used in ways that promote a re-traditionalization of the educational practice. He stated, 'Interactive whiteboards (and IT) should be used not only by the teacher, but also by students. A student at a school said that the boards are "a teacher thing" and that students may not use them, as the school is afraid that students will destroy them. In other schools students are allowed to use the interactive whiteboards, for example to hear music during breaks, and here it is the experience of teachers and pupils that such an approach [is] opening up for greater engagement and that there is no signs of vandalism. If the interactive whiteboards predominantly are used by the teacher, there is a risk that the board will contribute to a traditional one-way teaching style' (Student, first semester, our translation).

The participants of the discussions represented a varied spectrum of experiences and views on the use of interactive whiteboards. Besides extensively referring to their own practice, they also drew on theories and concepts with which to reflect practice. The discussions show the potential of educational designs that encourage students to reflect on their experiences from practice when discussing the subject matter of the course.

CONCLUSION

Educational designs based on problem- and project-based learning approaches emphasize the involvement of students in the actual unfolding of a learning environment. This may happen in courses where students are involved as co-designers in relation to which specific topics to focus on or in projects where students relate their experiences from practice to theoretical approaches. Teachers may interchangeably apply different strategies and positions as lecturers, facilitators or mediators in their daily practice of supervising students in their independent collaborative project work. For students to act and learn in modern, complex societies, they need to reflect on their knowledge in relation to new situations that develop. Thus, developing their information literacy as an integrated part of their study competence is a key area. Educational institutions and libraries can support this process by treating information literacy not in general terms, but as an integral aspect of the students' activities.

The traditions of problem- and project-based learning highlight the students' active role in co-designing the educational environment or acting as mediators during course activities. Coping with and engaging in real-world problems also promote the development of student engagement. In the present context with rapidly evolving new social media and active user involvement, problem- and project-based learning approaches gain new relevance in the interplay with new technological possibilities. It is part of the educational design to incorporate and allow these possibilities to develop.

The discussions of using synchronous and asynchronous online communication in learning processes show that not all types of e-learning activities can be designed and planned in advance, as the example of the study group's unorthodox use of Skype shows. Even though not easily planned for, such unplanned activities may be important parts of a study environment that supports students in meeting the expectations of an educational programme.

REFERENCES

American Library Association (Presidential Committee on Information Literacy). (1989). *Final report*. Chicago, IL: American Library Association. Retrieved from http://www.ala.org/acrl/publications/whitepapers/presidential/. Accessed on 30 March 2012.

Anderson, T. (2008). *Theory and practice of online learning* (2nd ed.). Edmonton: Athabasca University Press.

Anderson, T., & Dron, J. (2007). Groups, networks and collectives in social software for e-learning. In D. Remenyi (Ed.), *Proceedings of ECEL 2007. The 6th European conference on e-learning*, Academic Conferences, Copenhagen (pp. 15–24).

Andreasen, L. B. (2006). Weblogs as forums for discussion – An alternative to the computer conference as a standard in online learning? In M. Buhl, B. Meyer & B. Holm Sørensen (Eds.), *Media and ICT – Learning potentials*. Copenhagen: Danish University of Education Press.

Andreasen, L. B., Meyer, B., & Rattleff, P. (Eds.). (2008). *Digitale medier og didaktisk design [Digital media and educational design]*. Copenhagen: Danish University of Education Press.

Bakhtin, M. (1986). *Speech genres and other late essays*. Austin, TX: University of Texas Press.

Barrett, T., & Moore, S. (2011). *New approaches to problem-based learning: Revitalizing your practice in higher education*. New York, NY: Routledge.

Breen, E., & Fallon, H. (2005). Developing student information literacy skills to support project and problem-based learning. In T. Barrett, I. MacLabhrainn, & H. Fallon (Eds.), *Handbook of enquiry and problem based learning* (pp. 179–188). Galway: AISHE and CELT, NUI Galway. Retrieved from http://www.nuigalway.ie/celt/pblbook/. Accessed on 30 March 2012.

Buhl, M. (2008). New teacher functions in cyberspace: On technology, mass media and education. *Seminar.net: International Journal of Media, Technology and Lifelong Learning.* *4*(1). Retrieved from http://seminar.net/index.php/volume-4-issue-1-2008-previousissues-meny-122/89-new-teacher-functions-in-cyberspace-on-technology-mass-media-and-education. Accessed on 10 November 2012.

Buhl, M., & Flensborg, I. (2011). *Visuel Kulturpædagogik [Pedagogy of visual culture].* Copenhagen: Hans Reitzel.

Dillenbourg, P., Järvelä, S., & Fischer, F. (2009). The evolution of research on computer-supported collaborative learning: From design to orchestration. In N. Balacheff, S. Ludvigsen, T. de Jong, A. Lazonder & S. Barnes (Eds.), *Technology-enhanced learning: Principles and products* (pp. 3–19). Berlin: Springer-Verlag.

Dirckinck-Holmfeld, L. (2002). Designing virtual learning environments based on problem oriented project pedagogy. In L. Dirckinck-Holmfeld & B. Fibiger (Eds.), *Learning in virtual environments* (pp. 31–54). Frederiksberg: Samfundslitteratur.

Dirckinck-Holmfeld, L. (2010). Design of a networked learning master environment for professionals: Using the approach of problem based learning to establish a community of practice. In L. Dirckinck-Holmfeld, V. Hodgson, C. Jones, M. de Laat, D. McConnell & T. Ryberg (Eds.), *Proceedings of the 7th international conference on networked learning 2010*, University of Lancaster, Lancaster (pp. 551–557).

Dirckinck-Holmfeld, L., & Jones, C. (2009). Issues and concepts in networked learning. In L. Dirckinck-Holmfeld, C. Jones & B. Lindström (Eds.), *Analysing networked learning practices in higher education and continuing professional development* (pp. 259–298). Rotterdam: Sense Publishers.

Egeland, L. (2004). *Det handler om læring [It's all about learning].* Oslo: ABM-utvikling.

Engeström, Y. (1987). *Learning by expanding: An activity-theoretical approach to developmental research.* Helsinki: Orienta-Kunsultit.

Fibiger, B., Nielsen, J., Riis, M., Sorensen, E.K., Danielsen, O., & Sørensen, B.H. (2004). Master in ICT and learning – Project pedagogy and collaboration in virtual e-learning. In: D. Remeney (Ed.), *Proceedings from 3rd European conference on e-learning*, Academic Conferences, Reading (pp. 87–92).

Frank, M., & Barzilai, A. (2006). Project-based technology: Instructional strategy for developing technological literacy. *Journal of Technology Education, 18*(1), 39–53.

Hopmann, S., & Riquarts, K. (Eds.). (1995). *Didaktik and/or curriculum.* Kiel: Institut für die Pädagogik der Naturwissenschaften.

Illeris, K. (2004). *The three dimension of learning: Contemporary learning theory in the tension field between the cognitive, the emotional and the social* (2nd ed.). Frederiksberg: Roskilde University Press.

Kahiigi, E. K., Ekenberg, L., Hansson, H., Tusubira, F. F., & Danielson, M. (2008). Exploring the e-learning state of art. *Electronic Journal of e-Learning, 6*(2), 77–88.

Kim, A. J. (2000). *Community building on the web.* Berkeley, CA: Peachpit Press.

Kolmos, A., Fink, F., & Krogh, L. (Eds.). (2004). *The Aalborg PBL model – Progress, diversity and challenges.* Aalborg: Aalborg University Press.

Mahiri, J. (2004). New teachers for new times. The dialogical principle in teaching and learning electronically. In A. F. Ball & S. W. Freedman (Eds.), *Bakhtinian perspectives on language, literacy, and learning* (pp. 213–231). Cambridge, UK: Cambridge University Press.

Mercer, N. (2000). *Words and minds: How we use language to think together?* New York, NY: Routledge.

Nielsen, J. L., Andreasen, L. B., & Jørgensen, L. (2006). *Udvikling af informationskompetence i problemorienteret arbejde med brug af digitale værktøjer [Development of information literacy in problem-based work using digital tools]*. Copenhagen: DEFF.

Nielsen, J. L., & Danielsen, O. (2012). Problem-oriented project studies: The role of the teacher as supervisor for the study group in its learning processes. In L. Dirckinck-Holmfeld, V. Hodgson & D. McConnell (Eds.), *Exploring the theory, pedagogy and practice of networked learning* (pp. 257–272). New York, NY: Springer.

OECD/CERI. (2005). *E-learning in tertiary education: Where do we stand?* Paris: Centre for Educational Research and Innovation, Organisation for Economic Co-operation and Development (OECD).

Olesen, H. S., & Jensen, J. H. (Eds.). (1999). *Project studies – A late modern university reform?* Frederiksberg: Roskilde University Press.

Olsen, P. B., & Pedersen, K. (2005). *Problem-oriented project work – A workbook.* Frederiksberg: Roskilde University Press.

O'Malley, C. (Ed.). (1995). *Computer supported collaborative learning.* Berlin: Springer-Verlag.

O'Reilly, T. (2005). What is web 2.0. Design patterns and business models for the next generation of software. O'Reilly: Spreading the Knowledge of Innovators. Retrieved from http://oreilly.com/web2/archive/what-is-web-20.html. Accessed on 18 April 2012.

Poellhuber, B., & Anderson, T. (2011). Distance students' readiness for social media and collaboration. *International Review of Research in Open and Distance Learning, 12*(6), 102–125.

Rambe, P. (2012). Constructive disruptions for effective collaborative learning: Navigating the affordances of social media for meaningful engagement. *Electronic Journal of e-Learning, 10*(1), 132–146.

Rommetveit, R. (1996). Læring gjennom dialog: Ei sosiokulturell og sosio-kognitiv tilnærming til kunnskap og læring [Learning through dialogue: A sociocultural and sociocognitive approach to knowledge and learning]. In O. Dysthe (Ed.), *Ulike perspektiv på læring og læringsforskning [Various perspectives on learning and educational research]* (pp. 88–104). Oslo: Cappelen Akademisk Forlag.

Rostvall, A-L., & Selander, S. (2008). *Design för lärande [Design for learning].* Stockholm: Norstedts Akademiska Förlag.

Schön, D. A. (1983). *The reflective practitioner – How professionals think in action.* New York, NY: Basic Books.

Selander, S., & Svärdemo-Åberg, E. (Eds.). (2009). *Didaktisk design i digital miljö [Didactic design in digital environments].* Stockholm: Liber.

Siemens, G. (2005). Connectivism: A learning theory for a digital age. *International Journal of Instructional Technology and Distance Learning, 2*(1), 3–10.

Skov, A. (2004) Information literacy and the role of public libraries. *Scandinavian Public Library Quarterly, 37*(3). Retrieved from http://www.splq.info/issues/vol37_3/02.htm. Accessed on 30 March 2012.

Sundararajan, B. (2010). Emergence of the most knowledgeable other (MKO): Social network analysis of chat and bulletin board conversations in a CSCL system. *Electronic Journal of e-Learning, 8*(2), 191–208.

Sørensen, B. H., Audon, L., & Levinsen, K. (2010). *Skole 2.0.* Aarhus: Klim.

Wegerif, R., & De Laat, M. (2011). Using Bakhtin to re-think the teaching of higher-order thinking for the network society. In S. Ludvigsen, A. Lund, I. Rasmussen & R. Säljö (Eds.), *Learning across sites. New tools, infrastructures and practices.* Milton Park: Routledge.

Wenger, E. (1998). *Communities of practice – Learning, meaning and identity.* Cambridge, UK: Cambridge University Press.

Zemsky, R., & Massy, W. F. (2005). Stalled: e-learning as thwarted innovation. In A. A. Carr-Chellman (Ed.), *Global perspectives on e-learning. Rhetoric and reality* (pp. 241–256). London: Sage.

MOBILE LEARNING: DEFINITION, USES AND CHALLENGES

Jorge Brantes Ferreira, Amarolinda Zanela Klein,
Angilberto Freitas and Eliane Schlemmer

ABSTRACT

New mobile platforms, connected seamlessly to the Internet via wireless access, become increasingly more powerful as each day passes. Smartphones and tablet computers, as well as other ultraportable devices, have already gained enough critical mass to be considered mainstream devices, being present in the daily lives of millions of higher education students. Whole firms, devoted solely to developing high-quality and high engagement content to these devices, have emerged, populating an application market of thousands of teaching applications (apps) focused on diverse higher education topics, from physics and calculus to anatomy and law. Many universities throughout the world have already adopted or are planning to adopt mobile technologies in many of their courses as a better way to connect students with the subjects they are studying. These new mobile platforms allow students to access content anywhere/anytime to immerse himself/herself into that content (alone or interacting with teachers or colleagues via web communication forms) and to interact with that content in ways that were not previously possible (via touch and voice recognition technologies, for instance). The study of such technologies

Increasing Student Engagement and Retention using Mobile Applications:
Smartphones, Skype and Texting Technologies
Cutting-edge Technologies in Higher Education, Volume 6D, 47–82
ISSN: 2044-9968/doi:10.1108/S2044-9968(2013)000006D005

and their possible uses for higher education, as well as the impacts they can have on stimulating more active participation and engagement with the course subjects and research in higher education, while at the same time fostering collaboration among students and even different institutions, is the goal of the proposed chapter. Through the evaluation of the teacher/student acceptance and adoption of such mobile technologies, this chapter plans to provide a thorough overview of the possibilities and consequences of mobile learning in higher education environments as a gateway to ubiquitous learning – perhaps the ultimate form of learner engagement, since it allows the student to learn, access and interact with important content in any way or at any time or place she/he might want.

DEFINING MOBILE LEARNING (M-LEARNING)

Introduction

Mobile technologies have become commonplace in our society. The reduction in their cost is contributing to promote social change through new forms of interaction, particularly with younger adults who use their mobile phones to maintain relationships unbound by proximity (Peters, 2005). With the expansion of 3G and 4G technologies, smartphones (advanced mobile phones that combine telephony, computing, messaging, multimedia capabilities, higher storage capacities for podcasts, videos, photos, files) will probably be the preferred devices to access the Internet in the near future, easing interaction among peers and allowing huge exchanges of content and information (Johnson, Levine, & Smith, 2008).

As mobile connectedness continues to sweep across the landscape, the possibilities of using mobile devices for learning are endless. The value of deploying mobile technologies in the service of learning and teaching seems to be both self-evident and unavoidable. The use of portable technologies makes it easier for learners to study whenever and wherever they want. It also facilitates 'just-in-time' learning, where learners can often take advantage of unexpected free time, since they frequently have their devices with them. Learners can create, share, and adapt their own content and evaluate these in social media networks of peers, colleagues or others that are not necessarily sharing the same lesson or classroom, expanding the learning experience beyond the traditional teacher-centred classroom model. The interactivity afforded by mobile technologies creates a teaching and learning environment more suited to a constructivist approach where the device is a tool for information and direction, but the structure of the learning is created by the learner (Sharples, Taylor, & Vavoula, 2007).

In December 2011, a group of experts from all over the world participated in a meeting at the UNESCO headquarters in Paris to discuss the diffusion of mobile learning (m-learning). This expert meeting was a cornerstone, indicating that m-learning is no longer a buzz word, but a concrete opportunity to reach the UNESCO goal of "education for all" in 2015. This is due to the fact that the majority of the population today owns mobile phones, since there are more than 5 billion mobile phone connections in the world.[1]

One of the most ubiquitous technologies in the history of mankind so far, the mobile phone has transformed the lives of many people by providing them access to communication to get job opportunities, citizenship information and family and community care. Getting access to education via mobile devices is not only a necessity but also a real possibility already accomplished by many students, teachers and workers worldwide. It is no coincidence that m-learning is becoming a priority issue in educational technology research today (BJET, 2011). The number of articles on this subject has dramatically increased in academic databases, especially after 2010.[2] Hwang and Tsai (2011) affirm that scientific publications on the subject grew exponentially in the last 5 years. But as a relatively new phenomenon, the understanding of what exactly is m-learning is still unclear.

What is M-Learning?

In spite of the progress of possible uses of mobile and wireless technologies for learning in the last few years, a consensus has not been reached yet in the academic and professional community about a m-learning definition. According to Hwang and Tsai (2011), a commonly accepted definition of m-learning is "using mobile technologies to facilitate learning." Traxler (2009) believes m-learning is sometimes seen as an extension of e-learning (Internet-based distance education); in other words, it is seen as an e-learning initiative accomplished through the use of mobile devices. In other cases m-learning is deemed to be something different from e-learning exactly for trying to overcome some of its limitations, such as barriers of time and space imposed by a "fixed" technology, or one that uses desktop computers.

According to Traxler (2009), the first m-learning definitions initially focused on the technology itself, basically relating m-learning to learning with the use of mobile technologies. As m-learning evolved in the academic and business contexts, several different practices began to be seen as related to the m-learning concept, some of them are as follows:

- *Mobile e-learning*: current practices of e-learning which can be reproduced with the use of mobile and wireless technologies. With that, an already existent learning management system – LMS – could be accessed from mobile devices. An example of that is Mobile Moodle (http://www. mobilemoodle.org/momo18/).
- *Learning in a live classroom supported by use of mobile and wireless technologies*: many initiatives related to m-learning refer to a restricted mobility, for instance students using notebooks or tablets and wireless networks which would allow for greater flexibility inside classrooms or specific campus or company.
- *Mobile training and instruction*: a possible use of m-learning involving instruction and training practices of field workers.
- *Increasing access*: several projects tied to m-learning seek to use vastly spread mobile technologies, as cell phones, to provide access to education opportunities for less favoured social groups or to those groups who are at isolated places, as, for instance, rural communities, as well as groups with some sort of special need.

At this point, an important distinction should be made about what sets m-learning apart from other practices, such as e-learning. According to Wagner (2005), mobile learning should not be seen as e-learning transferred to mobile devices. Instead, he claims that the value of mobile devices as a learning tool resides in their capacity to allow people to connect to educational content anytime anywhere and to facilitate the connection between everyone at any time and place. So if e-learning takes students beyond the traditional classroom, m-learning takes them beyond the classroom and beyond a fixed location.

More than the simple use of mobile and wireless technologies for learning, it is important to differentiate m-learning from other practices or teaching-learning modalities. According to a group of authors (Kukulska-Hulme, Sharples, Milrad, Arnedillo-Sanchez, & Vavoula, 2011; Sharples, 2000; Traxler, 2009; Winters, 2007) m-learning can be characterized by its ability to help promote the following elements:

- *Increased sense of control and autonomy over one's learning* – learning centred in the individual.

- *Situational learning* – in the place, schedule and conditions judged to be most suitable by the student.
- *Continuity and connectivity among contexts* – for instance, while the student moves through a certain area or along an event.
- *Spontaneity, opportunity* – m-learning can provide the student with the possibility of taking advantage of moments, spaces and any given opportunity to learn in a spontaneous way, as best paired with their interests and needs.

In this sense, it is considered that m-learning refers to learning processes supported by the use of mobile and wireless information and communication technologies which have as a fundamental characteristic the students' mobility, who may or may not be physically or geographically distant from one another and also from formal educational spaces, such as classrooms, instruction and training rooms or work place. Also, the new generation of students has these mobile devices as part of their daily routine. These topics are discussed further in the following sections.

The Sense of Mobility

It is necessary to remark that the most important aspect of m-learning is not technology itself, but the perception of *mobility* added to the learning process. This mobility shouldn't be understood as physical mobility alone, but unfolded in many different types of mobility, as explained below (El-Hussein & Cronje, 2010; Kukulska-Hulme et al., 2011; Lyytinen & Yoo, 2002; Sharples, 2000; Sherry & Salvador, 2002; Sørensen et al., 2008):

- *The students' physical mobility*: people move about and they may want to take advantage of opportunities created during that displacement to learn, for instance during a trip or while waiting for transportation.
- *Mobility of the technology*: several mobile devices can be taken along and used while the student is on the move, depending on the student's needs and situations in the surrounding environment. For instance, if certain physical and comfort conditions are present, a notebook could be used, or perhaps something even more portable, carried closed to the body, like a cell phone or an MP3 player, could be used instead.
- *Mobility in conceptual space*: According to Sharples, Milrad, Arnedillo Sánchez, and Vavoula (2009), as we move, we encounter several opportunities for learning. In this process, we are always learning, and our attention span among several concepts and contents to which we are

exposed every day, creating numerous learning episodes. Our attention moves from one conceptual topic to another driven by curiosity, personal interest or commitment, increasing learning opportunities.

- *Social or interactional mobility*: We also learn as we interact with diverse social groups and ranks, including our family, company or classmates. While moving ourselves we can interact with one of these groups, or with more than one simultaneously, as we make use of certain technologies, like the cell phone.
- *Temporal mobility*: new technologies allow us not only to learn at different locations, but also at different moments. They may even weaken the boundaries between work or formal education schedule and leisure time, which brings both negative and positive consequences. One of the great advantages of these technologies is the possibility to transform eventual "downtimes" (for instance when one is in a waiting room) into learning opportunities. On the other hand, it has already been said that these same technologies lead us to attempt accomplishing several parallel activities that could quite possibly generate an overload.

Rather than assuming that learning occurs within a fixed location, such as a classroom, over a bounded period of time, it is the combination of these kinds of mobility that fosters learning experience. This is what constitutes mobile learning, which the learning process augmented by technology increases the process of gaining new knowledge, skills and experience.

The "Digital" Generation

These different kinds of mobility allied to the new possibilities afforded by m-learning are aligned with the ascension of the so called "millennial generation" or "generation Y," formed by "digital natives" (Prensky, 2001). This generation is composed of individuals who were born in a time when the use of computers was already disseminated among common users, when most of the digital technologies available today (especially the Internet) were already part of everyday life (Dede, 2005; Veen & Vrakking, 2008).

For this new generation, traditional education, centred on the teacher, linear in form, fundamentally based on texts and excessively expositive, in which the student is a passive subject of the learning process, does not make sense anymore. The new generation is accustomed to acting instead of passively watching – as can be clearly seen with the massive adoption of electronic games. Instead of simply absorbing content, this generation expects to produce it, both individually and in groups, and to share the product in social networks. The content accessed and produced is not limited to texts, but also involves images, sounds, videos and animations; in short, it entails movement and implies the use of multiple medias. It is a generation empowered by the massive use of technology. Previous studies demonstrate that the use of mobile technologies in learning processes generates great motivation among youngsters, particularly among students that usually are not engaged with the course or generally present a lack of performance (Dede, 2005; Goh, Seet, & Chen, 2011).

In the following sections of this chapter, we will discuss the main technologies that make m-learning practices possible and how they have been spread in higher education. Next we will proceed to discuss ways in which these technologies can be employed as a medium to stimulate the students and to provide innovative forms of teaching-learning, especially in higher education settings. Finally, we identify the challenges and consequences of its use, ending with the final remarks.

MOBILE COMPUTING TECHNOLOGIES

The Emergence of Mobile Computing Technologies

The mobile revolution is finally here. Look around at coffee shops, cars, trains and airports and the evidence of mobile devices' penetration and adoption is irrefutable: cell phones, smartphones, tablets, PDAs (personal digital assistants), MP3 players, portable game devices, laptops and netbooks abound (Martin-Dorta, Saorin, & Contero, 2011). Cell phones have evolved to smartphones with PDA features, web browsers, e-mail, cameras and video capabilities. Laptops have gotten lighter, with longer battery life, and are capable of connecting wirelessly to high speed networks at thousands of public Wi-Fi access points, called "hot spots," and increasingly in homes with wireless broadband.

Particularly, the diffusion of mobile phones in our society and their increasing capabilities to access the Internet are changing the face of our society. From children to seniors, nobody is immune to this phenomenon. It is estimated that by 2015, 80% of people accessing the Internet will do it through cell phones (Johnson, Smith, Willis, Levine, & Haywood, 2011), changing the way people will communicate in the future (Hsu, Rice, & Dawley, 2012). The advance of wireless environments and the increasing access to broadband worldwide have promoted socialization at any place and has become a powerful trend, especially among young people, inspiring social networking websites such as Blogs, Facebook, Twitter etc. The increase in socialization due to the Internet happens through nonverbal communication media such as multimedia audio-visual objects, images, pictures and other diverse media, improving close interpersonal relationships.

The growth of mobility and the advent of the social networks caused by mobile technologies suggest we are reaching a turning point in the way technology is used for learning. The available technologies, such as high bandwidth wireless communication-networking infrastructure and advanced handheld devices, promise to make learning experiences more exciting, engaging and accessible (Conole, de Laat, Dillon, & Darby, 2008).

Mobile Technology or M-Technology

Advances in mobile and wireless technologies have affected the entire society. Global Positioning System (GPS) means never getting lost again. Bluetooth technology makes it possible to create Personal Area Networks (PANs) among physically close devices. Radio Frequency Identification (RFID) transponders have revolutionized inventory and supply chain management. Instant messaging (IM) enables real-time and often simultaneous communication. The current technological development, however, is not happening without concerns. The anticipated arrival of WiMAX and LTE (wireless broadband technologies) raises questions regarding the liabilities of being "always on, always connected" (Wagner, 2005).

Although there are questions to be answered, one cannot deny that the advance of technology influences all aspects of everyday life. In this respect, it is important to understand the use of technology and the impact it causes on people's routine. But what encompasses mobile technology? Caudill (2007) divides mobile technology in the two key components: (1) the wireless networking and (2) hardware, representing the mobile devices.

Wireless Networking

Wireless networking is the first technological key component contributing to mobile technologies. The term wireless, in this case, is used to refer to technologies that enable communication without cables or cords, mainly through use of radio frequency or infrared rays (Wagner, 2005). The most prevalent and widely recognized mobile technology is the IEEE 802.11 specification, the official designation for the wireless protocol, commonly called Wi-Fi. This wireless technology uses a series of access points, which are transmitter/receiver stations that wireless devices can connect to via their own Wi-Fi networking capability.

Wireless communications are managed via networks. Networks can be categorized as sets of interconnected computers or other devices, and can be designed in many different ways. Wide Area Networks (WANs) cover large geographical areas. Local Area Networks (LANs) are networks that typically service a single organization, household or individual (via home Wi-Fi setups, for instance) and are often connected to WANs to communicate with users in other locations. Less commonly used today, but likely to be more frequent in the future, are PANs that use Bluetooth or infrared technologies, allowing devices to talk to each other over short distances (Peters, 2005).

Of these, the most available, widespread and known network technology is the Internet. The Internet is effectively a WAN for information and communication. Until a few years ago, Internet access was restricted to fixed telephone connections at desk-based work stations. However, with the advent of third-generation (3G) phones (third generation, or java/web enabled phones) and the new WiMAX and LTE 4G technologies, this scenario is rapidly changing. New Internet-capable mobile phones are now firmly settling in the market, selling as fast as they are produced.

Within this wireless environment, many different uses of mobile technologies, represented by the web 2.0, have become popular and widely accepted, such as blogs (Huang, Jeng, & Huang, 2009), podcasting (Evans, 2008; Harris & Park, 2008) and social networking, for example. Users can access the web via mobile device whenever or wherever the need arises, and publish their thoughts and experiences via blog articles, podcasts or social network updates. In this context, web 2.0 technologies tend to redefine the process chain of content creation, opening a wide avenue of possibilities for learning and collaboration (Westera, 2011).

Hardware
The second technological key component contributing to mobile technologies is hardware, particularly in the form of mobile devices. In terms of mobile devices, Peters (2005, p. 2) proposes following three criteria to determine whether devices should be classified as mobile technology:

1. capable of providing communication and/or information functions;
2. small enough to be easily carried;
3. can be used (at least part of the time) without a physical connection to fixed power or telecommunications services.

To be a mobile technology, hardware had to advance to a point that would enable people to carry and access the device on a regular basis. Devices such as mobile cell phones, smartphones, tablets, PDAs and MP3 players fit into the category of mobile devices (Mellow, 2005). Regarding laptops, notebooks and netbooks computers, sources disagree on their status as mobile devices. While they are capable of accessing wireless networks without plugging into a power source, due to their size, configuration and the fact that they take time to boot up and shut down would mischaracterize them as devices that people can carry everywhere and quickly access at any time (Mellow, 2005). However, with the new generation of laptops, the boundaries between what are considered a mobile device and what is not has become more tenuous. Because newer laptop computers are more portable and faster to boot up, it is still unclear whether those laptops could be considered mobile devices or not.

Most devices today include built-in Wi-Fi connectivity, being able to access public or private Wi-Fi hotspots (Balachandran, Voelker, & Bahl, 2003). This capability gives individuals the freedom to work at a wide variety of locations, but also to deliberately choose comfortable locations, such as a favourite coffee shop, from which to work.

Finally, a very promising family of mobile devices that could indeed leverage the mobile wireless experience is the tablet computer, such as Apple's iPad. Even though they are not designed to make phone calls such as a cell phone, their computational capacity, small size and access to 3G/4G networks opened up new possibilities of use for mobile devices. Coupled with the anticipated development of a new generation of mobile operating systems that will provide seamless synchronicity among phone/computing/PDA, together with longer battery life and expanded PAN capability, it is expected that many new mobile computing and communication opportunities will be created by tablets in the near future.

Mobile Technologies in the Learning Environment

Despite the fact that many technological devices are produced in portable form and people have become accustomed to them, the development and use of digital technologies so far has been limited to social communication, with few people regarding mobile learning as a core pedagogical activity in higher education institutions (El-Hussein & Cronje, 2010).

However, El-Hussein and Cronje (2010) point out that the growth of mobile technologies presents a huge opportunity for the delivery of learning via devices such as smartphones, mobile phones and tablets. The new generation of mobile devices has the capacity to connect to the Internet and deliver content and instruction that can enable learners to learn at anytime and anywhere in a format that is culturally prestigious among people in the same age group. With the recent advances in technology that incorporate features that support a portable, digital and wireless lifestyle, teaching and learning experiences of this kind tend to increase. Today, mobile devices, such as smartphones, are equipped with location information receivers, cameras, RFID readers and other environmental awareness sensors that can provide rich and interactive multimedia contents for educational purposes (Jeng, Wu, Huang, Tan, & Yang, 2010).

Nonetheless, given this scenario, what one should keep in mind is that all the enthusiasm about the potential for m-learning needs to be tempered with the recognition that mobile technologies do not necessarily substitute existing technologies or that its diffusion and adoption in higher education settings is guaranteed. The idea of using mobile technologies for teaching and learning environments is to use them to create rich, interactive experiences, tailored to the needs of the learner. The success of mobile learning depends on the confluence of several factors and experiences, which will rest, in turn, on a foundation of converged network, devices and wireless services. To be effective, mobile learning will require, in addition to new digital communication skills, new practices and, ultimately, new pedagogical approaches.

In this sense, to be effectively used, mobile learning should take aspects that involve rich social practices built around the technology, especially among teenagers and young adults (Rheingold, 2002). Technology can engage learners and help them have a learning experience more memorable and engaging than what they are used to. However, as pointed out by Wagner (2005), to get people to adopt and use mobile devices in education actually requires little extra effort. We delve into this discussion in the next section, discussing what factors influence the adoption and use of mobile technologies for learning.

THE ADOPTION AND DIFFUSION OF MOBILE LEARNING PLATFORMS

Widespread adoption of mobile technologies is a key requirement for the success and the future of mobile learning endeavours. Liu, Li and Carlsson

(2010) point out that the mobile learning market is growing, even though there is a lack of understanding about what factors drive the adoption of this form of education. While connected mobile devices have already impacted education on many levels, the idea of seamless learning, where every single student has a device (or even multiple devices), as exposed by Chan et al. (2006), would still require wider adoption and usage of mobile learning technologies and systems. Such availability and adoption could promote true one-to-one technology enhanced learning, with the usage of mobile learning systems being possible to every student at anytime, anywhere (Wong & Looi, 2011).

Despite the educational potential presented by mobile technologies, there are many challenges that might hinder mobile learning adoption. Bouwman, Carlsson and Walden (2008) showed that, while consumers are aware of the functionalities of their mobile devices, many choose not to use those features, opting to use the traditional voice and texting services instead. Similarly, Corbeil and Valdes-Corbeil (2007) argue that, even though students and faculty are familiar with mobile technologies, they might not be ready yet for m-learning. Pozzi (2007) discusses the occasional and supplemental nature of m-learning usage in education settings, alerting for the fact that mobile technology still needs to find its place as a core of learning tool for faculty and students alike. Despite the fact that it is still unclear what factors drive an individual's attitude towards accepting m-learning for educational purposes, in order to understand its adoption and use we briefly discuss the most common concepts investigated in the literature related to m-learning technology acceptance.

Usefulness, Ease of Use and Innovativeness

Quite a few studies in the literature evaluate the main drivers of m-learning usage and adoption. Liu, Han and Li (2010) analyse the current state of m-learning adoption research, pointing out possible applications and issues surrounding the acceptance of the technology. The authors note that m-learning requires autonomy and individual willingness to participate in the learning experience, which in turn could foster the engagement of the students with the content and activities provided. They emphasize the fact that as technology users, individuals might find perceived usefulness and perceived ease of use (Davis, Bagozzi, & Warshaw, 1989) to be important attributes in defining their attitudes and adoption intention towards m-learning services and systems. Thus, the more useful mobile learning technologies are perceived to be by students, be it by providing reading materials remotely, by offering new ways to communicate with fellow learners or instructors (Markett, Sanchez, Weber, & Tangney, 2006), by allowing access to course and campus information at all times or by any other means, the higher their willingness to engage in their use will be. By the same token, if mobile systems and devices are found to be easy to operate and mobile content is readily available with interfaces and interactivity that are easily figured out and employed, the greater would be the desire to use and interact with mobile learning technologies.

Liu et al. (2010) advise that perceived usefulness should be divided in short- and long-term perceptions, each of which are understood to have significant impacts on the intention of using information technologies. Long-term usefulness would reflect future results, while short-term usefulness would evidence immediate results. Such a division of the perceived usefulness concept seems to fit well with students' perceptions about mobile learning usage in higher education settings, given that, while short-term adoption of m-learning tools might be spurred by professors requiring students to use mobile courseware, true adoption, engagement and widespread use, even when not required, might only happen if positive long-term consequences are foreseen.

Additionally, Liu et al. (2010) propose that personal innovativeness (Agarwal & Prasad, 1999), the individual's disposition in trying any new information technology, should also influence m-learning usage, with individuals presenting higher levels of innovativeness being more prone to develop positive beliefs about innovations, compared to those that possess lower levels.

Mobility and Perceived Enjoyment

As discussed previously, one of the main aspects of m-learning is the sense of mobility. The notion of mobility itself, according to the user's perception, seems to be of particular importance to the adoption of mobile technologies, including mobile devices and services such as m-learning. Mallat, Rossi, Tuunainen and Oorni (2008) and Huang, Lin and Chuang (2007) state that a significant influence of perceived mobility over the adoption of mobile services and mobile learning could be found, strengthening the idea that freedom of space, time and context is indeed a key concept behind usage and acceptance of mobile learning.

Huang et al. (2007) also propose that perceived enjoyment (Teo & Noyes, 2011) could also promote further adoption and engagement of students with mobile learning, pointing out that the enjoyment and fun that can be associated with m-learning activities, together with perceived mobility, were the factors with the highest impact on students' intentions towards mobile learning usage.

Self-Efficacy and Subjective Norms

In regard to self-efficacy (Compeau & Higgings, 1995; Pituch & Lee, 2006), the concept represents a person's judgement about his/her capacity to organize and to execute a required course of action to achieve designated types of performance. Still, as Bandura (1977) describes, self-efficacy reflects beliefs about the individual's capacity to execute certain tasks with success. Since m-learning demands more individual autonomy, it is plausible to anticipate that self-efficacy might positively influence students' intention to use the technology, with the concept having already been validated for e-learning contexts via previous studies (Pituch & Lee, 2006).

Likewise, subjective norms, in the form of perceived social pressure from peers to engage in a specific behaviour (Ajzen, 1991), can be a key determinant of students' interest in using mobile learning technologies. If classmates, family or faculty members all utilize and say good things about mobile learning, a student is deemed more likely to be willing to try it and possibly adopt it. Since peer pressure is especially pronounced in higher education settings, the influence and importance of subjective norms for m-learning adoption might even be particularly high in comparison to its relevance for consumer or workplace technology adoption settings.

Compatibility

Another important concept that might affect students' intention to engage in mobile learning use is compatibility (as originally defined by Rogers, 2003) and represents the degree by which an innovation is perceived to be consistent with one's values, needs and previous experiences. It is believed that this concept is important in the adoption of m-learning, because, in order to be able to perceive advantages in using it as a learning instrument, the adopter must notice its compatibility with the learning/teaching process he/she is accustomed to, taking into account his/her beliefs and values.

Widely considered in technology adoption studies (Moore & Benbasat, 1991; Venkatesh, Morris, Davis, & Davis, 2003), compatibility might play an important role in the adoption of m-learning by both students and faculty members. To promote and take advantage of m-learning activities, faculty members should consider including mobile learning content and technologies in their course material as a way to promote more student engagement both in class (via games, interactive content or other activities) and outside class, in contexts such as laboratories, in the field or even at home. If m-learning practices are not seen as compatible with current teaching methods, leading professors resist its use, a great barrier to adoption might form. Failure to stimulate its use via integration with course materials promoted by faculty members might lead students to disregard m-learning as a whole.

Flow Theory

Flow theory (Csíkszentmihályi & Csíkszentmihályi, 1988; Csíkszentmihályi, 1990) states that if a user is truly focused and has all his/her attention directed to a particular experience, she/he might reach a state of mind in which he/she is not conscious of anything besides the focus of his/her attention. Flow is characterized by a narrowing of the focus of awareness, filtering irrelevant perceptions and thoughts out; a loss of self-consciousness; responsiveness to clear goals and unambiguous feedback and a sense of control over the environment, being said to be the holistic sensation that people feel when they act with total involvement. In this sense, Liu, Liao and Pratt (2009) and Lu, Zhou and Wang (2009) suggest that elements from flow theory could be used to advance the comprehension of m-learning adoption. Therefore, if mobile technologies can promote learning activities that truly engage students, managing to attract and focus their attention and concentration, m-learning adoption and usage might be enhanced.

Understanding Mobile Learning Adoption

Despite the euphoric discourse in relation to m-learning, knowledge about its practice and use is still in its infancy, and its theoretical foundations have not yet matured (Muyinda, 2007). Regardless of the high degree of insertion of mobile devices in current society, the mere availability of technology itself does not guarantee that its potential will be used for learning or accepted by all evenly. That translates into the perception that, up to this moment, m-learning still has not caused great impact in the educational context (Liu et al., 2010). Although there are already some studies that seek to understand what factors influence students' intentions to use m-learning, the understanding of the adoption of mobile technologies in educational environments is still incipient (Pozzi, 2007). In particular, questions about how to promote the acceptance of m-learning by users are still largely unresolved. Given that, many other variables, besides the ones discussed in this section, might be relevant to comprehend how students and faculty members decide to engage in the usage of mobile learning technologies. If the most important factors behind m-learning adoption can be pinned down and understood, m-learning's acceptance and impact on higher education practices could be more profound than first thought.

M-LEARNING IN HIGHER EDUCATION ENVIRONMENTS: STIMULATING LEARNING ENGAGEMENT AND PARTICIPATION

M-Learning Practical Applications

When reviewing the literature, it is possible to identify a number of different m-learning practices, from simple applications (like the use of SMS to support traditional teaching) to more sophisticated systems, specifically developed with this education modality in mind. It is also seen that m-learning has applications for all educational levels, from elementary schools to higher education settings (Hwang & Tsai, 2011). Current m-learning practices allow students to (Fig. 1)

- carry out activities using SMS, interacting with classmates and teachers in order to receive and send messages regarding class activities, notes of mixed nature, including delivery of essays, study meetings, doubts etc. It is also possible to participate in discussion forums or video classes via cell phones (see real examples in Goh et al., 2011; Grönlund & Islam, 2010; Hayati, Jalilifar, & Mashhadi, 2012; Motiwalla, 2007).
- answer to a "quiz" through a cell phone, containing questions to be answered after watching a video, listening to an audio track or accessing previously defined content in a mobile way (Gedik, Hanci-Karademirci, Kursun, & Cagiltay, 2012).

Fig. 1.   M – Learning Practices.

- access a learning management system designed for mobile devices in order to complete a course, interact with classmates, search for or post materials anywhere or whenever desired, sharing knowledge (Beckmann, 2010; Chen & Huang, 2010; Saccol, Barbosa, Schlemmer, & Reinhard, 2011).
- learn by using mobile games. Ardito et al. (2008) show how they created an educational game for archeological parks in Italy, using mobile devices carried by students during the exploration of the site. Brown et al. (2011), in his turn, created a system for route memorization employing location based services (LBS) intended to help people with intellectual deficiencies, while Liu and Chu (2010) developed a game with context sensibility for language learning.
- capture and organize information or lectures that occur in specific places. Vavoula, Sharples, Rudman, Meek and Lonsdale (2009) and Wishart and Triggs (2010) present applications for m-learning that allow students to

capture images/videos and access information about objects seen during a museum visit. Chu, Hwang, Tsai and Tseng (2010) developed an application using RFID that allows image capture of plants for students working in the field, providing instantaneous feedback. Hwang and Chang (2011) developed a mobile evaluation system intended to be used during visits to museums or other study places.

- access different Third Dimension Virtual Worlds (TDVW) via mobile devices. There are some mobile applications available that allow access to TDVW, such as Pocket Metaverse (http://www.pocketmetaverse.com/) which provides mobile access to Second Life, and Virtway (http://virtway.with/EN_index.php).
- access social networks (e.g. Facebook, Twitter etc.) to exchange information or for informal learning activities.
- listen to podcasts presenting comments or lecture syntheses recorded by a teacher or classmate, after a class (Beckmann, 2010; Evans, 2008).
- learn in context. For example, one can visit a historical place and receive specific information of important events that happened in that place, at each point of interest, as the learner walks around the site (Kukulska-Hulme et al., 2011).
- support in attendance teaching. For instance, some schools already demand that newly enrolled students possess a notebook or a tablet to attend the classes. De-Marcos et al. (2010) developed a self-evaluation system via m-learning as a support to teaching activities.

A less explored possibility for m-learning is its utilization in corporate training. Employees can use the same mobile devices they use to do their work as tools for m-learning. For instance, waiters that use mobile devices such as PDAs to take orders can also use them to access training sessions about hygiene norms, safety or products they should offer to customers. Salespeople that use mobile devices to access sales software can also use these same devices to receive training, such as accessing information regarding products by reading bar codes with their mobile devices. Thus, those professionals would not need to leave their work places in order to get further qualification or instruction (Brown & Metcalf, 2008; Peters, 2005). However, it is accurate to affirm that academic studies on corporate m-learning are still quite rare (Macdonald, Columbia, & Chiu, 2011; Saccol et al., 2011).

Kukulska-Hulme (2010, p. 8) affirms that "learners are actively using their cell phones, smartphones, PDAs and MP3 players to create, collect and access useful resources to communicate inventively in a variety of ways with other individuals and communities, and to make best use of time wherever they happen to be."

Following an extensive research, Kukulska-Hulme (2010) lists a series of daily life uses of m-learning in different countries. Therefore, it is possible to conclude that there are many possible applications of mobile technologies both to formal and informal learning. For further information about various already developed m-learning systems, see Hwang, Wu, Tseng and Huang (2011), Kukulska-Hulme et al. (2011) and Hwang and Tsai (2011).

Therefore, it is possible to conclude that there are many possible applications of mobile technologies both to formal and informal learning. For further information about various already developed m-learning systems, see Hwang et al. (2011), Kukulska-Hulme et al. (2011) and Hwang and Tsai (2011).

M-Learning in Higher Education: Pedagogical Assumptions

In spite of all current possibilities, m-learning diffusion in higher education is not a simple matter because it demands a series of cultural changes. First, it is necessary to change the institutions, where the teaching culture is, in general, strongly marked by traditional (face-to-face) environments (Grönlund & Islam, 2010). It is also necessary to change teachers' culture, whose pedagogic practices are, in their majority, ingrained with the notion that students assume a passive role, supported by traditional teaching methodologies that may reflect their own experiences as a student. That leads to a challenge in which teachers must learn new technologies and teaching methods with which they did not have any previous personal experience (Kukulska-Hulme et al., 2011). Moreover, it is essential to understand how to stimulate learning and engage students' participation. With that thought in mind, it is important to remember how different learning is from teaching.

For Piaget (1972), learning, in general, is incited by environmental situations but only occurs when there is, on the subject's part, an active assimilation: "the whole emphasis is placed in the subject's activity, and I believe that without that activity there is no possible didactical or pedagogical way to significantly transform the subject" (Piaget, 1972, p. 11). Piaget, when making this statement, points to the importance of the subject's action in order for learning to actually happen, attributing to the subject the main responsibility for the learning process.

In order to stimulate the active involvement of the subject, it becomes necessary to find a balance between the level of challenge in an activity and the subjects' abilities and competence levels in synchrony with playfullness. According to Csíkszentmihályi (1990), it is possible to identify some of the factors that contribute to the flow experience:

- *Clear objectives*: expectations and rules need to be evident and the objectives should be attainable and aligned with the group of competencies and abilities necessary to reach them.
- *Balance between competencies, ability and challenge levels*: the activity can neither be too easy nor too difficult for the subject.
- *Direct and immediate feedback*: successes and failures during the activity should be made evident, so that behaviour could be adjusted whenever necessary.
- Sense of personal control (dominance) over the experience.
- *Playfullness*: one must deem an activity as intrinsically gratifying so that there is an effort to perform the action.

It is necessary to engage students in a significant and sufficiently challenging learning situation to provoke them into action and stimulate interaction. In addition, the more entertaining the activity, the greater will be its ability to attract students' focus and involvement.

In that context, information represents one of the essential elements of learning, as a provocative external factor. However, learning does not consist only of receiving information by itself. There are other fundamental processes involved, such as action or interaction of subjects on it and with it. This way, the subject can assimilate and accommodate the information, adapting it to build new intellectual structures or broaden existing ones to compensate for the disturbance caused by the information.

Learning implicates much more than receiving information (contents). No matter how attractive those contents may be, they are just the first external incentive to rouse the subject's interest in learning. The subject must be able to analyse, contemplate, apply, discuss and, ultimately, act on the information to make sense of it, consequently constructing his/her own knowledge.

That does not mean that one can neglect content production or structured information stored and distributed by networks. Instead, it means drawing attention to what in fact constitutes the heart of learning, of education: the context in which the individual is inserted. Information, learning and knowledge can be bound to different contexts, making it important to develop learning processes that take these contexts into consideration.

Most actual applications for m-learning are designed to deliver contents via mobile devices (Grönlund & Islam, 2010) but m-learning practices can go quite beyond that simple use, helping creating 'relational spaces' (Maturana, 1993). According to Figueiredo (2005) and Figueiredo and Afonso (2005) a "learning context" is a group of relevant circumstances involved when someone needs to learn something. Until the eighteenth century, it was commonplace to learn from others present in the context of one's daily activities, solving problems and difficulties as they appeared. Towards the goal of becoming professionals, for instance, students developed their skills amidst the context of their master's workshop. However, the industrial revolution and principles such as Taylorism transformed educational environments, since schools started to be managed as production lines that generated workforce in large scale for the industrial society. This mechanized view of education perceives knowledge not as something that students can construct by themselves, in appropriate contexts, but as a "content" that can "be transferred" from teachers' minds to students'. As this transformation took place, real learning contexts gradually began to disappear from formal education.

The possibilities brought up by m-learning favour the "return" of contextual learning, as students can move or act in diverse environments to increase their qualifications and learn, maintaining as much access to contents for learning as interaction with teachers, instructors and with other students that can help them or enrich the learning process. Some authors coined the term Mobile Seamless Learning (MSL) to define a perspective in which "a learner can learn in a variety of scenarios" and in which "they can switch from one scenario or context (such as formal and informal learning, personal and social learning etc.) to another easily and quickly" (Wong, 2012, p. E19). That approach privileges the subject's contextualized action through different scenarios, integrating different types of learning in an active way, and not only passively receiving contents: "Mediated by technology, a seamless learner should be able to explore, identify and seize boundless latent opportunities that her daily living spaces may offer to her, rather than always being inhibited by externally defined learning goals and resources" (Wong, 2012, p. E19).

In this context, learning mediation is not carried out only by a teacher or instructor. It is possible to have a multiple pedagogic mediation (Okada & Okada, 2007). Individual learning can be supported by social networking in interactive virtual environments that enhance the exchange of information and share experiences with several people. Teaching is no longer centred in the teacher's role, but in the students, who can assist each other and directly interact with teachers or instructors. All individuals involved can lean on each other and learn together.

A Pedagogical Approach Proposal for M-Learning

M-learning can be related to the development of methodologies and practices that contribute to individualized learning but that also can promote cooperation and collaboration among engaged students. Both possibilities originate from an epistemological conception of the teacher and the institution, in other words, from how it is believed that a subject learns, in consonance with an analysis of the possibilities presented by different technologies and the objectives of each course.

Because m-learning is such a fresh concept, it still lacks research and, consequently, methodologies and pedagogic practices specifically developed for it. Taking current studies on human learning as reference, more specifically in regard to education theories, and seeking to apply them to m-learning, an interactionist-constructivist-systemic approach is proposed as a way to contemplate competence and interdisciplinary development.

Among the general characteristics of this approach, it is possible to mention mobility (physical, technological, conceptual, social/interactional and temporal) to access information, communicate, produce and display available knowledge, as much individually as collaboratively and cooperatively, by means of mobile devices and wireless networks. Considering the ubiquitous technologies that make context sensibility possible, it is feasible to supply information in a dynamic and autonomous way about the subject's situation and surrounding background, contributing to the subject's learning in the real world.

Students are seen, in this approach, as autonomous authors, agents of their own learning processes, possessing previous knowledge, as researchers, enabling them to be participative and collaborative. A teacher, instructor or facilitator, on his turn, exercises an accomplice's role, as explorer, investigator, arbiter and problem creator, besides guiding and aiding students in articulating information in order to produce knowledge and to establish relationships between the feedback of their actions and their objectives.

In m-learning, information is present in any time and space, as much in synchronous as in asynchronous ways, depending on the subjects' learning needs. Students can access or capture data wherever they are, transform it in information and publish it in the Internet at a very fast pace, or even cross that information with other knowledge databases to produce new insights. Subjects may also receive information more suitable to their momentary needs and in accordance with the conditions they find themselves in, via objects or devices that have environmental sensors and location mechanisms, that verify the subject's location and supply information (Huang, Yang, & Liaw, 2012).

Learning takes place in a mobility context, located in a real environment, and it is centred in the subject's needs, having as a starting point one's action and interaction with the physical, social and digital mediums, guided by one's perception of the surrounding ambient, exploration and experimentation, engaging in approaches and estrangements when necessary to achieve significance. Since it is autonomous, it allows students to find their own sources and strategies in order to enlarge their individual and group knowledge, providing an adaptable solution.

In such a learning approach, the development of competencies (OECD, 2005) is enhanced, becoming more effective due to contextual learning. Follow up and evaluation of learning need to be continuous and formative. It involves diagnosis, observation and the constant tracking of interactions of subjects' development, individually and in small groups, respecting their personal rhythms and learning needs. Given this approach, evaluation aims to reorient, giving directions to help subjects to overcome perceived difficulties and enhance their development. Evaluation of learning itself can be accomplished via initial or diagnostic evaluation, prognostic evaluation, formative evaluation, systematizing evaluation, self-evaluation and summative evaluation, which involves the teacher, classmates and the student being evaluated.

It is appropriate to emphasize that the success of an educational proposal for m-learning is directly related to the understanding of how the learning process takes place, the identification of the potential applications of the selected technology, the recognition of the learning context and the knowledge and fluency of the teachers in applying technology. It is from this reality that methodological choices and pedagogic practices to be adopted should appear. Although the technologies making m-learning possible evolve quickly, the same cannot be said regarding didactic-pedagogic issues such as those discussed here. However, these issues constitute a very important aspect, given that the main objectives are learning and the students' active engagement in the process.

MOBILE LEARNING: CONSEQUENCES AND CHALLENGES

When choosing m-learning as an educational modality, it is necessary to consider, initially:

- institutional culture;
- details of the area of knowledge where it shall be applied;
- previously developed m-learning experiences, as well as their results;
- characteristics of the public for whom the methodology is designed, including their familiarity with digital technologies;
- available digital technologies and applications.

This collection of information will be used to define methodologies, practices and pedagogic mediation processes, as well as follow-up forms and evaluation of learning, thus composing a pedagogic project for m-learning.

M-learning results will depend, largely, on the importance and articulation of these key pieces of information. Consequences of using m-learning can be unfolded in three types:

- epistemological and pedagogic issues;
- technological and economical issues;
- contextual and social issues.

Epistemological and Pedagogical issues

The several information and communication technologies available for m-learning today were not designed considering epistemological and pedagogical issues. They were developed and diffused before they were actually used in teaching and learning processes.

Thus, m-learning practices, as well as other practices that employ the use of different digital technologies, run the risk of having a fundamentally technological focus, without previously considering epistemological and pedagogic issues. So, it is necessary to be careful with the "charming" aspect of technology itself because that could compromise m-learning's efficiency and effectiveness.

The use of a new technology in teaching and learning processes does not guarantee educational innovation. It is necessary to link the use of new technologies to methodologies, practices and pedagogic mediation processes designed with the understanding of the nature and specific learning applications of those technologies, as previously discussed.

It is vital, for instance, to verify when and how m-learning is in fact the most appropriate educational modality, presenting superior results when confronted with other learning forms (for instance, face-to-face "traditional" teaching, or even "fixed" e-learning). For this same reason, it is essential that the use of new technologies promotes collaborative learning, fundamental to human development, because the use of mobile technologies (carried and used by each individual) does not replace the need for human contact, nor the sharing of ideas, experiences and different points of view.

We know that, in many contexts, distance education (in a general way) and e-learning are still seen with prejudice, distrust and safeguards (Dlouhá, Macháčková-Henderson, & Dlouhý, 2012). The same may happen to m-learning, which also makes learning possible without the constraints of proximity or physical presence. It is critical to develop and test new methodologies, practices and pedagogical mediation forms that utilize these new technologies. It is also important to ensure that professionals are qualified to utilize these new technologies in educating students.

For instance, in many institutions the use of cell phones is restricted due to social conventions. This policy needs to be rethought if this device is to be used for educational purposes. On the other hand, it is known that the probability that students will get distracted and interrupted by the use of mobile technologies is very high, and that needs to be managed.

Technological and Economic Issues

As seen, a vast range of technologies can be used for m-learning practices. Technological choices should be linked to the epistemological conceptions underpinning m-learning activities. It is important to understand how learning occurs and debate pedagogical issues such as methodologies, practices and mediation processes. For instance, if a constructivist, interactive approach is adopted, technologies that allow access to virtual environments where there is intensive interaction (through forums, chats, spaces for sharing of projects etc.) should be chosen. That will require devices with interface, memory and processing capacity adapted to the use of those tools, as well as bandwidth and network availability to support an intensive exchange of messages and content.

Technological choices should still be subordinated to accessibility and technology adaptation issues, as well as to economic criteria (costs and benefits). For instance, in underdeveloped or in-development countries, the cost of cellular telephony services is high (e.g. access to data), and Internet connections are not always available or reliable (Beckmann, 2010; Saccol et al., 2011). Local wireless networks are still unavailable in most places (in some places they can also have a high access cost) and can present some instability.

Another technological challenge is overcoming interface limitations regarding mobile devices. Due to the reduced screen and keyboard size of many mobile phones, it is usually difficult to read or create texts in such devices. Even learning objects based on animations and sounds need to be well adapted for mobile interfaces (Churchill & Hedberg, 2008). These devices were not specifically designed for educational activities. For that reason, when employed with educational purposes, their use must be well planned. It becomes necessary to build up resources using other friendlier medias or develop new more efficient interfaces (such as accurate voice recognition).

The degree of obsolescence of mobile devices is also high. Frequently, when a user begins to really dominate the use of a device (like a smartphone) it is exchanged for a more advanced model that demands a new learning curve (Kukulska-Hulme, 2007). That high obsolescence also generates a high cost to access the most advanced technology. It is also essential to observe maintenance costs and assess risks of loss, robbery or destruction of mobile devices. Since they are portable, they present more challenges.

Contextual and Social Issues

Taking the context surrounding learners into consideration is essential for m-learning practices, as already discussed. Besides having access to computational resources, some minimal physical conditions are necessary for the comfort of the student, for instance to sit down or find a surface in order to write or read; to have low levels of environmental noise and appropriate lighting conditions so screen visibility will not be compromised etc. Without minimal comfort conditions, learning can be impaired.

As for social context, it is important to be attentive to what is deemed adequate or not in the use of mobile and wireless technologies, depending on place or event where the student is interacting. This involves social rules of conduct and etiquette. For instance, a voice chat may offer a friendlier interface than text insertion in a miniaturized mobile device; however, depending on place or event, the use of this particular resource can be regarded as offensive and disrespectful. In the same way, interruptions caused by messages or calls originated from a teacher, instructor or other students can disturb and generate overload for the student that receives them. They can also cause embarrassment or disturb other important personal interactions.

In that sense, a fundamental issue is the possible invasion of privacy due to m-learning practices, which can blur the boundaries between work and personal life or formal education schedules and leisure time, for example. The flexibility found by the breaching of these borders needs to be counterbalanced by preserving the student's quality of life, which is a condition for the quality of the learning itself. Permanent accessibility and traceability can generate anxiety and an increased sense of urgency, generating overload and stress. Those issues need to be well contemplated when planning activities involving m-learning.

Studies as Kazlauskas and Robinson's (2012) demonstrate that people who concomitantly study in higher education institutions and have a full-time job usually have little time to access didactic resources via m-learning, such as podcasts with notes from a class in a MP3 device. Some people also prefer to use their MP3 devices only to access music content, not being used to accessing didactic materials, thus keeping the distinction between study and leisure time.

Another important social issue is digital inclusion. In underdeveloped or in-development countries, where cell phones have a superior degree of diffusion than personal computers among less favoured classes, a great opportunity is at hand to use that technology for educational purposes (Grönlund & Islam, 2010; Saccol et al., 2011). However, as already discussed, it involves a series of other economic and technological issues that need to be analysed. There is also need to develop competencies not only for the use of mobile and wireless technologies for learning, but also for other practices that are requirements for m-learning, as, for instance, knowledge and mastering of personal computation in a general way, reading abilities, interpretation and generation of content, researching, autonomy to learn in a continuous, collaborative form, authorship etc.

Table 1 proposes a series of benefits and limitations that need to be considered regarding the consequences of m-learning practices. As technology matures, probably becoming more accessible in terms of cost, with greater stability and friendlier interfaces, pedagogical practices related to m-learning should also mature, allowing new possibilities and opportunities.

Table 1.   Benefits and Limitations of M-Learning.

Benefits	Limitations
• Flexibility (learning anywhere/anytime)	• Learning activities duration and learning content accessed can be limited
• Situational learning (on field, at work etc.), stimulates exploration of different environments and resources and gives flexibility for learners	• Ergonomic barriers may limit the use of certain resources (e.g. text data entry)
• Student centred, personalized learning. It can stimulate individual autonomy	• Care should be taken to allow interaction and cooperation with other learners and educators, instructors, teachers etc., avoiding individual isolation
• Speedy access to information and interaction in real time, anywhere	• Quick and superficial interactions can impair complex learning processes and activities that demand intensive cooperation and reflection
• Use of "downtimes" for educational activities	• The student's attention can be displaced due to other activities or parallel environmental stimuli (e.g. noise, interruptions, other interactions etc.)
• Use of popular technologies (e.g. cell phone) as educational tools	• Mobile and wireless technologies are not yet mature, can present instability (e.g. wireless networks) and have fast obsolescence
• Attractiveness: exploration of new technologies and innovative practices	• There can be an excessive focus in technology (technocentrism) in detriment of real learning objectives
	• It is necessary for students and teachers (or instructors) to have good technological skills and also know how to use mobile technologies
• M-learning can allow educational activities in different social classes and geographical areas	• Connection costs can be high, and could be unavailable for certain individuals (e.g. poor, isolated communities)
	• Ergonomic limitations of mobile devices can be particularly impairing for users with special needs
• M-learning can be used to complement other forms of teaching (face-to-face, e-learning), enriching them	• A careful planning of each learning modality is needed, in order to not generate redundancy or information overload
• M-learning can provide learning opportunities to professionals or people who are on the move	• It is necessary that mobile professionals have the necessary contextual conditions (physical, temporal etc.) to learn in an effective way through m-learning

As Table 1 indicates, m-learning is not a panacea for all education goals. It brings a series of possibilities, but it also has limitations. Therefore, it is an educational modality that depends on

- the urgency of learning;
- The degree of students' mobility;
- how much learning is conditioned to the context where the student is (for instance, during fieldwork, in a museum, in an archeological site etc.);
- the availability of other educational modalities. For instance, in the case of mobile workers (salespersons, technicians, consultants etc.), every hour spent off the field incurs in income loss for the company and for the professional (if he is commissioned). In those cases, m-learning can allow training and instruction processes that would not happen in other ways (or that would incur additional business losses).
- *time availability*: the student can learn wherever and whenever he/she wants (lying on a bed, in a green area etc.), but he/she must find the time for that during a protentially busy daily schedule.

Considering all the different benefits and limitations of m-learning, one can also perceive that mobile technologies allow for many changes on how people see and interact with the world, each other and a plethora of contents. Those changes will be intensified as technologies become "smarter," more efficient and friendly, at the same time that users and students learn to dominate them and use their full potential.

Students are also demanding (and will probably demand even more) personalized learning forms that allow co-creation of value, where students and teachers or instructors will collaborate in different ways. As students have access to information in real time anywhere or anytime and have access to tools to create their own contents and register and complement their learning with greater autonomy, they can at the same time be connected and collaborate with classmates or other people that may even be out of their formal education circles. The "distance" between those that learn and those that teach will be reduced, demanding a reorganization of functions and roles.

Changes should happen even to physical infrastructures of teaching institutions. In the future, for instance, it will not make sense for an institution to offer a computer laboratory (Dede, 2005). Technology will be everywhere, and that will affect the conception we currently hold of what constitutes teaching or learning space and how it should be structured. Technical support for users of mobile devices, particularly those who move about and study at the most varied places, is also a new challenge in technical and pedagogic terms. In conclusion, formal educational spaces will not disappear, but they will change.

FINAL REMARKS

In summary, it is important to remember that, when proposing formative processes and training via m-learning, it is necessary to prioritize the didactic-pedagogic aspect to have in mind the different characteristics and aspects linked to each form of m-learning and to understand the different learning contexts where it can be utilized. It is essential to consider the goals of using mobile technologies and evaluate the possible impacts of the physical mobility of the subjects, as well as issues related to time and space. Ways must be found to adapt the learning experience to the subjects' context, enhancing their participation and, consequently, their acceptance of this new educational modality. "Time" also needs to be considered, since m-learning not only provides access to the contents anywhere but also at any moment. Students should have the required time to engage and adequately concentrate in m-learning activities, having access to comfortable learning environments where reading, studying, interacting and learning can take place.

Another aspect that needs to be considered is the offer of learning solutions customized to specific needs of certain subjects or groups, designed in a way to best serve different learning contexts. Given that, until now, there are no specific theories about m-learning and its uses, it is necessary to adapt existent pedagogical theories in relation to the technological choices to be made.

Digital technologies, by themselves, including mobile, ubiquitous and wireless technologies, do not change education. However, the way they are employed can have deep impact on how students learn. As individuals adopt and include different digital technologies in their daily lives, they re-invent (Rogers, 2003) the innovations to fit their needs and uses. These new applications can include the employment of mobile technologies in learning environments, with learning purposes, in a plethora of different ways.

New practices and manners to employ m-learning are being shaped right now. As Kukulska-Hulme (2010, p. 11) states: "Increasingly, learners will use mobility and awareness of their immediate context as starting points for keeping social contact alive (who is nearby?), accessing fresh content (what resources are available here?), getting local information (what's interesting here?) and becoming visible as creators and producers of content (what can I contribute?)."

However, the effective use of m-learning depends mainly on what it means for their users. Individuals and communities must define how deeply new technologies should be incorporated into their learning habits, and how. Therefore, it is necessary to always keep a critical and attentive assessment about the meanings and uses that these new learning technologies can have in each particular setting, seeking to better understand their potential and benefits, as well as their possible limitations.

NOTES

1. Source: http://www.bbc.co.uk/news/10569081
2. A simple search for articles and patents in Google Scholar with the keywords m-learning OR "mobile learning" between 1999 until 2009 shows 15,600 results in 11 years of research, whereas the same search between 2010 and 2012 shows 15,300 results over a span of 3 years only.

REFERENCES

Agarwal, R., & Prasad, J. (1999). Are individual differences germane to the acceptance of new information technologies? *Decision Sciences, 30*(2), 361–391.
Ajzen, I. (1991). The theory of planned behaviour. *Organizational Behaviour and Human Decision Processes, 50*(2), 179–211.
Ardito, C., Buono, P., Costabile, M. F., Lanzilotti, R., Pederson, T., & Piccinno, A. (2008). Experiencing the past through the senses: An m-learning game at archaeological parks. *IEEE Multimedia, 15*(4), 16–88.
Balachandran, A., Voelker, G., & Bahl, P. (2003). Wireless hotspots: Current challenges and future directions. In P. Kermani (Ed.) *Proceedings for WMASH'03.* 19 September, San Diego, CA, USA. Retrieved from http://research.microsoft.com/~bahl/Papers/Pdf/monet05.pdf. Accessed on 24 January 2012.
Bandura, A. (1977). Self-efficacy: Toward a unifying theory of behavioral change. *Psychological Review, 84,* 191–215.
Beckmann, E. (2010). Learners on the move: Mobile modalities in development studies. *Distance Education, 31*(2), 159–173.
BJET. (2011). Editorial: Trends in learning technologies. *British Journal of Educational Technology, 42*(6), 885–888.
Bouwman, H., Carlsson, C., & Walden, P. (2008). Trends in mobile services in Finland 2004–2006: From ringtones to mobile Internet. *Info, 10*(2), 75–93.
Brown, D. J., McHugh, D., Standen, P., Evett, L., Shopland, N., & Battersby, S. (2011). Designing location-based learning experiences for people with intellectual disabilities and additional sensory impairments. *Computers & Education, 56*(1), 11–20.

Brown, J., & Metcalf, D. (2008). *Mobile learning update*. Saratoga Springs, NY: The MASIE Center & The Leaning Consortium. Retrieved from http://masiecontent.s3.amazonaws. com/content/masie/pdf/MobileLearningUpdate.pdf. Accessed on 27 July 2010.

Caudill, J. (2007). The growth of m-learning and the growth of mobile computing: Parallel developments. *International Review of Research in Open and Distance Learning*, *8*(2).

Chan, T. W., Roschelle, J., Hsi, S., Kinshuk, K., Sharples, M., & Brown, T. (2006). One-to-one technology-enhanced learning: An opportunity for global research collaboration. *Research and Practice in Technology-Enhanced Learning*, *1*(1), 3–29.

Chen, H., & Huang, H. (2010). User acceptance of mobile knowledge management learning system: Design and analysis. *Educational Technology & Society*, *13*(3), 70–77.

Chu, H., Hwang, G., Tsai, C., & Tseng, J. (2010). A two-tier test approach to developing location-aware mobile learning systems for natural science courses. *Computers & Education*, *55*(4), 1618–1627.

Churchill, D., & Hedberg, J. (2008). Learning object design considerations for small-screen handheld devices. *Computers & Education*, *50*(3), 881–893.

Compeau, D. R., & Higgings, C. A. (1995). Computer self-efficacy: Development of a measure and initial test. *MIS Quarterly*, *19*(2), 189–211.

Conole, G., de Laat, M., Dillon, T., & Darby, J. (2008). Disruptive technologies', 'pedagogical innovation': What's new? Findings from an in-depth study of students' use and perception of technology. *Computers & Education*, *50*(2), 511–524.

Corbeil, J. R., & Valdes-Corbeil, M. E. (2007). Are you ready for mobile learning? *Educause Quarterly*, *30*(2), 51–58.

Csíkszentmihályi, M. (1990). *Flow: The psychology of optimal experience*. New York, NY: Harper & Row.

Csíkszentmihályi, M., & Csíkszentmihályi, I. S. (1988). *Optimal experience: Psychological studies of flow in consciousness*. Cambridge, UK: Cambridge University Press.

Davis, F. D., Bagozzi, R. P., & Warshaw, P. R. (1989). User acceptance of computer technology: A comparison of two theoretical models. *Management Science*, *35*(8), 982–1002.

Dede, C. (2005). Planning for neomillennial lerning styles. *Educause Quarterly 1*. Retrieved from http://www.educause.edu/EDUCAUSE + Quarterly/EDUCAUSEQuarterlyMaga-zineVolum/PlanningforNeomillennialLearni/157325. Accessed on 19 April 2012.

De-Marcos, L., Hilera, J., Barchino, R., Jiménez, L., Martínez, J., Gutiérrez, J., ... Otón, S. (2010). An experiment for improving students' performance in secondary and tertiary education by means of m-learning auto-assessment. *Computers & Education*, *55*(3), 1069–1079.

Dlouhá, J., Macháčková-Henderson, L., & Dlouhý, J. (2012) Learning networks with involvement of higher education institutions. *Journal of Cleaner Production*. Advanced online publication. Retrieved from http://www.sciencedirect.com/science/article/pii/S0959652612003034in3rd. Accessed on 3 July 2012.

El-Hussein, M. O. M., & Cronje, J. C. (2010). Defining mobile learning in the higher education landscape. *Educational Technology & Society*, *13*(3), 12–21.

Evans, C. (2008). The effectiveness of m-learning in the form of podcast revision lectures in higher education. *Computers & Education*, *50*(2), 491–498.

Figueiredo, A. D. (2005). Learning contexts: A blueprint for research. *Interactive Educational Multimedia* (11), 127–139.

Figueiredo, A. D., & Afonso, A. P. (2005). Context and learning: A philosophical framework. In A. D. Figueiredo & A. P. Afonso (Eds.), *Managing learning in virtual settings: The role of context* (pp. 1–23). Hershey, PA: Information Science Publishing.

Gedik, N., Hanci-Karademirci, A., Kursun, E., & Cagiltay, K. (2012). Key instructional design issues in a cellular phone-based mobile learning project. *Computers & Education, 58*(4), 1149–1159.

Goh, T., Seet, B., & Chen, N. (2011). The impact of persuasive SMS on students' self-regulated learning. *British Journal of Educational Technology, 43*, 624–640. doi: 10.1111/j.1467-8535.2011.01236.x.

Grönlund, Å., & Islam, Y. M. (2010). A mobile e-learning environment for developing countries: The Bangladesh virtual interactive classroom. *Information Technology for Development, 16*(4), 244–259.

Harris, H., & Park, S. (2008). Educational usages of podcastint. *British Journal of Educational Technology, 39*(3), 548–551.

Hayati, A., Jalilifar, A., & Mashhadi, A. (2012). Using short message service (SMS) to teach English idioms to EFL students. *British Journal of Educational Technology*. doi: 10.1111/j.1467-8535.2011.01260.x.

Hsu, Y., Rice, K., & Dawley, L. (2012). Empowering educators with Google's Android App Inventor: An online workshop in mobile app design. *British Journal of Educational Technology, 43*(1), E1–E5.

Huang, Y., Jeng, Y., & Huang, T. (2009). An educational mobile blogging system for supporting collaborative learning. *Educational Technology & Society, 12*(2), 163–175.

Huang, J., Lin, Y., & Chuang, S. (2007). Elucidating user behavior of mobile learning: A perspective of the extended technology acceptance model. *Electronic Library, 25*(5), 586–599.

Huang, A., Yang, S., & Liaw, S. (2012). A study of user's acceptance on situational mashups in situational language teaching. *British Journal of Educational Technology, 43*(1), 52–61.

Hwang, G., & Chang, H. (2011). A formative assessment-based mobile learning approach to improving the learning attitudes and achievements of students. *Computers & Education, 56*(4), 1023–1031.

Hwang, G., & Tsai, C. (2011). Research trends in mobile and ubiquitous learning: A review of publications in selected journals from 2001 to 2010. *British Journal of Educational Technology, 42*(4), E65–E70.

Hwang, G., Wu, C., Tseng, J., & Huang, I. (2011). Development of a ubiquitous learning platform based on a real-time help-seeking mechanism. *British Journal of Educational Technology, 42*(6), 992–1002.

Jeng, Y., Wu, T., Huang, Y., Tan, Q., & Yang, S. (2010). The add-on impact of mobile applications in learning strategies: A review study. *Educational Technology & Society, 13*(3), 3–11.

Johnson, L., Levine, A., & Smith, R. (2008). *The 2008 horizon report*. Austin, TX: New Media Consortium. Retrieved from http://www.nmc.org/pdf/2008-Horizon-Report.pdf. Accessed on 24 January 2012.

Johnson, L., Smith, R., Willis, H., Levine, A., & Haywood, K. (2011). *The 2011 horizon report*. Austin, TX: The New Media Consortium.

Kazlauskas, A., & Robinson, K. (2012). Podcasts are not for everyone. *British Journal of Educational Technology, 43*(2), 321–330.

Kukulska-Hulme, A. (2007). Mobile usability in educational contexts: What have we learnt? *International Review of Research in Open and Distance Learning, 8*(2).

Kukulska-Hulme, A. (2010). Learning cultures on the move: Where are we heading? *Educational Technology & Society, 13*, 4–14.

Kukulska-Hulme, A., Sharples, M., Milrad, M., Arnedillo-Sanchez, I., & Vavoula, G. (2011). The genesis and development of mobile learning in Europe. In D. Parsons (Ed.), *Combining e-learning and m-learning: New applications of blended educational resources* (pp. 151–177). Hershey, PA: IGI Global.

Liu, T., & Chu, Y. (2010). Using ubiquitous games in an English listening and speaking course: Impact on learning outcomes and motivation. *Computers & Education, 55*(2), 630–643.

Liu, Y., Li, H., & Carlsson, C. (2010). Factors driving the adoption of m-learning: An empirical study. *Computers & Education, 55*(3), 1211–1219.

Liu, S. H., Liao, H. L., & Pratt, J. A. (2009). Impact of media richness and flow on e-learning technology acceptance. *Computer & Education, 53*(3), 599–607.

Liu, Y., Han, S., & Li, H. (2010). Understanding the factors driving m-learning adoption: A literature review. *Campus-Wide Information Systems, 27*(4), 210–226.

Lu, Y. B., Zhou, T., & Wang, B. (2009). Exploring Chinese users' acceptance of instant messaging using the theory of planned behavior, the technology acceptance model, and the flow theory. *Computers in Human Behavior, 25*(1), 29–39.

Lyytinen, K., & Yoo, Y. (2002). The next wave of nomadic computing. *Information Systems Research, 13*(4), 377–388.

Macdonald, I., Columbia, B., & Chiu, J. (2011). Evaluating the viability of mobile learning to enhance management training. *Canadian Journal of Learning & Technology, 37*(1), 1–12.

Mallat, N., Rossi, M., Tuunainen, V. K., & Oorni, A. (2008). An empirical investigation of mobile ticketing service adoption in public transportation. *Personal and Ubiquitous Computing, 12*(1), 57–65.

Markett, C., Sanchez, I. A., Weber, S., & Tangney, B. (2006). Using short message service to encourage interactivity in the classroom. *Computer & Education, 46*(3), 280–293.

Martin-Dorta, N., Saorin, J. L., & Contero, M. (2011). Web-based spatial training using handheld touch screen devices. *Educational Technology & Society, 14*(3), 163–177.

Maturana, H. R. (1993). Reflexiones: Aprendizaje o deriva ontogénica. In M. R. Maturana (Ed.), *Desde la biologia a psicologia. Santiago de Chile: Editorial Mitech Ltda. Ediciones Synthesis.*

Mellow, P. (2005). The media generation: Maximize learning by getting mobile. In *Proceedings for ASCILITE 2005 conference: Balance, fidelity, mobility: Maintaining the momentum?* 4–7 December, Brisbane, Australia. Retrieved from http://www.ascilite.org.au/conferences/brisbane05/blogs/proceedings/53_Mellow.pdf. Accessed on 24 January 2012.

Moore, G., & Benbasat, I. (1991). Development of an instrument to measure the perceptions of adopting an information technology innovation. *Information Systems Research, 2*, 192–222.

Motiwalla, L. (2007). Mobile learning: A framework and evaluation. *Computers & Education, 49*(3), 581–596.

Muyinda, P. (2007). MLearning: Pedagogical, technical and organizational hypes and realities. *Campus-Wide Information Systems, 24*(2), 97–104.

OECD. (2005). *The definition and selection of key competencies (DeSeCo).* Retrieved from http://www.oecd.org/edu/statistics/deseco. Accessed on 27 July 2010.

Okada, A., & Okada, S. (2007). *Novos paradigmas na educação online com a aprendizagem aberta. V Conferência Internacional de Tecnologias de Informação e Comunicação na Educação*Braga: Universidade do Minho.

Peters, K. (2005, November). *Learning on the move: Mobile technologies in business and education.* Canberra: Commonwealth of Australia. Retrieved from http://pre2005.flexiblelearning. net.au/projects/resources/2005/Learning%20on%20the%20move_final.pdf. Accessed on 19 September 2010.

Piaget, J. (1972). *Development and learning.* New York, NY: Hartcourt Brace Janovich.

Pituch, K. A., & Lee, Y. (2006). The influence of system characteristics on e-learning use. *Computer & Education, 47*(2), 222–244.

Pozzi, F. (2007). In C. Stephanidis (Ed.), *The impact of m-learning in school contexts: An 'inclusive' perspective.* Berlin: Springer-Verlag.

Prensky, M. (2001). Digital natives, digital immigrants, Part 1. *On the Horizon, 9*(5), 1–6.

Rheingold, H. (2002). *Smart mobs: The next social revolution.* Cambridge, MA: Perseus.

Rogers, E. (2003). *Diffusion of innovations* (5th ed.). New York, NY: Free Press.

Saccol, A., Barbosa, J., Schlemmer, E., & Reinhard, N. (2011). Mobile learning in organizations: Lessons learned from two case studies. *International Journal of Information and Communication Technology Education, 7,* 11–24.

Sharples, M. (2000). The design of personal mobile technologies for lifelong learning. *Computers & Education, 34,* 77–193.

Sharples, M., Milrad, M., Arnedillo Sánchez, I., & Vavoula, G. (2009). Mobile learning: Small devices, big issues. In N. Balacheff, S. Ludvigsen, T. de Jong, A. Lazonder & S. Barnes (Eds.), *Technology enhanced learning: Principles and products* (pp. 233–250). Heidelberg: Springer.

Sharples, M., Taylor, J., & Vavoula, G. (2007). A theory of learning for the mobile age. In R. Andrews & C. Haythornthwaite (Eds.), *The Sage handbook of elearning research* (pp. 221–247). London: Sage.

Sherry, J., & Salvador, T. (2002). Running and grimacing: The struggle for balance in mobile work. In B. Brown, N. Green & R. Harper (Eds.), *Wireless world: Social and interactional aspects of mobile age* (pp. 108–120). London: Springer-Verlag.

Sørensen, C., Al-Taitoon, A., Kietzmann, J., Pica, D., Wiredu, G., Elaluf-Calderwood, S., & Gibson, D. (2008). Exploring enterprise mobility: Lessons from the field. *Information Knowledge Systems Management, 7*(1–2), 243–271.

Teo, T., & Noyes, J. (2011). An assessment of the influence of perceived enjoyment and attitude on the intention to use technology among pre-service teachers: A structural equation modeling approach. *Computers & Education, 57*(2), 1645–1653.

Traxler, J. (2009). The evolution of mobile learning. In R. Guy (Ed.), *The evolution of mobile teaching and learning* (pp. 103–118). Santa Rosa: Informing Science Press.

Vavoula, G., Sharples, M., Rudman, P., Meek, J., & Lonsdale, P. (2009). Myartspace: Design and evaluation of support for learning with multimedia phones between classrooms and museums. *Computers & Education, 5*(2), 286–299.

Veen, W., & Vrakking, B. (2008). *Homo zappiens: Educando na era digital.* Porto Alegre: Artmed.

Venkatesh, V., Morris, M. G., Davis, G. B., & Davis, F. D. (2003). User acceptance of information technology: Toward a unified view. *MIS Quarterly, 27*(3), 425–478.

Wagner, E. (2005). Enabling mobile learning. *EDUCAUSE Review, 40*(3), 40–53.

Westera, W. (2011). On the changing nature of learning context: Anticipating the virtual extensions of the world. *Educational Technology & Society, 14*(2), 201–212.

Winters, N. (2007). What is mobile learning. In M. Sharples (Ed.), *Big issues in mobile learning. Report.* University of Nottingham. Retrieved from http://www.lsri.nottingham.ac.uk/

Publications_PDFs/BIG_ISSUES_REPORT_PUBLISHED.pdf. Accessed on 27 July 2010.

Wishart, J., & Triggs, P. (2010). Museum scouts: Exploring how schools, museums and interactive technologies can work together to support learning. *Computers & Education*, *54*(3), 669–678.

Wong, L. (2012). A learner-centric view of mobile seamless learning. *British Journal of Educational Technology*, *43*(1), E19.

Wong, L. H., & Looi, C. K. (2011). What seams do we remove in mobile-assisted seamless learning? A critical review of the literature. *Computers & Education*, *57*(4), 2364–2381.

BRINGING IT ALL TOGETHER: INTERDISCIPLINARY PERSPECTIVES ON INCORPORATING MOBILE TECHNOLOGIES IN HIGHER EDUCATION

Christina M. Partin and Skyler Lauderdale

ABSTRACT

In this chapter, we offer a thorough research compendium that bridges together theories and perspectives from various disciplines including adult and higher education, psychology and social psychology, sociology, and women's and gender studies in order to help instructors think about ways to expand on existing activities by incorporating mobile technologies in the learning process. Based on this review of literature, we discuss the importance of motivation, participation, community, voice, and learning in higher education and offer our Interdisciplinary Model for Student-Centered Classrooms *as a guide for helping instructors who want to use mobile technologies in their own classes. In the second half of the chapter, we discuss suggestions for achieving this model through the use of mobile*

Increasing Student Engagement and Retention using Mobile Applications:
Smartphones, Skype and Texting Technologies
Cutting-edge Technologies in Higher Education, Volume 6D, 83–114
ISSN: 2044-9968/doi:10.1108/S2044-9968(2013)000006D006

technologies, provide several opportunities for critical reflection of this model through problem-based scenarios to stimulate applications of our model, and consider the process of infusing mobile technologies into current pedagogical techniques. Overall, this chapter provides a theoretical basis and mandate for further research and implementation of mobile technologies as useful pedagogical tools in higher education capable of increasing student retention, engagement, and positive learning outcomes in higher education.

INTRODUCTION

The use of electronic devices during class meetings is not allowed. Cell phones must be silenced, laptops must be put away, and all other electronic devices (iPads, mp3 players, etc.) are not allowed. The use of these devices is distracting to me and other students. Students in violation of this policy will be dismissed from class unless special accommodations have been requested.

How often have you seen statements similar to the one above included in syllabi – perhaps you include one in your own courses? In the higher education classroom, these commonly restricted technologies are considered bothersome at best or downright disrespectful and distracting at worst (Burns & Lohenry, 2010). Still, in our constantly evolving and increasingly technologized world of iPhones, Blackberrys, iPads, and future unknown technologies, mobile Internet browsing and social networking capabilities have forever changed the way that people connect and learn about each other and their worlds.

Critics worry that allowing students to bring in mobile electronic devices leads to untimely distraction from students' learning outcomes. We use a multidisciplinary framework to argue in this chapter that the benefits from their structured and guided use outweigh any possible adverse effects and that numerous possibilities for increasing learner engagement and improving learning outcomes ensue. These devices feature high computing power, large displays, robust graphics, capable digital cameras, location-based services, and high-speed Internet access – to name a few – which we see as particularly useful for students' learning.

Outside of the classroom, our students have access to a great wealth of information and technology to increase productivity and assist in daily living. In addition to these changes in the daily lives of individuals, there have also been changes to the way we perceive higher education and the processes of learning in general. For instance, there has been a shift in perception about the implementation of curriculum in higher education away from a banking model of education (Friere, 1970). This model embraces a top-down approach to teaching and learning where the instructor is the sole authority and the students are passive recipients of knowledge. While some instructors continue to embrace this method, many others are moving toward a student-centered environment that encourages critical thinking and active inquiry over memorization and routinization (Fink, 2003).

Education researchers are beginning to realize that simply providing students with facts is not preparing them to enter the post-industrial workforce (King, 2003). Many instructor-led (Stockwell, 2010) or institutionally based (Parchoma, 2008) initiatives demonstrate the onset of a shift in attitudes about technology in higher education. We assert, based on this literature, that educators and institutions of higher education should continually search for fruitful ways to incorporate existing and emerging innovations such as mobile technologies in their pedagogical strategies to increase learner engagement. We see incorporation of mobile technologies as particularly relevant given the unfolding trend of young people using their mobile devices in increasingly sophisticated ways and in many aspects of their personal lives (Carter, Thacher, Applefield, & Mcalpine, 2011).

Prior research indicates that the introduction of multimedia is one method of encouraging a student culture of active learning (Mayer, 2008), which we discuss in more depth in our literature review. For instance, research on "clickers" indicates that the introduction of these devices into the classroom is a useful pedagogical practice for engaging students in the learning processes (Mollburn & Hoekstra, 2010). However, these single-use devices are often expensive or even cost prohibitive. We recognize the potential that clickers have for classroom participation but instead focus on seeking transferable technologies with applications to real-world settings outside of the classroom.

In addition to building skills inside the classroom, understanding ways to use mobile technologies for educational purposes gives students a skill for seeking out information and an increased comfort level with emergent technologies for cogent participation in a learning society (Edwards, 1997) – a trait important to the process of lifelong learning (Candy, 1991; Tough, 1971). By examining research from diverse bodies of literature and our own exploratory action-based research, it has become clear to us that students enjoy incorporating mobile devices into classroom activities, and learning outcomes are increased as a result (Lauderdale & Partin, 2012; Partin & Lauderdale, 2011).

This theoretically based chapter connects literature across disciplines in order to promote student engagement, retention, and learning through the introduction of mobile technologies. To that end, we provide a rationale and introduce our *Interdisciplinary Model for Student-Centered Classrooms*. Acknowledging the continual changes in society due in part to transformative implications of technological innovation for students in and out of the classroom, our work empowers educators and serves as a mandate for continuous evaluation and purposive inclusion of new technologies in higher education.

We thought it helpful to end our introduction with the parameters of this chapter. We consciously and purposefully use the term "mobile technology" in a vague manner. Since we hope to foster readers' creativity to envision the use of any variety of emerging or future technologies, we felt that limiting our discussion to any specific technology denies the reader the opportunity to consider ways to effectively incorporate technology to their pedagogical strategies. Further, we recognize that technology may generate or perpetuate new or existing classroom challenges. As such, we do not recommend replacing or eliminating the traditional classroom, rather we see the inclusion of technology as a way to enhance it. In line with the focus of this volume, we offer our suggestions for using mobile technologies to augment the traditional class environment.

The prospect of a co-constructed learning community, created through the use of any number of specific mobile devices, bolsters courses by increasing student engagement and retention. Upcoming chapters in the application section of this volume offer the reader-specific case studies and detailed accounts of the use of various technologies and provide readers the opportunity to consider their respective uses and benefits. In contrast, this chapter explores the theory and logic behind the inclusion of mobile technology. The inclusion of mobile technologies reshapes and reframes pedagogical techniques to increase classroom participation and bring classroom materials into the twenty-first century.

WHY INCORPORATE MOBILE TECHNOLOGIES? WEAVING TOGETHER DISCIPLINARY KNOWLEDGE

Johnson, Smith, Levine, and Haywood's (2010) *Horizon Report* identifies five key trends in K-12 education that are applicable to the development and implementation of strategies for incorporating innovative technologies such as mobile technologies in higher education. The five trends noted by Johnson et al. as having an influence on the direction of education today are listed as follows:

1. Technology is increasingly a means for empowering students, a method for communication and socializing, and a ubiquitous, transparent part of their lives.
2. Technology continues to profoundly affect the way we work, collaborate, communicate, and succeed.
3. The perceived value of innovation and creativity is increasing.
4. There is increasing interest in just-in-time, alternate, or non-formal avenues of education, such as online learning, mentoring, and independent study.
5. The way we think of learning environments is changing. (2010, p. 4).

Taking these trends into consideration begs the question – if technology truly is impacting education in these various ways, would it not be possible to develop and implement this medium for the purpose of increasing collaboration and active learning in higher education?

We address this question by reviewing literature from multiple disciplines to establish an integrative interdisciplinary framework that perforates through academic silos. Specifically, we connect prominent theories and bodies of knowledge from adult and higher education, psychology and social psychology, sociology, and women's and gender studies to illustrate the ways that different disciplines can contribute to more student-centered outcomes in the classroom. After discussing each body of literature, we examine its linkages and theoretical impacts as they relate to the inclusion of emerging and future mobile devices in higher education.

We recognize that the literature review we offer originates from incongruous points across academic spatiotemporality, across micro- or macro-levels of analysis, or whether or not technology was initially a central focus. Additionally, we recognize that the academic distinctions drawn to provide background and context in this chapter are artificially rigid; however, the literature we use represents our best effort to give credit to the many scholars and academic disciplines that can inform the introduction of mobile technologies in higher education.

ADULT AND HIGHER EDUCATION

Lifelong Learning

As Field (2005) notes, "the concept of learning is very different from the concept of education, and people's active engagement in the wider social context is an extremely important aspect of distinction between the two" (p. 3). No single definition for lifelong learning exists in the literature. However, even among disconcordant definitions, we recognize common attributes of lifelong learners. For instance, the term *lifelong learner* generally encompasses a wider range of students than strictly the traditional-aged, full-time students often referred to as "typical college students."

In these difficult economic times, higher education is often seen as a means to gain the skills necessary for reemployment of recertification to ensure continued employment. Contemporary college students are seeking more from their classes than facts or knowledge. They also need the skills to apply this knowledge to their specific contexts and the ability to transform their knowledge as new applications inevitably arise. An individual cannot (and should not have to) return to school each time a new technology emerges. Students need to learn how to learn and sustain and reframe their knowledge to novel situations when needed (Edwards, 1997).

Learning Society

In fact, many researchers assert that our society has evolved into a learning society that not only values, but mandates the ability to gain new skills as new technologies and innovations emerge (Edwards, 1997; Merriam, Caffarella, & Baumgartner, 2007). This is evidenced in industrial and post-industrial workplaces. For instance, when typesetting was replaced with computer-based alternatives, tradespeople were forced to learn the new technologies or sit back and watch as their skills became outdated and unnecessary. In a twenty-first century learning society, lifelong learning is more than a skill – it is requisite for success in the workplace.

Based on previous research (Merriam, Caffarella, & Baumgartner, 2007), not only has our society changed in terms of radical technological innovation, it has also seen a shift in the way that people think about work and working, as well as expectations of employees. Further, some social philosophers note that we are living in a postmodern society (Lyotard,

1984). What this means is that due to the continually changing nature of our society, constant change is the new status quo.

Some postmodern scholars hold the belief that the development of technology provides the venue for rapid social change. Further, as the cost of technology falls, the way that people use technology to interact with their environments rises. As such, some postmodernists may refer to this era as being defined by "digitality," a term coined by Nicholas Negroponte (1995) that refers to the condition of living in a digital culture. Although not all scholars agree that digitality emerged in our society in conjunction with postmodernity, it is difficult to deny the various ways that technology helped to shape a more participatory society (Jenkins, 2006). If it is the case that the new social norms include a participatory society, it becomes vital for educators to think about the ways that they communicate information to their students.

Constructivist Learning Environments

Constructivist learning environments provide an epistemological view of learning that embraces student knowledge and input as valuable to the learning process. This emerging educational paradigm has impacted the field of instructional design, where designers are rethinking the traditional classroom in order to accommodate constructivist beliefs and practices related to learning (Jonassen & Rohrer-Murphy, 1999).

Further, Jonassen and Rohrer-Murphy state that this is important because constructivist learning environments are based on different epistemic and pedagogical assumptions than classical approaches to instructional design (1999). Especially in the context of the college classroom, students are seeking more than data. They want to see how data are applied practically to their own ideas and existing knowledge, lives, and lived experiences (Hand, Treagust, & Vance, 1997). Constructivist learning environments are designed to provide these very opportunities to students.

Active Learning

Apart from constructivist approaches, active learning is a teaching style that encourages students to look beyond their books and develop their critical thinking skills. Students are not recipients of knowledge – they are asked to seek out the answers they look for and to question their own thoughts and beliefs, as well as to question the rhetoric presented by their instructors. Active learning ties inquiry into the classroom, and, in conjunction with collaborative learning, helps students realize their full potential as students and as thinkers.

Many books and articles have been written to encourage interactive classroom activities which feature active learning strategies (Fink, 2003; Meyers & Jones, 1993; Parry, 1996; Silberman, 1996), and clear attempts have been made to bring these activities into classrooms. For instance, one activity that has grown in popularity in recent years is the think-pair-share activity (Parry, 1996) which asks students to think in isolation about a topic for a short period of time. Next, they turn to a person nearby to discuss their thoughts, and finally students share their joint discoveries with their classmates. Pedagogically, this activity is meant to encourage collaboration among peers and open a dialogue in the classroom.

While this activity is a great ice-breaker and serves to get students talking, it is fraught with problems. For example, there is often little accountability because even in the "share" time not all pairs get the opportunity to have their voices heard. Additionally, there is little incentive for students to "pair" and discuss the topic sincerely. Students realize any sharing that occurs may not include their thoughts and may not be representative of their true feelings since there is no anonymity (students have to take ownership of their ideas, which is problematic when discussing sensitive or controversial topics).

According to Ames (1992), the structure of the class or of class activities can encourage or discourage motivation for participation. Educators know this from anecdotal evidence – they ask students to signal their agreement or disagreement on a topic and a few might respond in each case, but dozens sit idle. Fassinger (1995) has noted this concern and asserts that there are student traits, professor traits, and class traits that can encourage or discourage participation. Some of these traits are difficult to control, but one trait that encourages participation is giving students the impression that participating will *positively* impact their grade. This demonstrates that motivation and structure influence students' willingness to actively contribute.

Applications of Adult and Higher Education to Mobile Technologies

Knowing that we are living in a learning society wherein lifelong learning skills become valuable assets, it is pertinent that educators imagine ways to give students practical skills that are applicable in other spheres of students' present and future lives. The literature establishes that these skills can be fostered through constructivist learning environments where students get the opportunity to explore and create knowledge relevant to their lives and pertinent to their goals.

Mobile technologies also have the capacity to provide transferable workplace skills to students in higher education. Apart from increasing user comfort with technology, the novel implementation of mobile technologies in the classroom gives students the skills necessary to implement technology in innovative ways throughout their lives – a lifelong learning skill. In line with the literature we review above in the field of adult and higher education, the structured implementation of mobile devices can accomplish existing classroom goals such as creating a constructivist learning environment or engaging students in active learning. Through the use of mobile technologies, students can connect, interact, and explore their educational environment in entirely new ways.

PSYCHOLOGY AND SOCIAL PSYCHOLOGY

Motivation

Beyond the interpersonal advantages to using mobile technologies in the classroom, motivation is another reason to engage students with their devices. Additionally, motivation can increase when students are engaged in structured inclusion of class activities (Ames, 1992), which can be implemented through structured inclusion. Without recognizing the importance of the task and without being engaged, students often lack motivation to participate. Pintrich and De Groot (1990) discuss three integral components in examining student motivation:

1. an expectancy component, which includes students' beliefs about their ability to perform a task;
2. a value component, which includes students' goals and beliefs about the importance and interest of the task; and
3. an affective component, which includes students' emotional reactions to the task (p. 33).

Students, according to Pintrich and De Groot (1990), are more likely to be motivated to participate or learn when they have a sense of self-efficacy regarding their ability to succeed in their education. Further, they argue, students are more motivated when they feel tasks are important to their goals or educational values. Finally, students who feel good about a task express more motivation. Still, motivation is not enough to ensure successful task completion or student learning outcomes. "Students," they argue, "need to have both the 'will' and the 'skill' to be successful in classrooms" (1990, p. 38).

Groups and Cooperative Learning

One way instructors might attempt to motivate students is by assigning group work or cooperative learning exercises. Group projects can help students develop interpersonal skills which often prove useful when they enter the workforce. Group projects might also enable students to collectively produce a final product much larger than they could accomplish on their own. However, intra-group dynamics can often hinder group performance or decision making: students may disagree on an appropriate course of action to complete the assignment, complain of incongruent working styles among the members, or disengage from the project altogether (Kerr & Tindale, 2004).

When accomplished successfully, however, cooperative learning groups can lead to a firestorm of learning. Three major theories in psychology have provided the basis for cooperative learning: (a) social interdependence theory, which states that successful cooperation results from "positive interdependence among individuals' goals, (b) cognitive-development theory "views cooperation as an essential prerequisite for cognitive growth," which is centered on an idea that groups who are working to attain common goals develop coordinated perspectives, and (c) behavioral learning theory, where it is posited that students "will work hard on tasks for which they will secure a reward of some sort and will fail to work on tasks that yield no reward or yield punishment" (Johnson, Johnson, & Smith, 1998).

Further, Zajonc (1965) suggests that students perform differently in group settings based on what attributes they bring with themselves into the group. In his drive theory of social facilitation, Zajonc argues that students who are adequately prepared and already comfortable with the material will be more likely to exert confidence in a stressful situation such as working in a group where they are likely to receive judgment of their peers (Zajonc, 1965). The students who have already mastered or nearly mastered the content, according to Zajonc's theory, will benefit from the situation and perform well in the social setting (Zajonc, 1965). Unfortunately, in a group environment students who are struggling with the material may become distressed and find that their learning is stifled.

In fear of being judged harshly by classmates or appearing incapable, students who may be most in need of practice in the group setting may be less likely to participate. Further, because they now have a direct (but skewed) basis for comparing their depth of knowledge to that of their classmates, these students run the risk of mentally withdrawing from the course (Pintrich & De Groot, 1990; Zajonc, 1965). While they may remain enrolled on the roster, in an extreme case, a student's esteem would plummet, her expectations for her own performance would fall, and her performance in all aspects of the class would drop. To counteract these possibilities, some instructors have tried using group work sparingly or not at all. Of course, this also absolves the possibility of a benefit for some students, so it leads us to wonder how group work can take place in a way that alleviates the negative aspects of social presence in a group setting.

Self

We can infer from the research by Zajonc (1965) that students' selves (especially in terms of self-esteem and self-worth, as well as their general self-identities) might be impacted by the use of group work. This is not to say that students who did not prepare well for a particular class session will leave with an irreparable sense of self-loathing. We are simply suggesting that students who tend to perform on average or below that of their peers may, over time, develop concerns about their future potential.

These students might find alternative ways to complete their educational pursuits; for instance, self-regulated learners might seek out classes that afford greater autonomy or less dependence on group learning environments (Pintrich & De Groot, 1990). Although some self-regulated learners may find a way to succeed despite less than ideal learning conditions (Zimmerman, 1990), a "sink or swim" mentality on the part of the instructor can be detrimental in any case: It can prevent some students from success or drive other students away from potentially beneficial learning opportunities. Instructors, then, must find innovative ways to promote positive learning experiences for all students.

Educators sometimes neglect to see the connection between students' selves and their electronic devices. Since students see themselves as technologically "wired," technology becomes fully integrated into their self-schemas. Since self-schemas are used by people to organize and process information about their experience of the world, technology then would become a vital aspect of the individuals' self-concepts. In fact, mobile devices are so important to the self-concept of some people that they can be seen as extensions or even as part of the body (Oksman & Rautiainen, 2003). Educators can easily realize that it is incredibly difficult to write without arms or see without eyes, yet the same educators metaphorically take away their students' eyes and arms the second they walk into the classroom. As a result, students may see their professors as "others" through a process of social comparison (Festinger, 1954).

Teske (2002) asks the question: "To what extent might increasing internet usage affect not only with whom we interact and the kinds of relationships we form, but also how we ultimately understand ourselves as social beings, including the incorporation of close relationships into self-understanding?" (p. 686). By implication, the kinds of electronic relationships we have or sustain with others would also impact the ways we feel appropriate to interact with others as well as the way that we view ourselves.

Technology has changed human relations and relationships. Electronic relationships alter the way in which we view other people. For example, we may start to think of others not as humans, but as e-mail addresses, LinkedIn connections, or Facebook timelines (or Facebook's terminology du jour for equating human beings to online user profiles).

Applications of Psychology and Social Psychology to Mobile Technologies

By looking at aspects of classroom dynamics through the lens of psychology and social psychology, we can see how the use of these devices increases students' motivation to participate. In the classroom, when instructors simply seek compliance during class activities, there is no "buy-in" from students. Through the use of mobile technologies, instructors can demonstrate to the students that they want to help students learn through the incorporation of tools that matter to the students. Students, then, are less likely to simply comply or conform to the instructor's wishes, but rather identify with her goals.

Thinking creatively, it becomes possible to envision ways that mobile technologies can assist in group environments that provide the benefits of learning and working together while alleviating concern of performance in front of peers in groups and cooperative learning contexts. Additionally, when considering the impact that technology has on the sense of self for many students, it becomes relevant and beneficial to consider how students might be better prepared to learn when the tools that have become a vital part of their self-schemas are incorporated into the classroom.

SOCIOLOGY

Consumerism

Social programs such as scholarships, the Federal Pell Grant (Seftor & Turner, 2002), and the G.I. Bill (Bound & Turner, 2002) have opened access to higher education to individuals who historically would have been denied such opportunities. However, the rising cost of college continues to be a prohibitive factor for many individuals who wish to attend such an institution. In these tight economic times, students are, at least in part, equating success in a class as a cost-benefit analysis: determining if they get enough from the class, considering what they invested in time and money after their decision to enroll (Heller, 1997). In a capitalist-based consumer society, it would be remiss not to discuss the ways in which economy has impacted higher education classrooms.

Since it has been demonstrated that students are sensitive to the price of tuition and it affects their probability of college or university matriculation (Heller, 1997), we believe students want to be assured that their investment (of economic capital, time, and effort) will generate a profitable return, and students who are dissatisfied with classes see the impact as a financial loss. In our service industries, many companies advertise that "the customer is always right" and "people should get what they pay for."

In many ways, this model has been paralleled in higher education, and students feel entitled to a degree because they have paid for it and not because they have earned it. Administrators are becoming more and more burdened with complaints from unsatisfied students, and they "may cut back on the number of courses or drop out of college completely" as a result (DeShields, Kara, & Kaynak, 2005, p. 129). This trend, while relatively standard in industry, is a newer issue in higher education that indicates that the students seek something substantial and concrete that they can take away from their courses (DeShields, Kara, & Kaynak, 2005).

While this issue may have educators or institutions of higher education concerned about the negative impacts of student satisfaction on retention, there is another side to this story: Students are feeling empowered to ask for information that they feel is applicable to their lives. As a result of the steep investment that students feel they are making, they are looking for ways to take the knowledge they acquire in the classroom and put it to work for themselves out in the "real world." The goal of providing students with transferable knowledge is what many educators sought to reach all along.

Community

Since sociologists are inherently interested in interactions, ranging from those that transpire in social settings to those that take place in the classroom, it becomes worthwhile to consider the ways that educators can successfully teach their students within the confines of the social context. Often, the classroom emulates a microcosm of society with individuals vying for limited resources in the higher education marketplace including attention, individualized instruction, and grades (especially when the instructor employs a competitive class environment by grading on a bell curve, for instance).

As an alternative to this competitive individualized classroom environment, some instructors have tried to create a sense of community in their classrooms. This may be ideal, as previous research has established that there is a positive correlation between student success and school environments (Hughes, 1986). Further, Halawah (2006) writes that the amount of and degree to which a student has interpersonal interactions with teachers and peers can predict student success and intellectual as well as personal development. These studies show that students are more content and more likely to succeed in learning environments where they feel that they are supported by faculty and classmates.

While the idea of classroom community seems promising, in some classes this environment is difficult to achieve. For example, much research has been conducted on ways to engage students in a large class setting (Kuh, Kinzie, Shuh, Whitt, & Associates, 2010; Nicol & Boyle, 2003; Stanley & Porter, 2002). Researchers tend to agree that there are several possible problems in this setting: Students feel anonymous (and often, students really are anonymous), their individual presence is not accounted for, they are not missed in the times that they do not attend, their instructor may not know their name, or they feel isolated as they are unable to make friends or participate in such a large setting. In other contexts, students may feel a lack of support from instructors or classmates because the class material does not generate discussion, the instructor does not seem to care about the students' input, or the students feel that their input is disparaged by the instructor or classmates.

The problems mentioned above have a common thread binding them into one larger problematic category: Students feel a lack of support from instructors or classmates when the class lacks *community*, which we operationalize for the purposes of this chapter as connective social ties – either in face-to-face learning environments or in online courses. This sense of community becomes especially important in higher education, as we move from the top-down, banking model of education to a model that seeks the voices of all students and validates their experiences as relevant to the course content. In doing this, students are better able to apply the course materials to their lives and gain the critical skills needed for success in the workplace.

Communicative Rationality

One critical skill needed for success in higher education and the workplace is the ability to articulate a position, listen to the position of another, and discuss the differences in a way that does not demean or diminish the input of the other. Habermas, a pragmatic sociologist who comes from a background rooted in critical theories, refers to the concept of communicative action. Habermas uses this term to describe the process of *mutual argumentation*, or the back-and-forth debate process of delivering ideas and receiving counterpoints that is undertaken by individuals in the pursuit of knowledge and understanding.

In his work *The Theory of Communicative Action*, Habermas (1984) argues the importance for communicative rationality – a self-reflexive, open dialogue between participants wherein a disagreement or argument can help an individual learn from others as well as gain insights about themselves through the reflexive process needed to justify one's own perspectives in a public arena. This is revolutionary for participants because most often, an individual's own beliefs are free to go unquestioned or unchecked until they are brought to light in the presence of someone who disagrees. Habermas (1984), however, notes the central tenets for success of this process are the absence of coercion, the mutual quest for knowledge, and the ability to listen for the better truth to gain better understandings of life.

Applications of Sociology to Mobile Technologies

Using mobile technologies as a tool for teaching and learning can assist in resolving each of these issues. Related to consumerism, we see that students may approach higher education with the expectation that they should leave with tangible skills that will help them compete in the job market. Through the introduction of mobile technologies, they will learn to use tools that are readily available in new and innovative ways. Students will discover that their mobile devices can provide access to data and information that can inform their daily lives at school, at home, or at work.

Additionally, through the use of mobile technologies, students in class will be able to experience a sense of community in the classroom. According to Mazzolini and Maddison (2007), there are several ways to build a sense of community in a group through the use of technology; however, Mazzolini and Maddison (2003) find that consistent involvement is the key to encouraging successful student participation. Students are invigorated when they have the opportunity to help others and take pride in the skills that they bring to the classroom, as most students will have great familiarity with the devices they possess.

This sense of community is augmented by the increased discussion and variety of voices that are heard. Students who are generally uncomfortable speaking aloud, afraid that they have the minority perspective, or disinterested due to a feeling of disingenuous engagement will find a rekindled interest in being involved in the class. While it is important for students to learn this technique without facilitation through technology, college students are often still acquiring communication skills (Ellis, 1995). Purposeful inclusion of mobile technologies, then, enables students to minimize the social isolation that they may experience from being in a learning environment without knowing or personally interacting with the instructor or fellow classmates.

We have already established that students want to be supported in classrooms by instructors and classmates. Yet, in the context of communicative rationality, students also need to be able to argue with classmates in order to learn to strengthen their arguments and listen to others. The question remains, how can we possibly generate an inviting and supportive environment while using arguments as a means of communication? This is exactly the kind of paradox suited for the introduction of technology. We feel the most important aspect gained based on Habermas' perspective is that students will be able to see a variety of perspectives presented through the use of mobile technologies in the classroom. Using mobile technologies with established ground rules creates a context using Habermas' (1984) tenets, as it provides an environment free of coercion, interested in the mutual quest for knowledge, and affording students the ability to listen for the better truth to gain better understandings of life. Students will be able to engage in lively but respectful academic debates without fear of being silenced by an instructor or classmates.

WOMEN'S AND GENDER STUDIES

Feminist Pedagogy

As discussed previously, one key trend in education is the use of technology as "increasingly a means for empowering students" (Johnson, Smith, Levine, & Haywood, 2010, p. 4). Women's and gender studies has traditionally been concerned with issues of inequality based on sex or gender. Feminist pedagogy is a development from within this discipline, but it is important to note that feminist pedagogy does not advocate for the success of women over men. Rather, it focuses on educating students about issues of social justice, bringing subjectivities into the classroom, recognizing social privileges, and providing equitable educational experiences for *all* students. Simply providing opportunities for activities may not give an equal voice to students who are often marginalized or disenfranchised in the classroom. Prior research shows privilege in classroom participation can be related to social characteristics of the students, such as gender, race, ethnicity, or ability/disability, among others (Erevelles, 2011; Maher, 1999; Morris, 2007; Noble & Davies, 2009; Rocca, 2010).

Today, feminist pedagogies seek to empower all students regardless of race, disability, age, or especially gender or sexual orientation by forming a student-centered learning environment (Crabtree & Sapp, 2003). Scholars of feminist pedagogy have noted that some of the problems associated with classroom inequity can be overcome through activities which rely on active learning principles (e.g. McIntosh, 1988/2004; Parry, 1996, discussed previously in this chapter). These activities often provide opportunities for students to engage in critical thinking and challenge students to consider their own privileges and the perspectives of the "other" (McIntosh, 1988/2004).

Organizing the Feminist Classroom

According to Gleason (1986), students are less likely to participate in larger classes – especially those which meet in auditorium-style classrooms. This presents a challenge to educators because these classes are likely most common in introductory level courses. Students who take these classes are likely to be in their freshman year, where they are forming their identities as college students and classroom participants (Upcraft, Gardner, & Barefoot, 2004). In a classroom that implements feminist pedagogy, it is not uncommon to find instructors advising their student to arrange their desks in a circle during class discussions. In a large auditorium class, asking students to rearrange their desks and form a circle or small groups to explore or discuss a topic would likely not be possible since the seating is often bolted to the floor in rows. The physical space of these classrooms actually discourages any kind of conversation besides teacher-to-student. This does not mean that the principles of active learning no longer apply. It simply means that a different mechanism should be used to implement the activities.

Applications of Women's and Gender Studies to Mobile Technologies

Previous studies suggest that classroom participation is critical to promoting an active learning environment and helping students develop critical thinking skills (Cohen, 1991), unfortunately student participation is not inherent to all classes. It has to be fostered by the instructor and nurtured by all participants. Our own research shows that appropriate activities which incorporate mobile technologies give students the voice necessary to generate a further, more engaged, classroom conversation inclusive of all students (Lauderdale & Partin, 2012). That is, activities using mobile technologies, we argue, can accomplish goals in feminist pedagogy of increasing communication, student empowerment, and classroom equity (Lauderdale & Partin, 2012).

Another central tenet of feminist pedagogy is reflection on classroom activities including goals and means for students' learning. We do realize the possibility that problems of inequality may be further hindered by unequal access to technology or unequal technological literacy (Brown, Campbell, & Ling, 2011). However, Brown, Campbell, and Ling (2011) also note that the so-called digital divide is closing as the cost of technology decreases and access becomes more readily available to the general population or ubiquitous. We feel strongly that steps can be taken when using mobile technologies to ensure all students are able to share their voice in a safe and supportive environment.

Instructors must find ways to ensure students – especially those without automatic privilege based on their demographic or physical attributes – feel empowered and have a voice in the classroom. In the digital age, mobile technologies, including assistive technologies (Dell, Newton, & Petroff, 2011), have the potential to become a strong mechanism for rapid and inclusive communication and response in the classroom (Lauderdale & Partin, 2012; Partin & Lauderdale, 2011). While the feminist classroom could traditionally be achieved by rearranging seats or using other mechanisms to encourage conversation, in the digital classroom, mobile technologies can enable the instructor to achieve the desired effect without a wrench!

INTEGRATIVE MODEL FOR STUDENT-CENTERED CLASSROOMS

Based on our review of the literature from a variety of disciplines, we see that various theories of learning and education triangulate the premise that students are more genuinely engaged in the classroom if they are able to incorporate their mobile devices into their learning. Combining these areas to discuss the rationale for implementation and integration of innovative teaching ideas has provided much insight on the ways that technology can help students in their educational goals. Additionally, the potential impact on classroom dynamics leads us to believe that students who are given these opportunities will generate increased job skills, report higher satisfaction, feel more motivated, feel empowered to have their voices heard in the classroom (through active engagement with course material, peers, and instructors), and reap many other benefits. We believe that these factors additionally will provide students with more opportunities to retain information, see the application of material to their lives, and thus, perform better on assessments.

Drawing from our interdisciplinary literature review, we have located several aspects of a student-centered learning environment. With these in mind, we propose an *Interdisciplinary Model for Student-Centered Classrooms* (Fig. 1).

This model illustrates how aspects of the theories discussed from different disciplines can create a more inclusive, student-centered environment. This model shows the evolution of the classroom environment as aspects such as motivation, participation, community, and voice are included for a positive learning outcome.

We argue that when an instructor's goal is learning, the likelihood of achieving that goal is increased by motivating students. When students are motivated, they are more likely to participate. When a critical mass of participation is reached, the classroom begins to demonstrate characteristics that make students feel that they are part of a community. This environment helps students come to feel like their contributions are important to the larger classroom dynamics, and they are more able to view course materials

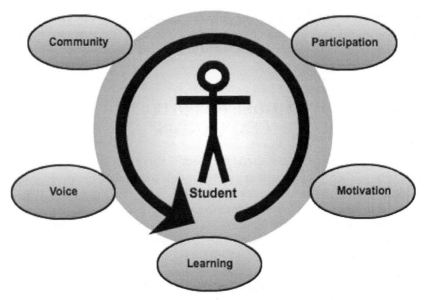

Fig. 1.   Interdisciplinary Model for Student-Centered Classrooms.

in light of their lives and experiences, and thus students are empowered with a voice in the classroom. Ultimately, the combination of these elements creates a classroom environment more suitable for learning. Fig. 1, therefore, is intended to demonstrate how these various aspects begin with and complete the cycle of learning.

In fact, since it is likely that students are more familiar with emerging technologies than their instructors, the inclusion of students' preferred technologies into the classroom can be a powerful way for students to become active agents in the formation of the student-centered classroom. After all, using ubiquitous technologies can simultaneously engage students through active learning principles, develop a constructivist learning environment, exercise lifelong learning skills, express their sense of self through technology, and promote feminist pedagogy – some of the facets identified in the literature review as integral for the formation of a student-centered classroom. It is important to note that our model does not explicitly require any technology to be enacted; however, we see the structured use of mobile technologies as a powerful way to construct a student-centered classroom by increasing motivation, participation, community, voice, and learning.

INFUSING TECHNOLOGY IN THE
STUDENT-CENTERED CLASSROOM

There are a variety of ways that the Interdisciplinary Model for Student-Centered Classrooms can be integrated to create a student-centered classroom. For instance, Alavi (1994) conducted an empirically based study on computer-mediated collaborative based learning, where face-to-face classes were supplemented with collaborative learning activities, and these activities made use of various technologies. Alavi found that students who used technology "in support of their group learning activities perceived higher levels of skill development, learning, and interest in learning relative to students who did not use the technology. Furthermore, students who used technology had a more positive evaluation of the classroom experience and the group learning activities relative to students who did not use technology to support their group learning process. While it was only noted as an interesting aside, an intriguing finding from this study is reported in the final course grades. While there were no significant differences in students' midterm grades, the fact that a significant difference did materialize over the course of the semester suggests that these activities may have a cumulative effect and value over time (Alavi, 1994).

Overall, Alavi (1994) suggests that using technology in the classroom can increase the positive effects of collaborative learning. Alavi's finding has spawned more current studies on ways that technology-inclusive collaborative learning has been facilitated. For instance, Koh and Lim (2012) show that technological design affects online collaboration and group assignments. Additionally, other researchers show that technology influences participation and procrastination dynamics in e-learning (Michinov et al., 2011) and that participation styles vary in technology-supported collaborative learning (Cho et al., 2007). While it cannot be doubted that technology has the potential to transform learning and student engagement in higher education, we do realize that technology is continually shifting and evolving. Still, the implications of Alavi's (1994) study are far reaching – the breadth of recent scholarship demonstrates the applicability of Alavi's (1994) study on ongoing research in educational technology.

As the aforementioned studies demonstrate, the structured and successful infusion of mobile technologies is one way of creating a student-centered classroom. Since students see their mobile devices as integral to their lives, encouraging them to bring in and use their devices in novel ways can increase motivation. As Fig. 2 illustrates, the specific mobile technology is

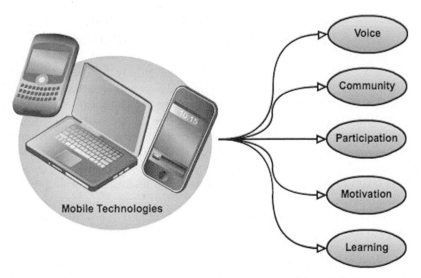

Fig. 2. Infusing the Student-Centered Classrooms Model with Mobile Technologies.

not as important as its capability to provide students with the ability to bring their technological applications to the classroom. For this reason, our figure accounts for existing technologies as well as those which have not yet been invented. In our previous research (Lauderdale & Partin, 2012; Partin & Lauderdale, 2011), data analysis of student perceptions revealed that the incorporation of mobile technologies is an effective learning tool in higher education. In this section, we demonstrate how mobile technologies give students a voice, help establish a community, increase participation, and motivate students to learn. Fig. 2 demonstrates that introducing technology can help an instructor and students create this environment. The scenarios outlined in the proceeding section invite readers to ask themselves whether infusing mobile technologies can enhance the course dynamics.

Still, the question remains: "How do I infuse mobile technologies in my own courses to develop a student-centered classroom?" In the following paragraphs, we provide several scenarios across multiple classroom venues and academic disciplines to provide readers with opportunities to consider how infusing technology can create student-centered classroom environments and enable learning. Although these particular scenarios are completely fictitious, they represent issues real instructors may face in a variety of course settings in higher education. Rather than follow each scenario with our own suggestions for integrating mobile technologies and creating a student-centered classroom, the scenarios are meant to encourage readers to consider how the introduction of mobile technologies might augment their own courses or help alleviate problems. Proceeding chapters in this volume provide in-depth examination of specific strategies for incorporating mobile technologies to provide solutions to classroom issues and learner engagement.

Scenario #1: Large-Enrollment, Face-to-Face Course

Dr. Ramirez is a fantastic teacher. In fact, he is so popular with the students, that last semester the department asked him to teach a large section of his course since the small sections fill up so quickly. He agreed, but now finds himself in unfamiliar territory – the students do not want to talk. It seems that the class size has intimidated the students, and his usual method of calling students to speak by name will not work, because he does not know all of the students' names! Placing the students in small groups is difficult because the room has theatre seating and the desks are affixed to the floor. Many activities he used in class will not work because the acoustics in the room make conversations so loud. Last week, Dr. Ramirez became frustrated during his lecture. He was covering interactive and engaging material, but the students did not want to discuss the topic. Additionally, as he circulated around the classroom he noticed that many students were browsing the Internet on their computers and sending and receiving text messages on their phones. How could Dr. Ramirez use the resources already in the room to turn this situation around?

Scenario #2: Small-Enrollment, Face-to-Face Course

Professor Carlson is teaching a small class in the Women's Studies department. The class is very close, with all students knowing their classmates, and generally feeling open to comment on and discuss class topics. One class session is dedicated to domestic violence, and the students are prepared for class but the atmosphere tells Professor Carlson that the students are timid due to the difficult nature of the material. At the beginning of the class session, a student, Sam, raises his hand and says, "Why do we even have to cover this topic? Domestic violence stopped happening years ago." Many students in class became visibly frustrated by his comment. Another student, Bethany, even went so far as to lambaste her classmate: "Are you serious? There is more domestic violence today than ever before! I bet half the people in this class have been victims of violence. In fact, we should have a show of hands!" Professor Carlson stops the conversation in its tracks. Of course, it would be unreasonable to ask students to identify themselves as domestic violence victims. However, in the back of her mind, Professor Carlson knows that Bethany has a great point. It would really drive home the message if her students could see that people – real people in their classes – have been victimized. Maybe an anonymous survey would work, but by the time the results come back, the students will have moved on to another topic. Sam speaks out again: "Well, if that's true, what are the statistics for our city?" Again, Professor Carlson is wishing she had anticipated that question, since she did not bring the regional statistics with her. How can she help her students connect with the material in a way that will not compromise their personal information or sense of security or comfort in the classroom? How can the students get engaged with the sensitive topic?

Scenario #3: Hybrid Course with Face-to-Face and Online Class Meetings

Mr. Green teaches a hybrid Twentieth Century American History course where students meet in person monthly but meet together online every Thursday evening for weekly lectures. Before the semester began, Mr. Green planned for students to write a paper based on an interview with a family member about their experiences of life in the 1970s. However, several students complained about this assignment because they would not be able to hear about the data collected by their peers. This struck a chord with Mr. Green, who recognized that this was a valuable perspective, especially after he noticed that several of the students come from diverse backgrounds and live in different regions of their state. How can Mr. Green find a way for students to record their interviews and share them with the class online? How might doing so make the assignment more valuable to the students than preparing their responses in isolation?

Scenario #4: Asynchronous, Online Course

Dr. Mills is teaching an architecture course online for the first time this semester. In her previous face-to-face classes, she often asked students to write a short reflection about the various architectural styles they observe in their neighborhoods. Dr. Mills has always enjoyed learning about the various kinds of architecture that the students write about finding in their neighborhoods. She would have loved to have students share their findings; however, there was just never enough time in class for students to do so. Now that she is teaching this course online, she thinks that students can read each other's posts on their course site without the constraints of allotted time that she encountered in her face-to-face classrooms. Still, she wonders if there is a way for students to collaborate so that they can discuss the architectural styles of their homes with one another in the online discussion board. Then another problem dawns on her: "How will students be able to envision their classmates' findings?" Since her online course is an introductory course, she realized that some students are still learning about common home architectural styles. Is there a way that students can share pictures of the houses in their respective neighborhoods? Would students benefit from the exposure of the various houses that they might not otherwise have seen?

APPLICATION OF SCENARIOS AND FIGURES

The preceding scenarios provide a few opportunities for reflective thinking about ways that technology can enhance classroom learning in a variety of class settings. For further reflection and specific outcomes, consider other hypothetical examples such as (a) an environmental science course, where, instead of arguing with each other about whether global climate change is a problem, students form groups and instead share reasoned points and counterpoints with their peers via text messages displayed for the entire class to see; (b) an urban studies course, where students can be tasked to use their mobile devices to photograph specific examples of the key terms in their local settings and write about what they find to help them understand abstract concepts from their textbooks; or (c) an education course in which students use their mobile devices to keep field notes of classroom observations and share mini-reflections with their classmates to generate class discussion and solidify budding research skills.

Without a doubt, cutting-edge technologies enable students to create and share information with their classmates and instructors in novel and effective ways. The implementation of mobile devices presents many opportunities to increase student engagement. The technological, photographic, and audio capabilities – to name a few – of mobile devices enable students to engage with course content away from the confines of the classroom and view the world as a learning laboratory. A simple web search yields dozens of free tools compatible with mobile technologies any of which can be incorporated or adapted for cogent use in higher education, and many more will surely be developed in the coming years.

These examples are intended to show how mobile technologies, when coupled with the *Interdisciplinary Model for Student-Centered Classrooms*, can provide transformations in classrooms that engage students and promote learning. To further demonstrate the process needed for this transformation, we introduce our vision of the process that instructors might take as they come to evaluate and incorporate mobile technologies in their own courses (Fig. 3). We see the formation of a student-centered classroom (Fig. 1) as the starting point to increasing learner engagement, retention, and learning while

Fig. 3. Processual Model for Innovating Student-Centered Classrooms to Enrich Learning.

producing enriching educational experiences through technology (Fig. 2). As such, this processual model (Fig. 3) is not intended to offer a step-by-step guide, unidirectional instructions, or any rigid structure to what we envision as a continual process of evaluation and reevaluation. The "steps" along the way to increasing learner engagement through the inclusion of technology are sometimes meandering or accomplished gradually or abruptly depending on the specific context of any given course.

INSTITUTIONAL CONSIDERATIONS AND CURRICULUM CHANGE

While it is easy to make these assertions based on the literature, we realize that implementation is often "easier said than done." By using feminist pedagogy, active learning, or other methods in their classrooms, some instructors have produced modest change in the curriculum of specific courses. Additionally, faculty with interests in the application of educational technologies have found ways to engage their students through innovative classroom activities. However, change will never exceed isolated cases of innovation without institutional support. To make lasting curriculum change, it is imperative to have institutions that support change, as well as faculty who are willing to innovate. According to Partin and King (2012), environmental variables such as ethics and respect, motivation, the consideration of academic freedom, and faculty input are requisites for creating an atmosphere where faculty feel supported and encouraged to try new teaching strategies without fear of reprisal.

Once these environmental factors are in place, Partin and King (2012) propose that an Integrative Innovation Model for Higher Education (IIMHE) can be implemented to encourage faculty innovation through institutional change. This four-stage model moves dynamically back and forth among (1) changes in policy, (2) changes of management, (3) change in culture, and (4) faculty development for student success and innovative teaching (Partin & King, 2012).

Essentially, this demonstrates that institutions need to consider policies (such as reduced teaching loads or class sizes as faculty try implementing new strategies) or other policy interpretations or changes that offer incentives and show value for teaching. Additionally, management (from department chairs to higher levels of administration) should consider the ways in which they are agents of the institution. They can provide the faculty with venue and voice for their ideas or concerns, and have a substantial role in the interpretation and implementation of existing institutional policies. Further, Partin and King suggest that once individuals within the institution take notice of the changes in policy and management of policy, a change in organizational culture will ensure, and will include, a positive view of faculty who teach and strategize about ways to improve. Lastly, within the newly formed context and culture, faculty will reap rewards for seeking out professional development opportunities to improve their teaching through innovative methods. Faculty, then, will be able to build a new repertoire of skills without concern for their performance evaluations, perceived value to the institution, or sense of self (Partin & King, 2012).

Organizational culture within the institution affects the perception and function of centers designed to promote or enhance excellence in teaching. In the prevailing culture, these centers often exist as a place to send 'bad teachers" for remediation or punishment after receiving low teaching evaluations. Increasingly, perceptions of these teaching centers are shifting. In the emerging paradigm, interested faculty use these centers to acquire new teaching skills, enhance their current teaching strategies, or learn to incorporate new technologies without fear of reprisal – in line with Partin and King's (2012) model. Despite the slow change in organizational culture, the increased institutional support for these centers is shown through the influx of funding (Darling-Hammond, 1997) demonstrates that administrators perceive these centers as vital for achieving institutional goals.

DISCUSSION

In this chapter, we bridge together perspectives from various disciplines including adult and higher education, psychology and social psychology, sociology, and women's and gender studies in order to help instructors think about ways to expand on existing activities by incorporating mobile technologies in the learning process. In doing so, the benefits we discussed throughout our review of the literature become tangible. Through the successful arrangement of our *Interdisciplinary Model for Student-Centered Classrooms* and the calculated incorporation of mobile technologies, instructors create great potential for their courses to allow for the voices of all students rather than a select, privileged few. This model, as based on our findings, can help educators transform their traditional classrooms from a structure in which students are merely passive consumers of education to one in which all students feel empowered to actively participate in classroom activities and discussions.

In an effort to provide lifelong learning, workforce skills to students in a learning society, instructors who opt to incorporate mobile technologies into their classes provide more than content to students. They offer students a practical use for an existing tool that they can take from the classroom to their homes or jobs. Students may not have access to all of their textbooks when they encounter an issue on the job (nor might their textbooks have answers). However, students who know how to use their mobile devices for educational purposes can find, access, and evaluate information as needed.

Our *Interdisciplinary Model for Student-Centered Classrooms* acknowledges the continual technological changes in society as well as the implication for students. By applying the principles herein, and considering the scenarios we provided as well as the specific examples provided in forthcoming chapters of this volume, educators can consider ways to include new technologies in higher education in order to promote student engagement, retention, and learning. We encourage instructors to continually evaluate their pedagogical techniques in an effort to connect with their students and to take advantage of the myriad opportunities available to the twenty-first century educator. Finally, we argue that institutions should invest in and support instructors as they endeavor to innovate in their classrooms to provide the highest quality education to their students.

REFERENCES

Alavi, M. (1994). Computer-mediated collaborative learning: An empirical evaluation. *MIS Quarterly, 18*(2), 159–174.

Ames, C. (1992). Classrooms: Goals, structures, and student motivation. *Journal of Educational Psychology, 84*, 261–271.

Bound, J., & Turner, S. (2002). Going to war and going to college: Did World War II and the GI Bill increase educational attainment for returning veterans? *Journal of Labor Economics, 20*(4), 784–815.

Brown, K., Campbell, S. W., & Ling, R. (2011). Mobile phones bridging the digital divide for teens in the US? *Future Internet, 3*, 144–158.

Burns, S., & Lohenry, K. (2010). Cellular phone use in the classroom implications for teaching and learning: A pilot study. *College Student Journal, 44*(3), 805–810.

Candy, P. C. (1991). *Self-direction for lifelong learning: A comprehensive guide to theory and practice.* San Francisco, CA: Jossey-Bass.

Carter, M., Thatcher, J. B., Applefield, C., & McAlpine J. (2011). What cell phones mean in young people's daily lives and social interactions. *Southern Association for Information Systems 2011 Proceedings.* Paper 29.

Cho, H., Gay, G., Davidson, B., & Ingraffea, A. (2007). Social networks, communication styles, and learning performance in a CSCL community. *Computers & Education, 49*(2), 309–329.

Cohen, M. (1991). Making class participation a reality. *Political Science & Politics, 24*, 699–703.

Crabtree, R. D., & Sapp, D. A. (2003). Theoretical, political, and pedagogical challenges in the feminist classroom: Our struggles to "walk the walk". *College Teaching, 51*(4), 131–140.

Darling-Hammond, L. (1997). *Doing what matters most: Investing in quality teaching.* New York, NY: National Commission on Teaching & America's Future.

Dell, A. G., Newton, D., & Petroff, L. (2011). *Assistive technologies in the classroom: Enhancing the experiences of students with disabilities* (2nd ed.). Boston, MA: Allyn & Bacon.

DeShields, O., Kara, A., & Kaynak, E. (2005). Determinants of business student satisfaction and retention in higher education: Applying Herzberg's two-factor theory. *International Journal of Education Management, 19*(2), 128–139.

Edwards, R. (1997). *Changing places? Flexibility, lifelong learning and a learning society.* New York, NY: Routledge.

Ellis, K. (1995). Apprehension, self-perceived competency, and teacher immediacy in the laboratory-supported public speaking course: Trends and relationships. *Communication Education, 44*(1), 64–78.

Erevelles, N. (2011). 'Coming out crip' in inclusive education. *Teachers College Record, 113*(10), 2155–2185.

Fassinger, P. (1995). Understanding classroom interaction: Students' and professors' contributions to students' silence. *Journal of Higher Education, 66*(1), 82–96.

Festinger, L. (1954). A theory of social comparison processes. *Human Relations, 7*(2), 117–140.

Field, J. (2005). *Social capital and lifelong learning.* Bristol, UK: The Policy Press.

Fink, L. (2003). *Creating significant learning experiences: An integrated approach to designing college courses.* San Francisco, CA: Jossey-Bass.

Freire, P. (1970). *Pedagogy of the oppressed.* New York, NY: Continuum.

Gleason, M. (1986). Better communication in large classes. *College Teaching, 34*, 20–24.

Habermas, J. (1984). *The theory of communicative action, Vol. 1: Reason and the rationalization of society* (T. McCarthy, Trans.). Boston, MA: Beacon Press.

Halawah, I. (2006). The impact of student–faculty informal interpersonal relationships on intellectual and personal development. *College Student Journal, 40*(3), 670–678.

Hand, B., Treagust, D., & Vance, K. (1997). Student perceptions of the social constructivist classroom. *Science Education, 81*(5), 561–575.

Heller, D. (1997). Student price response in higher education: An update to Leslie and Brinkman. *Journal of Higher Education, 68*(6), 624–659.

Hughes, R. (1986). *A study of the relationship of school climate, managerial system, public control ideology, and student academic achievement in selected Kentucky secondary schools.* Doctoral dissertation. University of Kentucky.

Jenkins, H. (2006). *Fans, bloggers, and gamers: Exploring participatory culture.* New York, NY: New York University Press.

Johnson, D., Johnson, R., & Smith, K. (1998). Cooperative learning returns to college what evidence is there that it works? *Change: The Magazine of Higher Learning, 30*(4), 26–35.

Johnson, L., Smith, R., Levine, A., & Haywood, K. (2010). *2010 horizon report: K–12 edition.* Austin, TX: The New Media Consortium.

Jonassen, D. H., & Rohrer-Murphy, L. (1999). Activity theory as a framework for designing constructivist learning environments. *Educational Technology Research and Development, 47*(1), 61–79.

Kerr, N. L., & Tindale, R. S. (2004). Group performance and decision making. *Annual Review of Psychology, 55*, 623–655.

King, K. P. (2003). *Keeping pace with technology: Educational technology that transforms. Vol. 2: The challenge and promise for higher education faculty.* Cresskill, NJ: Hampton Press.

Koh, E., & Lim, J. (2012). Using online collaboration applications for group assignments: The interplay between design and human characteristics. *Computers & Education, 59*(2), 481–496.

Kuh, G., Kinzie, J., Shuh, J., Whitt, E., & Associates. (2010). *Students success in college: Creating conditions that matter* (2nd ed.). San Francisco, CA: Jossey-Bass.

Lauderdale, S., Partin, C. (2012, March). *I got to speak without being judged!.* Unpublished paper presented at The Southern Sociological Society, New Orleans, LA.

Lyotard, J. (1984). *The postmodern condition: A report on knowledge.* Manchester, UK: Manchester University Press.

Maher, F. (1999). Progressive education and feminist pedagogies: Issues in gender, power, and authority. *Teachers College Record, 101*(1), 35–59.

Mayer, R. E. (2008). Applying the science of learning: Evidence-based principles for the design of multimedia instruction. *American Psychologist, 63*, 760–769.

Mazzolini, M., & Maddison, S. (2003). Sage, guide or ghost? The effect of instructor intervention on student participation in online discussion forums. *Computers & Education, 40*(3), 237–253.

Mazzolini, M., & Maddison, M. (2007). When to jump in: The role of the instructor in online discussion forums. *Computers & Education, 49*, 193–213.

McIntosh, P. (1988/2004). White privilege: Unpacking the invisible knapsack. In P. S. Rothenberg (Ed.), *Race, class, and gender in the United States* (6th ed., pp. 189–192). New York, NY: Worth Publishers.

Merriam, S. B., Caffarella, R. S., & Baumgartner, L. M. (2007). *Learning in adulthood: A comprehensive guide* (3rd ed.). Hoboken, NJ: Wiley.

Meyers, C., & Jones, T. (Eds.). (1993). *Promoting active learning: Strategies for the college classroom.* San Francisco, CA: Jossey-Bass.

Michinov, N., Brunot, S., Le Bohec, O., Juhel, J., & Delaval, M. (2011). Procrastination, participation, and performance in online learning environments. *Computers & Education, 56*(1), 243–256.

Mollborn, S., & Hoekstra, A. (2010). A meeting of minds: Using clickers for critical thinking and discussion in large sociology courses. *Teaching Sociology, 38*(1), 18–27.

Morris, E. (2007). 'Ladies' or 'loudies'? Perceptions and experiences of black girls in classrooms. *Youth Society, 38*, 490–516.

Negroponte, N. (1995). *Being digital.* New York, NY: Vintage Books.

Nicol, D., & Boyle, J (2003). Peer instruction versus class-wide discussion in large classes: A comparison of two interaction methods in the wired classroom. *Studies in Higher Education, 28*(4), 457–473.

Noble, J., & Davies, P. (2009). Cultural capital as an explanation of variation in participation in higher education. *British Journal of Sociology of Education, 30*(5), 591–605.

Oksman, V., & Rautiainen, P. (2003). "Perhaps it's a body part": How the mobile phone became an organic part of everyday lives of Finnish children and teenagers. In J. E. Katz (Ed.), *Machines that become us: The social context of personal communication Technology* (pp. 293–310). New Brunswick, NJ: Transaction Publishers.

Parchoma, G. (2008). *Adoption of technology enhanced learning in higher education: Influences of institutional policies and practices.* Saarbrücken, Germany: VDM Verlag.

Parry, S. (1996). Feminist pedagogy and techniques for the changing classroom. *Women's Studies Quarterly, 3,* 45–54.

Partin, C., & King, K. (2012). Technology and its impact on higher education. In B. Ran (Ed.), *Contemporary perspectives on technological innovation, management and policy.* Charlotte, NC: Information Age Publishing.

Partin, C., Lauderdale, S. (2011, November). *If you can't beat 'em, text 'em: Digital natives, mobile devices, and active learning in the twenty-first century learning community.* Unpublished paper presented at The Association for Educational Communications and Technology, Jacksonville, FL.

Pintrich, P., & De Groot, E. (1990). Motivational and self-regulated learning components of classroom academic performance. *Journal of Educational Psychology, 82*(1), 33–40.

Rocca, K. (2010). Student participation in the college classroom: An extended multidisciplinary literature review. *Communication Education, 59*(2), 185–213.

Seftor, N., & Turner, S. (2002). Back to school: Federal student aid policy and adult college enrollment. *Journal of Human Resources, 37*(2), 336–352.

Silberman, M. (1996). *Active learning: 101 strategies for teaching any subject.* Des Moines, IA: Prentice Hall.

Stanley, C., & Porter, M. (Eds.). (2002). *Engaging large classes: Strategies and techniques for college faculty.* Boston, MA: Anker.

Stockwell, G. (2010). Using mobile phones for vocabulary activities: Examining the effect of the platform. *Language Learning & Technology, 14*(2), 95–110.

Teske, J. A. (2002). Cyberpsychology, human relationships, and our virtual interiors. *Zygon, 37*(3), 677–700.

Tough, A. (1971). *The adult's learning projects: A fresh approach to theory and practice in adult learning.* Toronto, ON: Institute for Studies in Education.

Upcraft, M., Gardner, J., & Barefoot, B. (2004). *Challenging and supporting the first-year student: A handbook for improving the first year of college.* San Francisco, CA: Jossey-Bass.

Zajonc, R. B. (1965). Social facilitation. *Science, 149,* 269–274.

Zimmerman, B. (1990). Self-regulated achievement and academic achievement: An overview. *Educational Psychologist, 25*(1), 3–17.

ENGAGING STUDENTS IN ONLINE COURSES THROUGH THE USE OF MOBILE TECHNOLOGY

Audeliz Matias and David F. Wolf II

ABSTRACT

Mobile technology can offer new opportunities for online learning that extends beyond the learning management system. Advancing a teaching strategy that incorporates mobile technology for online classes does not need to require a large budget. Two adoption strategies are presented here: leveraging of mobile web 2.0 tools and use of native mobile tools. The paradigm of mobile learning brings new pedagogical affordances to context for authentic learning. We demonstrate an activity-based approach to provide learners with additional tools to create meaningful learning experiences anytime, anywhere. This approach fits nicely into learner-centered and constructivist environments because students are learning through their own active involvement. At the same time, it allows students to get excited about what they are learning. In addition, we discuss the institutional, architectural, and pedagogical challenges arising from the use of mobile technology in online courses.

Increasing Student Engagement and Retention using Mobile Applications:
Smartphones, Skype and Texting Technologies
Cutting-edge Technologies in Higher Education, Volume 6D, 115–142
ISSN: 2044-9968/doi:10.1108/S2044-9968(2013)000006D007

INTRODUCTION

The rapid changing landscape of the web and other technologies are disrupting what many consider the conventional practice of teaching and learning. Faculty and administrators all over the educational spectrum are questioning their pedagogical practices and, importantly, if these practices should change.

During the last decade, with both interest and skepticism, an increasing number of higher education institutions across the world have incorporated online courses into their curriculum (Allen & Seaman, 2011; Kirschner, 2012).This shift does not simply imply a different way of delivering education but rather a new approach to curriculum design and strategies. In a world where learners want easy and timely access to connect with course materials, we are uniquely positioned to advocate for the responsible use of digital access in pedagogy. As distance learning keeps evolving, and more technology is available, we need to consider how to engage students beyond providing access and content through online courses.

Properly integrated technology foster student engagement in the learning process (Bransford, Brown, & Cocking, 2000; Ramli, 2010; Revere & Kovach, 2011).Technology such as smartphones and tablets are widely accessible and educators ought to leverage these tools to engage students in active learning. Mobile, "always-connected" devices – as defined by Johnson, Smith, Willis, Levine, and Haywood (2011) – have the potential to promote a learner-centered environment by addressing mobility and availability issues that affect students and instructors alike. The flexibility of the wireless web is substantially altering learning spaces with and through technology. This chapter explores the concept and practice of how mobile technology can aid learning opportunities and provide learners with additional tools to create meaningful learning experiences.

Mobile Technologies

Mobile technologies are a familiar part of our daily lives. Current affordability of mobile devices and increased network reliability enable ubiquitous access to information and tools for learning and productivity. Many see these devices replacing computers for numerous online tasks in the near future. For a third year in a row, The New Media Consortium's *Horizon Report* for higher education places the adoption of mobiles as an important emerging technology trend for the next year or less (Johnson, Adams, & Cummins, 2012; Johnson, Levine, Smith, & Stone, 2010; Johnson et al., 2011).

A recent survey conducted by the Pew Research Center's Internet and American Life Project in the Unites States revealed 45% of adults 18 and older own a smartphone (Smith, 2012), up from 35% in 2011 (Smith, 2011). This overall increase in smartphone ownership is relative widespread globally and across age groups. It is also estimated that by 2015, 80% of people accessing the web will be doing so from cell phones, tablets, or similar always-connected devices (Johnson et al., 2011).The findings from the Educause Center for Applied Research (ECAR) survey of under-graduate students reflect the rapid growing use of mobile web (Smith & Caruso, 2010). For example, tablets quickly rose in popularity during the last year (comScore, Inc., 2012) and tablet ownership among undergraduate students has more than tripled in the last year, with 25% of students now owning a tablet compared to 7% in 2011 (Pearson Foundation, 2012).

Importantly, according to Smith (2011), non-white and low-income level smartphone users are most likely to go online using their phones. The implications for education are many as mobile devices have the potential to reshape students' learning experience in a time of increasing globalization and diversity (Cobcroft, Towers, Smith, & Bruns, 2006; Corbeil & Valdes-Corbeil, 2007). It is imperative that as educators we embrace the use of mobile devices in our teaching.

Mobile Technologies and Higher Education

Many colleges and universities have already jumped into the mobile learning trend by creating mobile-friendly sites and applications to provide access to their institutions' resources and information. Campus mobile applications ("apps") facilitate access to campus news and maps, transportation information, calendar of events, self-guided tours, searchable directories and even course registration (e.g., iStanford, by Stanford University). Apps also provide a platform to attract future students (e.g., StudyAtOU, by The Open University), engage students in course material (e.g., Star Walk, by Vito Technology Inc.), create opportunities for informal lifelong learning (e.g., Leafsnap, by Columbia University, the University of Maryland, and the Smithsonian Museum), and aid learning support (e.g., GoodReader, by Yuri Selukoff).

The challenge as teachers and curriculum designers is to understand and explore how to best use these resources to support learning by increasing student engagement. Here we provide a summary of recent findings and development in the area of mobile learning. We also present an activity-based approach to considering learning with mobile technology and how they contextualize learning for students. In addition, the chapter discusses the possible challenges arising from the use of mobile technology in courses. Ultimately, the goal of this chapter is to show readers the pedagogical potential of mobile technology as a tool.

Mobile Learning

As discussed in previous paragraphs, the use of mobile technology has received a lot of attention in recent years. However, the meaning of "mobile learning," or "m-learning," is highly controversial and varies among communities. Leung and Chan (2003) defined it as a "new paradigm" that provides another form of electronic learning. Others, such as Cochrane and Bateman (2010), define mobile learning purely in terms of its technologies and its hardware, namely that it is learning delivered or supported solely or mainly by mobile devices, such as smartphones. These definitions, however, lack the connection to the learner and the learning experience. Mobile learning is not just about using or learning with a mobile device (Wang, Wiesemes, & Gibbons, 2012). The appeal of mobile learning is about learning across contexts such that the nature of the learning is mediated through the portable technology. According to Sharpless, Taylor, and Vavoula (2005), a key factor of mobile learning relies on the mobility of the learner. They also argue that mobile learning is an active process of building knowledge through practice and it embraces learning that takes place within informal settings such as work.

In this chapter, mobile learning focuses on affordances of mobile devices within the online environment. The term "affordance," originally presented by Gibson (1977), refers to the relationship between the physical properties of a tool or object and the user's characteristics which enables interactions among them. The "affordances" of mobile technology have, then, become an important attribute behind promoters of the use of mobile technology for learning. Despite its prevalent use, and similarly to the definition of mobile learning, there is no clear agreement on the definition of affordance among researchers (Wright and Parchoma, 2011). Some place the primary affordance of mobile devices in their portability (e.g., Orr, 2010), whereas others argue the affordances unique to mobile devices are intrinsic to the technical features, such as built in geotagging, media recording capabilities, and communication tools (e.g., Cochrane & Bateman, 2010). It is important to note that both "mobile learning" and the "affordance for learning" in this chapter should be taken in a broad sense.

INCORPORATING MOBILE TECHNOLOGY IN ONLINE COURSES

When developing for a mobile environment, we are faced with a dilemma of choosing how to deliver content and/or tools to students. The mobile market is a multi-platform environment and several platforms are incompatible with one another. Nevertheless, advancing a teaching strategy that incorporates mobile technology for online classes does not need to require a large development budget and/or connections to mobile technology providers.

For instance, utilizing an instructional design that employs already established mobile-friendly technology allows students to learn with and through mobile devices without the need to invest heavily in research and development of these tools. This approach to the integration of mobile technology provides two viable, independent possibilities for educators. First, the adoption of learning tools that either can be accessed by mobile devices or have free apps enables their use by learners without posing extra work for faculty and instructional designers. Second, courses can also be augmented with tools developed specifically for mobile devices. Despite the fact that these are two different options, there are significant advantages of bringing together mobile-friendly and mobile-specific technology to easily scaffold mobile learning. These two opportunities are discussed in the following paragraphs.

Mobile Web 2.0 Tools

The emergence of web 2.0 nearly a decade ago ushered a new paradigm of web development. Previously the web mostly consisted of static content controlled by a small set of publishers. With web 2.0 tools, the web became a dynamic environment where users contribute to its content. These tools allow for participatory document creation and sharing, social bookmarking, communication app, user-generated content, and interactive presentations (e.g., mashups) among others. Thus, web 2.0 tools engage learners in innovative ways. Like mobile technology, these tools allow for collaborative interaction that coincides with constructivist instructional design for online courses.

Fortunately, many web 2.0 apps are mobile compatible which facilitates harnessing their collective power to improve online courses while offering a mobile element for learners. Using services that already accommodate mobile devices, hence, allows for a curriculum accessible and adapted for mobile technology. For example, Dropbox is a service that lets you access and share files easily. Users are able to access photos, documents, and videos from multiple computers and mobile devices. Synchronizing data with this mobile-friendly tool on multiple computers can indeed have a lot of uses in online learning. Part of what makes Dropbox a great mobile utility for education is its technological simplicity yet powerful collaboration capabilities. With the access of files anytime, anywhere both faculty and students are able to share files and engage in collaborations. By offering a public folder, the Dropbox enables users to share their documents with others, even if they do not have a Dropbox account. An added benefit of the Dropbox experience is that it expands the capability of mobile devices by enabling them to open files, such as those created with Microsoft Office, which mobiles may otherwise not have the software capability to accommodate.

Most social networks, such as Facebook and Twitter, have also adopted a mobile functionality to take advantage of its accessibility and features. Apps exist across architectural platforms that allow users of various mobile devices to have a seamless and efficient mobile virtual interface for social networking. Even as there may be privacy concerns for adopting social networking for teaching, effective implementation of these tools augment learning by enabling faculty and students to connect and communicate as needed, on-the-go. By harnessing the social networks' ability to foster conversation and information sharing, such as video or hyperlinks, the mobile social network community can inspire topical discussions and assist students through collaboration on assignments (Wolf, Beckem, & Matias, 2011). This method of integrating mobile web 2.0 tools is a great way to generate collaborative project-based opportunities for online learners. Further, if your courses are using a social networking element, chances are that several students are already using a mobile interface to access this element or even your course. The most important aspect, perhaps, of utilizing a mobile social networking element in courses is the familiarity students already have with these communities, which eliminates unnecessary technical stress. Being involved in social media allows students to personalize their learning.

In addition to be prevalent in today's society, social networks, as well as many other web 2.0 tools, make use of Really Simple Syndication, better known as RSS feeds. RSS feeds refer to a group of standardized web feed formats used to publish regularly updated work, such as blogs, headlines, or media channels. They are traditionally used by other apps and tools for aggregation (e.g., Vuvox, AideRSS, Feed Mingle), syndication (e.g., Word-Press, Facebook Pages, YouTube), or a combination of both (e.g., Yahoo-Pipes, Dipity). Feed readers, also called aggregators, detect feeds and present them much like a television can display a station. Using them allows course designers to collect resources and present changing content to students. RSS feeds have several benefits for mobile learning in course design. They allow courses to present content such as podcasts, YouTube videos, and professional journals in an easily accessible format that is embedded within a course and can be accessed through a computer or mobile device.

As more web services are developed, we should expect to see their mobile interface become ubiquitous in web design. For example, the personal publishing platform of WordPress offers a specific mobile interface for its blogging service. Users can access and edit their websites or blogs from mobile devices with several options, including a mobile plug in and mobile apps. Additionally, the implementation of web tools that work well on mobile platforms is not just a good strategy to engage online learners, but it also demonstrates the foresight to prepare online higher education institutions for the future maximizing available resources.

In spite of the collaborative and social nature of web 2.0 apps that benefits mobile and online learning, they could also be considered a double-edged sword. Several of these apps rely heavily on the Adobe Flash Player platform and, unfortunately, most mobile devices are not Flash compatible. Jobs (2010) explained that Adobe Flash causes several problems for mobile computing including excessive demand of battery power and security issues, and, most importantly, it cannot account for touchscreen interaction as its design is based on a static pointer device. These and other innate properties make the display of Flash-based integrative learning objects impossible to be accessible through mobile devices. Unfortunately, waiting for mobile devices to be Flash Player compatible is not an option, as Adobe has abandoned the development of their Mobile Flash Player (Arthur, 2011; Winokur, 2011).

With the majority of people using mobile devices as a primary way to accessing the Internet by 2015 (Johnson et al., 2011), instructional designers and faculty want to develop courses with tools that the most students have access to. While some web 2.0 tools may be excellent for teaching, if they remain heavily entrenched in the Adobe Flash Player, they will soon become obsolete. Most successful web 2.0 services have already adapted accordingly or offer mobile apps.

Mobile-Specific Tools

We need to address the potential learning benefits or pedagogical affordances of investing and using mobile-specific tools when considering the integration of mobile technology in online course. These affordances include the facilitation of tasks that lead to greater opportunities for learning, increased motivation/engagement, improved contextualization of learning, and richer collaborative experiences within any context. Tools such as e-publications, mobile apps, and websites designed with mobile technology in mind have become more prevalent in today's society. Beyond the basic phone features, texting, and camera capabilities, the average learner use smartphones for Internet search, games, social networking, navigation, shopping, and other personal affairs (Purcell, 2011). Perhaps more important, educators can gain from the proliferating world of mobile-specific tools as well as their growing popularity among college students of all ages.

eBooks

There are several formats for articles and content readable by mobile devices, but the two most common types are the portable document format (PDF) and the electronic publication (ePub). Both of these allow students to download content to their devices for future access independently from data connection. This portability, consequently, supports students demands for anytime, anywhere access to course materials. Both file formats can be employed across platforms. Nonetheless, there are several advantages to using ePubs over PDF for educational purposes. The ePub format emulates the feel of a traditional textbook while being viewable on tablets, eReaders, smartphones, and computers. Unlike textbooks, electronic books can contain hyperlinks and animations to assist learning. In addition, this format allows readers to search, bookmark, annotate, and highlight text within their own electronic copies to help individualize learning (Fig. 1). What is more, text in ePub format can be resized and the background colors changed to support optimal reading conditions.

Mobile Apps

Mobile native apps, applications developed specifically for mobile architecture, are tailored to harness benefits specific to the architecture of the phone and may be able to function even without an Internet connection. This feature, similar to ePubs, allows for practical use of these tools for students on the go. According to the Pew Research Center's Internet and American Life Project, in 2010, 35% of adult cell phone users had mobile apps on their phones (Purcell, Entner, Practice, & Henderson, 2010). Mobile app use is even greater among tablet owners, with 75% of them report downloading apps to their tablets (Purcell, 2011).

Developing native apps requires technical expertise that may not be available within the institution and could be cost prohibitive. While some

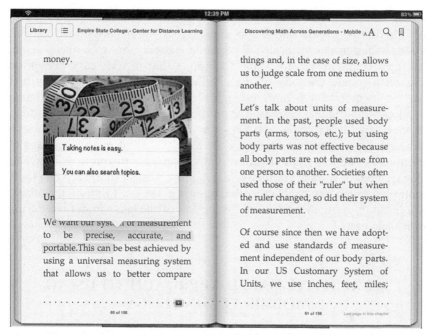

Fig. 1. Snapshot of the Electronic Book in ePub Format Created for the Lower Level Math Course, Discovering Math Across Generations. This Format Allows Students to Download the Content on Several Different Mobile Devices, Such as Kindle, Android phone, or iPad. Learners Have the Ability to Highlight, Annotate, Bookmark, Resize Texts, and Change the Background Color.

free app building tools exist, they often follow templates and do not provide unique architecture utilization needed to reach learners utilizing different mobile platforms (e.g., Android, Blackberry, and iOS). The need to develop several versions of one same app would require a great amount of institutional resources. Conversely, using third-party mobile apps in course design can help keeping up with rapidly evolving hardware. The cost per app is minimal and many of these are available free. They are becoming more than tools for "doing" things on-the-go. Instead, they are taking part of the knowledge process (Scolari, Aguado, & Feijoo, 2012). Apps have found their way into almost every academic subject and area. Useful apps for online learning also include those that help students and instructors communicating, sharing documents, collecting data, documenting results, and creating interactive projects.

Mobile Sites
An alternative to the native-app approach is mobile web development, websites designed specifically for mobile devices. As such their design leverages common web tools and techniques that provide easy navigation and often mimic the look of the interface of a native app. The current interest in mobile web apps using HTML5 elements is growing among developers and higher education institutions. Android, iOS, and Windows phones can access these app-like sites as well as computer browsers, although browser features can vary. Perhaps this is the main advantage of creating mobile web apps instead of native apps. Furthermore, editing and management of content from mobile web apps is easier to upkeep due to its centrally located nature. Making the changes in the one location, the server, will instantly push changes to all future uses of the site without interfering with their users.

AN ACTIVITY-BASED APPROACH TO USING MOBILE TECHNOLOGY

The mobile revolution professed by researchers such as Prensky (2001) and Wagner (2005) has arrived. Traditional approaches to teaching and learning are typically based on static, unidirectional tasks and criteria with fixed deadlines even when employing the use of a learning management system (LMS) to provide full or partial distance education. Today students, however, are demanding greater control of their learning (Allen & Seaman, 2011; Siemens, 2004; Vandewaetere & Clarebout, 2011).

As discussed in previous sections, the paradigm of mobile learning brings new pedagogical affordances to context for authentic learning (Cochrane & Bateman, 2010; Parry, 2011). This authentic learning experience is important as it focuses on real-world problems and solutions allowing students to explore and meaningfully connect concepts and relationships relevant to the real world (Donovan, Bransford, & Pellegrino, 1999; Lombardi, 2007). As Keskin and Metcalf (2011) summarized, there are many theories and approaches supported by the use of mobile technology as an extension of learning.

One of the most widely used learning theories when designing courses is the constructivism theory. Technology such as mobiles is transforming the constructivist framework. Constructivism, derived mainly from the works of Piaget (1970) and Vygotsky (1978), states that learning takes place in context and the learners construct much of what they learn through experiences. In addition, numerous studies have shown that students benefit positively in their academic and social development through active learning (e.g., Elby, 2000; Zhu, Valcke, & Schellens, 2010), social collaborations (e.g., Ford, Bowden, & Beard, 2011; Powell & Kalina, 2009), and the integration of technology (e.g., Alexander, 2006; Conole, de Laat, Dillon, & Darby, 2008; Ramli, 2010). The mobile learning advent supports teaching and facilitates greater learner autonomy with inquiry-based, collaborative, and socio-constructivist learning approaches by enabling the learner to construct understandings.

In 2005, Prensky stated that effective learning processes such as listening, observing, reflecting, and practicing among others are supported through the use of cell phones. Nonetheless, he made clear that using these devices as tools requires a change in practices as learning can only be supported when we "design it right" (Prensky, 2005). The Educause Center for Applied Research (ECAR) Study of Undergraduate Students and Information Technology, 2010 revealed 3 out of 10 students are using social networking technologies and nearly half of them were using them collaboratively in courses during the term of the survey (Smith & Caruso, 2010). It is clear that by using mobile web, students are actively producing knowledge (Klamma, Cao, & Spaniol, 2007) and they highly value the ability to access course materials through their mobile devices to augment the classroom setting (Gomez, 2007).

An initial attempt to provide design criteria that accounts for mobility and learning process was given by Sharpless et al. (2005). Despite the use of an identified theoretical perspective, Herrington, Herrington, and Mantei (2009) presented 11 principles recommended for the incorporation of mobile technology into higher education. More recently, from a broader perspective, Keskin and Metcalf (2011) discussed pedagogical theories in the context of mobile learning. But even so, there is no clear conceptual framework for mobile learning best practices.

The Study

The most effective way to view the use of mobile technology for online learning is, perhaps, within the context of pedagogical best practices in an activity-based approach. Our activity-based empirical study of the use of mobile technology in online courses took place during January 2010 to December 2011. Five courses across disciplines were selected to research a valid instructional design method to incorporate mobile technology. The intent of thinking about the use of mobile technology as activities rather than as a whole course is to support experimental learning for teachers and students beyond what is achieved with traditional online methods. Thus, mobile tools should be approached not just in terms of "accessing content" but also as a function of the nature of the learning activities they can support.

In this study, with the exception of one course, the students were not required to engage in the mobile-enhanced activities but rather were invited to utilize their mobile devices to interact with course material and assignments. Therefore, the conditions of the study were what you would expect for a fully asynchronous environment. In Discovering Math Across Generations, however, students in one out of the three sections simultaneously running during the fall of 2011 were required to have a mobile device such as a smartphone, a tablet, or an Internet-enabled MP3 player. For this course, the content material was the same in all sections but the learning activities in the mobile section integrated mobile tools.

This study utilizes collaboration interaction and mobile access to resources, which presents learners with opportunities for learning by doing anytime, anywhere. It essentially interweaves concepts and technology. We believe that mobile technology should not be the driver behind its use for online learning but rather the activities that involve the task or concept to be learned. This approach fits nicely into learner-centered and social-constructivist environments because students are learning through their own active involvement. At the same time, it allows students to get excited about what they are learning.

DISCUSSION

As we have noted, the inherent characteristics of collaboration, communication, and creation can be easily leveraged using mobile technology. Faculty and instructional designers must work together toward achieving balance between content, activities, and the mobile tools. An important step is to identify a topic, expected learning outcomes, and the mobile technology that is best suited for the activity. Support of learners, for both technical and learning issues, and scaffolding within the course should also be considered.

Learning activities traditionally viewed as passive have the opposite effect when accomplished with or through mobile technology. Several examples of these learning activities and the potential use of mobile technology to engage students in online learning are summarized in Table 1. For instance, the availability of robust mobile apps for smartphones and tablets that can

Table 1. Examples from Activity-Based Approach to Mobile Learning.

Learning Activity	Pedagogical Method	Mobile Activity and Tool
Evaluate content and other readings	Student-centered learning	Read, discuss, highlight, and take notes: *GoodReader, ezPDF* Text to speech converter: SpeakText
Write a collaborative (small group) essay	Collaborative learning	Blogging platform: *WordPress* File sharing: *Dropbox* Notes taking: *Evernote* Social bookmarking: *Delicious* Group communication: *Facebook, Twitter, Skype, Google +* Group meeting and sharing of screen: *Join.me*
Collect data relevant to their community and interests in a particular topic	Active learning; social constructivism; situated learning	Audio recording: voice recorder from device, *Audioboo, Voxie, Voice Recorder* Digital photo capture: camera from device, *360 Panorama* Scan and share handwritten notes and other documents: *JotNot* Geo-locate events and photos using built in GPS
Participate in synchronous group discussion with the instructor	Collaborative learning	Group texting messenger (without incurring in cost): *Kik* Group meeting and sharing of screen: *Join.me* Group communication: *Facebook, Twitter, Skype, Google +*
Peer review of classmates' written work	Collaborative learning; social constructivism	One-stop platform that provides functionality and allows to create groups, upload documents, posts discussions, and exchange of ideas with peers, calendar sharing, and grading: *Edmodo*
Create an interactive presentation	Student-centered learning; active learning; project-based learning	Video slideshows creation: *Animoto* Video streaming with social network interactivity: *Flixwagon* Mind mapping: *MindJet*
Practice and learn foreign languages	Student-centered learning	RSS feeds with YouTube videos Podcasting Mobile flashcards: *Mental Class* Group practice: *Facebook* -

handle large text files and electronic books (eBooks) in different formats have revolutionized the way students evaluate course content and other readings. With apps such as GoodReader and ezPDF, they not only have the ability to read anytime, anywhere but also the capacity to highlight content, draw lines and arrows, and perform a text search. Other tools (e.g., SpeakText) allow students with busy lives to convert text files into MP3 files and listen to them on the go. With mobile tools, students can take ownership of their reading. Fig. 1 shows a snapshot of the electronic book in ePub format created for the Discovering Math Across Generations course. It contains all the content pages normally hosted in the LMS as well as hyperlinks and pictures emulating the content pages in the course (Fig. 1). To avoid compatibility problems with the LMS, the eBook was uploaded into Dropbox and the link was shared with the students.

The range of mobile technologies that encourages communication, collaboration, and active learning are astonishing. The importance of student-faculty contact and cooperation among students for effective undergraduate education was noted by Chickering and Gamson (1987). Some companies have specifically designed mobile spaces that provide functionalities where students and faculty have the opportunity to engage. Of course, widely used social networking sites (e.g., Facebook) also have mobile apps that allow for ubiquitous interaction.

Social networking as a communication tool can strengthen faculty-student communication (Helvie-Manson, 2011). In March 2010, one section of the business course Diversity in the Workplace adopted the use of Facebook as a discussion tool. We embedded a live stream widget for the social networking site within the LMS to provide students with a one-stop, easy access to the tool. Students were highly encouraged, but not required, to participate in a term-long discussion by sharing resources and experiences through Facebook. The instructor also shared resources as well as course announcements. We found that students' sense of community within the online environment improves with the use of this mobile-social networking tool (Wolf et al., 2011). One thing has been clear from our observations, when given the choice students chose to use their mobile devices to access social tools for course assignments.

Harnessing of RSS feeds for mobiles from podcasts, news sources, and social networks also gives students access to a wealth of information at their fingertips. We developed two mobile sites based on HTML5 architecture with RSS feeds to allow students to practice foreign languages anytime, anywhere (Fig. 2). The Introductory Chinese: Language and Culture and French 1 courses take advantage of mobile sites with such aggregators to

Fig. 2. Two Snapshots of the Mobile Site Created Using RSS Feeds for the French 1 Online Course. The Image to the Left Shows the Main Menu of the Mobile Site Where Students Access Podcasts, Video Tutorials, News Resources and Social Networking Tools. The Image to the Right Shows a Detail of the Facebook Page Option. Here Students Can Read Posts from Native Speakers as well as Opt to Join the Conversation.

assist students with language practice. We simulated the look of a mobile app and included a unique icon to appear when the site is bookmarked to the mobile device's home screen. These mobile sites are a single source of supplementary resources which offers video tutorials to strengthen their vocabulary, inflection, and pronunciation skills. An added benefit of the mobile site is that students who do not have smartphones could still use the site with Chrome and Safari browsers.

Looking at the mobile sites usage for these two courses, we discovered that a significant number of students access them through Android and iOS devices as well as computer browsers. This confirms the challenge faculty and instructional designers face when trying to reach the maximum number of students. Unfortunately, for the Chinese course the information about the mobile tool was not openly visible to students in the LMS. Thus, students were not taking advantage of it until the instructor informed them of the tool. Still, a quick poll of users' opinion about the mobile site featured in the Chinese course revealed a desire for more mobile tools. Overall, our pilot project using mobile-friendly sites confirmed that: any mobile learning strategy should accommodate multiple platforms; students respond positively to the incorporation of mobile tools in online course; and, the effectiveness of mobile learning depends on instructional design.

Finally, there are apps for mobile devices catering to nearly every concentration in academia, ranging from basic facts related to highly interactive interfaces. Apps have become the most popular, and affordable, way of incorporating mobile learning in higher education. A wide variety of apps were investigated throughout the various projects, some with more success than others. Fig. 3 presents some of the most useful and popular general apps for teaching and learning based on functionality in their specific category. This affordance of mobile technology offers vast opportunities for assignments that involve researching topics and sharing resources learners find.

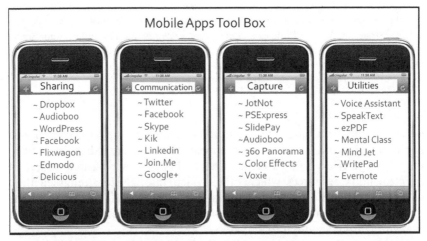

Fig. 3. The Mobile Apps Tool Box Lists Some of the Most Useful and Popular General Apps for Teaching and Learning Based on Functionality Within Four Categories: Sharing, Communication, Capture, and Utilities. Each of These Work Across Several Platforms; However, They May Not be Available on all Platforms.

Mobile math apps were integrated throughout each learning module in Discovering Math Across Generations to increase engagement and promote creative, experimental learning. This course is designed for interaction with children between the ages of 6 and 12, called a Math Exploration Partner (MEP), through a series of hands-on activities. The iChoose app, for example, provides an opportunity for authentic learning in the area of probability through coin toss, dice roll, and random number activities. Other course activities give students the opportunity to also find their own math-related apps. Importantly, students complete an online journal throughout the term in which they reflect on their mobile math activities based on the concepts, the apps, and their experience.

Further, mobile videos and pictures can be directly streamed from smartphones with apps such as Flixwagon and Flickr, respectively. The built-in camera on most cell phones can record audio and video and capture photos providing with additional ways to engage in active learning. As demonstrated by Ferry (2009) and Hoban (2009), the use of mobile devices to take pictures and videos is convenient for group projects as well as case-study assignments where learners collect data from their communities. The same applies to the Global Positioning System (GPS) most mobile devices currently have. The GPS provides latitude and longitude information that enables sharing of spatial information relevant to field-related experiences, including geotagging of photos and maps. Learners, thus, can engage in active and situated learning using their devices and apps. Students in the lower-level science course, GPS, and the New Geography are encouraged to collect ecological field data using mobile devices and share with the rest of the class.

Currently, we are also working on incorporating apps for group projects. Group projects are a great collaborative learning experience that can take place synchronously and asynchronously when using mobile devices. Apps such as Join.me allow instructors and students to share a computer screen with multiple users remotely when working in group projects. Another activity that encourages student-student interaction and could be aided with mobile technology is peer review of student-generated content. Peer review encourages collaboration and reduces the time faculty spend evaluating each assignment. Edmodo is a one-stop platform that provides functionality and allows creation of groups, uploading of documents, discussion posting, and exchange of ideas with peers, calendar sharing, and grading. This tool is accessible through the browser and several mobile platforms.

CONSTRAINTS AND CHALLENGES OF MOBILE LEARNING

It is true that many college students have regular access to smartphones, tablets, and other mobile devices. As a result, more educators are looking for ways to utilize this technology in their distance, online courses. Despite the potential of mobile devices for online teaching and learning, we need to understand the possible constraints and challenges that come with the pedagogical use of such devices. Any systemic approach to the transformation of online education to embrace mobile affordances can hardly avoid struggles along the way. We catalogue potential challenges of mobile learning implementation into three main types: institutional, architectural, and pedagogical (see Table 2 for a summary of mobile learning challenges).

It is important to recognize the limitations of mobile learning associated with the institution, such as the established infrastructure, demand on faculty members, training needs, and technical support. Likewise, every technology has limitations. Mobile technology has shown some architectural problems including the difference in platforms and the need for wireless connection via a data plan or a WiFi hotspot. It is important to note that we did not include the physical attributes of mobile devices in this category as we believe they are negligible; rapid advances in technology continues to improve their memory, screen size, and battery life as well as network reliability and speed. Literature review shows that the most important constraint of utilizing mobile devices to engage students in education, regardless of the instructional setting, is undoubtedly the lack of best practices for effective instructional design. Notably, none of these challenging elements exists in isolation.

Institutional

Institutionally driven issues are, most likely, the first thing that comes to the minds of many educators when thinking about hurdles of mobile learning. Weak or no infrastructure support could seriously hamper any mobile learning initiative even before it is envisioned. Inadequate policies about what faculty and professionals can test or have in their computers hold back the integration of mobile technology in courses. The traditional hierarchical organizational structure of colleges and universities frequently determines the organization's technological needs and its vision for the future. It is crucial that efforts are made by administrators to decentralize decision making of technology implementation as it relates to teaching and learning.

Table 2. Summary of Challenges of Mobile Learning.

Category	Challenge	Description
Institutional	Established Infrastructure	Weak or no institutional infrastructure support, including inadequate policies, human resource capacity, technological services, and funding constrain the integration of mobile technology in courses
	Demand on faculty	The lack of time is systematic and one of the most important, pressing constraints affecting faculty innovators. Course load and other demands on full-time and part-time faculty time hinders the amount of time they can allocate to explore the use of new technologies in their pedagogy
	Training and technical support	Generally, most faculty do not receive training to stay abreast of new technologies. If they want to make use of innovative tools, they need to learn on their own. This is extremely important for online education models that heavily rely on part-time faculty
Architectural	Cost of data plans	Although the affordability of mobile devices such as smartphones has been steadily increasing as technology advances, the cost of data plans for these devices could limit their usage by students.
	Mobile platforms	One important technical challenge of engaging in mobile learning is the mobile technology itself. Students own a wide range of devices supported by different platforms, such as Apple's iOS, Android, and Windows. In addition, mobile platforms not always support web tools (e.g. Flash interactive objects)
Pedagogical	Effective learning design	Learning style differs among students. Thus, instructional designers and faculty need to take these differences into account when adding mobile technology tools to online courses
	Learning assessment	Faculty and instructional designers are encountering difficulties implementing effective assessment methods when using tools such as mobile apps
	Capturing student work	It is important to use mobile technology to supplement learning as used in conjunction with a learning management system in order to create a repository of student work

Additionally, the current economic crisis in most higher education institutions worldwide also limits and prevents changes needed for innovation in the advent of new technology and learners' interests. The lack of human resources, technological services, and equipment could cause the most innovative players to stagnate. An approach that has proven beneficial at the Center for Distance Learning, State University of New York Empire State College is the administration's support for the creation of a temporary group formed for the purpose of carrying out an exploratory phase around an affinity topic like mobile learning tools. The membership of such a task force needs to include faculty, instructional designers, and administrators that are early adopters and should engage on small-scaled projects. Encouraging collaborations among early adopters could significantly improve negative views of institutional commitment to the advancement of pedagogical practices.

We also need to recognize that carrying out innovation in teaching places extraordinary demands on faculty members. The lack of time is systematic among faculty and one of the most important, pressing constraints affecting those more inclined to become innovators. Course load and other demands on full-time and part-time faculty reduce the amount of time they can allocate to explore the use of new technologies in their pedagogy. Unless faculty are given release time to fully engage in the development of mobile learning materials, very few faculty will be willing to embrace the use of mobiles in their online courses. Furthermore, sponsorship of faculty reassignment that provides release from regular activities (e.g., teaching) to support the creation of projects utilizing mobile technology shows faculty that their institution is invested in teaching and learning. Similarly, providing recognition and rewards for the effective use of mobile learning as well as other technology in teaching and learning convey the message that taking on the demanding task of harnessing technology to enhance student learning is valuable. General promotion and tenure criteria should make explicit the recognition for effective integration of technology within the context of teaching and scholarship, thus creating an institutional culture that supports an organic evolution of teaching and learning.

At the same time, many people are uneasy about engaging in innovative, technology-based endeavors for teaching and learning regardless of their personal interest. Generally, most faculty do not receive training to stay abreast of new technologies. If they want to make use of innovative tools, they need to learn on their own. Training and technical support is particularly important for online education models that heavily rely on instructors hired to teach courses for a particular length of time, often part-time. The strong growth of part-time instructors, also known as adjunct faculty, teaching online courses over the last decade has been primarily the result of increasing enrollments in online education (Allen & Seaman, 2008). However, many institutions have yet to develop a sustainable model for training of adjunct faculty beyond the basic learning management tools, which causes lack of interest in technology integration in their courses. Administrators should, perhaps, strongly advocate for an online collaborative environment where all faculty and instructional designers can learn about and share resources of mobile-enhanced online learning to support continuous professional development. Just like with students, increasing access to resources could translate into increasing faculty and administrators buy-in and interest. Of course, many may argue, this is true for any pedagogical approach.

Architectural

Another important challenge of using mobile technology to support learning is that it assumes students' ownership of these devices and, in some cases, data plan coverage. Hence, using mobile technologies as an optional supplemental resource for teaching helps to overcome this obstacle and reduces inequalities that new educational technology could create. As mentioned in the previous section, the inherent differences between platforms make it especially difficult to maximize infrastructure as the platform determines the type of possible media usage. Therefore, we need to incorporate these parameters in order to ensure that learners effectively engage with the technologies without many problems.

Mobile technology in itself provides a barrier as students own a wide range of devices supported by different platforms, such as Apple's iOS, Android, and Windows. Unfortunately, these mobile platforms do not always support web tools. For instance, as discussed, interactive objects created using Adobe's Flash Player are not supported by Apple's iOS and the Windows Phone. In fact, in November 2011, Adobe announced the end of Flash Player for mobile devices after recognizing that it cannot become ubiquitous on these devices (Winokur, 2011). In addition, several design considerations need to be taken in order to provide easy use of mobile web or apps by students. We must pay particular attention to user input and needs. Also, technical focus should be given to layout of any in-house developed mobile tool. Content, for instance, must be broken up into appropriate chunks and be viewable without extensive downward scrolling in order to facilitate viewing on smaller mobile devices such as smartphones. Finally, we consider physical attributes of mobile devices, such as screen size, negligible as new technology keeps revolutionizing them.

Pedagogical

Perhaps the most serious issue facing educators exploring mobile learning is the need of effective instructional design practices. As we all know not all learners are alike. The integration of mobile learning for different learning styles during course design is imperative. Effective course design takes into account students' excitement when exposed to learning experiences that go beyond information assimilation to create authentic learning experiences. Project-based collaboration and guided inquiry evoke increased learner motivation. The inclusion of mobile technology during course design leads to ubiquitous, active, and collaborative learning activities.

A literature review confirms that mobile technologies empower learners to construct and guide their own knowledge (e.g., Cochrane & Bateman, 2010; Herrington, 2009; Jeng, Wu, Huang, Tan, & Yang, 2010; Kervin & Mantei, 2009; Lim, Fadzi, & Mansor, 2011; McConatha, Praul, & Lynch, 2008; Park, 2011; Ramli, 2010). However, a central concern is the need for best practices to develop mobile enhanced learning in online higher education. In a practical sense, online courses should structure learning activities to foster interaction and collaboration among all students and instructors. Regardless of the different approaches, theories, and practices that encompass mobile learning, we need to make sure that our online courses use students' digital strengths and interests accordingly.

An additional concern about mobile learning is assessment, particularly when using a student-centered approach to course design. To achieve an effective match between learners' assessment and technology, online course should have clear alignment with the learning activities, outcomes, and assessment (McNeill, Gosper, & Hedberg, 2010). It is, however, not always easy to develop measurable learning outcomes. The identification of learning needs and goals is essential to the effective implementation of mobile technology. The difficulty, then, is to find ways to assess students even when they are learning actively, asynchronously, anywhere, and across different contexts. Recent research (e.g., Hwang & Chang, 2011; Vavoula & Sharples, 2009) suggests that when evaluating online learning, a formative-based approach allows greater potential and flexibility due to the ubiquities of mobile learning.

Related to assessment is the challenge of tracking learners' progress and capturing student work. Commonly available LMS, such as Blackboard and Moodle, are capable of hosting multimedia content created with and for mobile devices. Yet, material submitted by students should be archived in the LMS for future reference and legal purposes. This poses a significant challenge to faculty. Faculty need to rely more on a combination of data collected and reports from students. For example, we have found that when using mobile-enabled social networking tools to facilitate informal group discussions, these are more effective when coupled with a self-reflection about the learning submitted through the LMS. This approach decreases time spent by the instructor finding ways to digitally capture student work and learning.

FINAL REMARKS

Mobile technology is growing at an exponential rate. Many of us have regular access to smartphones and tablets and use them to talk, connect through text messaging, and to take pictures and search the web. In a few years the vast majority of Internet users will be accessing it with a mobile device. These devices can do everything computers and books can do as well as incorporate other features such as camera, voice recording, and GPS capabilities. Educators should take into account this transformation when engaging students in a range of different learning processes. Mobile devices cannot be the ultimate solution to encourage students' participation in online courses. However, good educators will see the opportunity in using this technology to enhance the learning process and facilitate student engagement.

Currently, students are using technologies extensively in a combination of ways to find, manage, and produce content. The average learner is becoming more comfortable with switching between media, tools, and content. Mobile technologies provide learners with more flexibility in terms of being able to undertake learning anytime, anywhere. Of course, there will always be a few students who are resistant, or for whom mobile learning is not the best approach to teaching and learning. Therefore, instructional design must take into consideration the learning conditions of students without mobile devices or that do not wish to utilize these devices for course work. The learning for these students should be equal to those engage through- and with mobile devices.

Mobile learning affords numerous active, collaborative, and social learning opportunities. The prevalence of mobile technologies as well as students' familiarity with these tools offers us a platform rich with possibilities. Mobile devices provide a convenient platform for anytime, anywhere learning including outside of the online LMS. Importantly, the use of technology known to our students eliminates technological barriers and helps create authentic learning experiences relevant to each of them.

Perhaps the most powerful use of mobile technology in online courses is to supplement rather than replace the utilization of computers and the LMS in learning. The first logical step for faculty and instructional designers who would like to engage students with mobile technology in online courses, then, is to make course materials accessible to students in mobile-friendly formats, such as eBooks.

In summary, we need to remember that using mobile technology to engage students in online learning is not just about using the devices but rather about learning across contexts anytime, anywhere. As seeing in our various projects undertaken, mobile technology immersed students within a constructivist environment and has the potential to greatly improve active learning, teamwork, critical thinking. Regardless of the theoretical framework used when developing the learning activities, the instructional design should help in enriching the learner's experience and learning. The effectiveness of the use of mobile technology in learning requires conceptualization of online course design in a different way. Instructional design approaches must foster students' learning styles and opportunities for knowledge construction. A key factor to successful integration of mobile technology in higher education is the close collaboration between faculty and instructional designers with the support of administrators. The advantages of using mobile technology in online learning are innumerable both for students and faculty, and the disadvantages generally stem from not knowing how to incorporate them.

ACKNOWLEDGMENTS

We thank Thomas Mackey (SUNY Empire State College) for his instrumental support. We would also thank Pauline Carrico (SUNY Empire State College) and the anonymous reviewers for their valuable comments and suggestions.

REFERENCES

Alexander, B. (2006). Web 2.0: A new wave of innovation for teaching and learning? *Educause Review, 41*, 32–44.

Allen, I. E., & Seaman, J. (2008). *Staying the course: Online education in the United States, 2008.* Needham, MA: Babson Survey Research Group and the Sloan Consortium.

Allen, I. E., & Seaman, J. (2011). *Going the distance: Online education in the United States, 2011.* Needham, MA: Quahog Research Group LLC, Babson Survey Research Group, and the Sloan Consortium.

Arthur, C. (2011, November 9). Adobe kills mobile Flash, giving Steve Jobs the last laugh. *The Guardian*. Retrieved from http://www.guardian.co.uk/technology/2011/nov/09/adobe-flash-mobile-dead

Bransford, J. D., Brown, A. L., & Cocking, R. R. (Eds.). (2000). *How people learn: Brain, mind, experience, and school: Expanded edition*. Washington, DC: The National Academies Press.

Chickering, A. W., & Gamson, Z. F. (1987). Seven principles for good practice in undergraduate education. *American Association of Higher Education Bulletin, 39*, 3–7.

Cobcroft, R. S., Towers, S., Smith, J., & Bruns, A. (2006). Mobile learning in review: Opportunities and challenges for learners, teachers, and instructors. In *Proceedings of the online learning and teaching (OLT) conference 2006*. Queensland University of Technology, Brisbane, Australia (pp. 21–30).

Cochrane, T., & Bateman, R. (2010). Smartphones give you wings: Pedagogical affordances of mobile web 2.0. *Australian Journal of Education Technology, 26*, 1–4.

comScore, Inc. (2012). *2012 mobile future in focus*. Retrieved from http://www.comscore.com/Press_Events/Presentations_Whitepapers/2012/2012_Mobile_Future_in_Focus

Conole, G., de Laat, M., Dillon, T., & Darby, J. (2008). 'Disruptive technologies', 'pedagogical innovation': What's new? Finding from an in-depth study of students' use and perception of technology. *Computers & Education, 50*, 511–524.

Corbeil, J. R., & Valdes-Corbeil, M. E. (2007). Are you ready for mobile learning? *Educause Quarterly, 2*, 51–58.

Donovan, M. S., Bransford, J. D., & Pellegrino, J. W. (1999). *How people learn: Bridging research and practice*. Washington, DC: National Academy Press.

Elby, A. (2000). What students' learning of representations tells us about constructivism. *Journal of Mathematical Behavior, 19*, 481–502.

Ferry, B. (2009). Using mobile phones to enhance teacher learning in environmental education. In J. Herrington, A. Herrington, J. Mantei, I. Olney & B. Ferry (Eds.), *New technologies, new pedagogies: Mobile learning in higher education* (pp. 45–55). New South Wales: Faculty of Education, University of Wollongong.

Ford, N., Bowden, M., & Beard, J. (2011). Learning together: Using social media to foster collaboration in higher education. In L. A. Wankel & C. Wankel (Eds.), *Higher education administration with social media (Cutting-edge technologies in higher education)* (Vol. 2, pp. 105–126). Bingley, UK: Emerald.

Gibson, J. J. (1977). The theory of affordances. In R. Shaw & J. Bransford (Eds.), *Perceiving, acting, and knowing: Toward an ecological psychology* (pp. 67–82). Oxford: Oxford University Press.

Gomez, S. (2007, February 9). Scroll to 'E' for education. *Times Higher Education*. Retrieved from http://www.timeshighereducation.co.uk/story.asp?storycode=207730

Helvie-Manson, L. (2011). Facebook, "friending," and faculty-student communication. In L. A. Wankel & C. Wankel (Eds.), *Teaching arts and science with the new social media (Cutting-edge technologies in higher education)* (Vol. 3, pp. 61–87). Bingley, UK: Emerald.

Herrington, A. (2009). Using smartphones to create digital teaching episodes as resources in adult education. In J. Herrington, A. Herrington, J. Mantei, I. Olney & B. Ferry (Eds.), *New technologies, new pedagogies: Mobile learning in higher education* (pp. 28–35). Faculty of Education, University of Wollongong, New South Wales, Australia.

Herrington, A., Herrington, J., & Mantei, J. (2009). Design principles for mobile learning. In J. Herrington, A. Herrington, J. Mantei, I. Olney & B. Ferry (Eds.), *New technologies,* new pedagogies: Mobile learning in higher education (pp. 129–138). Faculty of Education, University of Wollongong, New South Wales, Australia.

Hoban, G. F. (2009). Using mobile phone cameras to capture images for slowmations: Student-generated science animations. In J. Herrington, A. Herrington, J. Mantei, I. Olney & B. Ferry (Eds.), New technologies, new pedagogies: Mobile learning in higher education (pp. 110–119). Faculty of Education, University of Wollongong, New South Wales, Australia.

Hwang, G-J., & Chang, H-F. (2011). A formative assessment-based mobile learning approach to improving the learning attitudes and achievements of students. Computers & Education, 56, 1023–1031.

Jeng, Y-L., Wu, T-T., Huang, Y-M., Tan, Q., & Yang, J. H. (2010). The add-on impact of mobile applications in learning strategies: A review study. Educational Technology & Society, 13, 3–11.

Jobs, S. (2010, April). Thoughts on flash, Apple. Retrieved from http://www.apple.com/hotnews/thoughts-on-flash/

Johnson, L., Adams, S., & Cummins, M. (2012). The NMC horizon report: 2012 higher education edition. Austin, TX: The New Media Consortium. Retrieved from http://www.nmc.org/publications/horizon-report-2012-higher-ed-edition

Johnson, L., Levine, A., Smith, R., & Stone, S. (2010). The 2010 horizon report. Austin, TX: The New Media Consortium. Retrieved from http://wp.nmc.org/horizon2010/

Johnson, L., Smith, R., Willis, H., Levine, A., & Haywood, K. (2011). The 2011 horizon report. Austin, TX: The New Media Consortium. Retrieved from http://wp.nmc.org/horizon2011/

Kervin, L., & Mantei, J. (2009). Collaborative gathering, evaluating and communicating "wisdom" using iPods. In J. Herrington, A. Herrington, J. Mantei, I. Olney & B. Ferry (Eds.), New technologies, new pedagogies: Mobile learning in higher education (pp. 99–109). New South Wales: Faculty of Education, University of Wollongong.

Keskin, N. O., & Metcalf, D. (2011). The current perspectives, theories and practices of mobile learning. The Turkish Online Journal of Educational Technology, 10, 202–208.

Kirschner, A. (2012, April 8). Innovations in higher education? Hah!. The Chronicle Review. Retrieved from http://chronicle.com/article/Innovations-in-Higher/131424/

Klamma, R., Cao, Y., & Spaniol, M. (2007). Watching the blogosphere: Knowledge sharing in Web 2.0. In N. Nicolov, N. Glance, E. Adar, M. Hurst, M. Liberman, J. H. Martin & F. Salvetti (Eds.), Proceedings of the international conference on weblogs and social media. Retrieved from http://www.icwsm.org/papers/2-Klamma-Cao-Spaniol.pdf

Leung, C.-H., & Chan, Y.-Y. (2003). Mobile learning: A new paradigm in electronic learning. In V. Devedzic, J. Spector, D. Sampson & Kinshuk (Eds.), Proceedings of the 3rd IEEE conference on advanced learning technologies, July 2003 (pp. 76–80).

Lim, T., Fadzi, M., & Mansor, N. (2011). Mobile learning via SMS at Open University Malaysia: Equitable, effective, and sustainable. International Review of Research in Open and Distance Learning, 12, 122–137.

Lombardi, M. M. (2007, January 1). Authentic learning for the 21st Century: An overview. Educause Learning Initiative (ELI) White Paper. Retrieved from http://www.educause.edu/library/resources/authentic-learning-21st-century-overview

McConatha, D., Praul, M., & Lynch, M. J. (2008). Mobile learning in higher education: An empirical assessment of a new educational tool. Turkish Online Journal of Educational Technology, 7, 2.

McNeill, M., Gosper, M., & Hedberg, J. (2010). Aligning technologies and the curriculum: A snapshot of academic practice. In Kinshuk, D.G. Sampson, M. Spector, P. Isaias, D. Ifenthaler, & R. Vasiu (Eds.), *Proceeding of the IADS international conference in cognition & exploratory learning in digital age*, January 2010 (pp. 153–160).

Orr, G. (2010). A review of literature in mobile learning: Affordances and constraints. In U. Hoppe, R. Pea, & C.-C. Liu (Eds.), *Proceedings of the 6th IEEE international conference on wireless, mobile, and ubiquitous technologies in education* IEEE Computer Society Press, Kaohsiung, Taiwan (pp. 107–111).

Park, Y. (2011). A pedagogical framework for mobile learning: Categorizing educational applications of mobile learning technology into four types. *International Review of Research in Open and Distance Learning, 12*, 78–102.

Parry, D. (2011). Mobile perspectives: On teaching mobile literacy. *EDUCAUSE Review, 46*. Retrieved from http://www.educause.edu/EDUCAUSE + Review/EDUCAUSEReview-MagazineVolume46/iMobilePerspectivesOnteachingi/226160

Pearson Foundation (2012). *Pearson foundation survey on students and tablets*. Retrieved from http://www.pearsonfoundation.org/great-learning/Survey-Students-and-Tablets.html

Piaget, J. (1970). Piaget's theory. In P. H. Mussen (Ed.), *Carmichael's manual of child psychology* (3rd ed., Vol. 1, pp. 703–732). New York, NY: Wiley.

Powell, K. C., & Kalina, C. J. (2009). Cognitive and social constructivism: Developing tools for an effective classroom. *Education, 130*, 241–250.

Prensky, M. (2001). Digital natives, digital immigrants, Part 1. *On the Horizon, 9*, 1–6.

Prensky, M. (2005). What can you learn from a cell phone? Almost anything!. *Innovate, 1*(5). Retrieved from http://www.innovateonline.info/pdf/vol1_issue5/What_Can_You_Learn_from_a_Cell_Phone__Almost_Anything!.pdf

Purcell, K. (2011, November 2). *Half of adult cell phone owners have apps on their phones*. Pew Internet & American Life Project. Retrieved from http://pewinternet.org/Reports/2011/Apps-update.aspx

Purcell, K., Entner, R., Practice, T., & Henderson, N., (2010, September 15). *The rise of apps culture*. Pew Internet & American Life Project. Retrieved from http://pewinternet.org/Reports/2010/The-Rise-of-Apps-Culture.aspx

Ramli, R. (2010). Technology enhanced learning: Fostering cooperative learning through the integration of online communication as part of teaching. *World Academy of Science, Engineering and Technology, 69*, 611–614.

Revere, L., & Kovach, J. V. (2011). Online technologies for engaged learning: A meaningful synthesis for educators. *The Quarterly Review of Distance Education, 12*, 113–124.

Scolari, C. A., Aguado, J. M., & Feijóo, C. (2012). Mobile media: Towards a definition and taxonomy of contents and applications. *International Journal of Interactive Mobile Technologies, 6*, 29–37. Retrieved from http://www.online-journals.org/index.php/i-jim

Sharpless, M., Taylor, J., & Vavoula, G. (2005). Towards a theory of mobile learning. In H. van der Merwe & T. Brown (Eds.), *Proceedings of mLearn 2005*. Retrieved from http://www.mlearn.org.za/CD/papers/Sharples-%20Theory%20of%20Mobile.pdf

Siemens, G. (2004). *Connectivism: A learning theory for the digital age*. Retrieved from http://www.elearnspace.org/Articles/connectivism.htm

Smith, A. (2011, July 11). *Smartphone adoption and usage*. Pew Internet & American Life Project. Retrieved from http://pewinternet.org/Reports/2011/Smartphones.aspx

Smith, A. (2012, March 1). *46% of American adults are smartphone owners.* Pew Internet & American Life Project. Retrieved from http://pewinternet.org/Reports/2012/Smartphone-Update-2012.aspx

Smith, S. D., & Caruso, J. B. (2010). The ECAR study of undergraduate students and information technology, 2010. *Research Study,* 6. Boulder, CO: EDUCAUSE Center for Applied Research. Retrieved from http://www.educause.edu/library/resources/ecar-study-undergraduate-students-and-information-technology-2010

Vandewaetere, M., & Clarebout, G. (2011). Can instruction as such affect learning? The case of learner control. *Computer & Education, 57,* 2322–2332.

Vavoula, G., & Sharples, M. (2009). Meeting the challenges in evaluating mobile learning: A 3-level evaluation framework. *International Journal of Mobile and Blended Learning, 1,* 54–75.

Vygotsky, L. S. (1978). *Mind in society: The development of higher psychological processes.* Cambridge, MA: Harvard University Press.

Wagner, E. D. (2005). Enabling mobile learning. *EDUCAUSE Review, 40,* 40–53.

Wang, R., Wiesemes, R., & Gibbons, C. (2012). Developing digital fluency through ubiquitous mobile devices: Findings from a small-scale study. *Computers & Education, 58,* 570–578. Retrieved from http://dx.doi.org/10.1016/j.compedu.2011.04.013

Winokur, D. (2011). Flash to focus on PC browsing and mobile apps; Adobe to more aggressively contribute to HTML5. *Adobe Feature Blogs,* Retrieved from http://blogs.adobe.com/conversations/2011/11/flash-focus.html

Wolf, D., Beckem, J., & Matias, A. (2011). Interactive technologies: Enhancing academic learning and stimulated student engagement with social media. In T. Bastiaens & M. Ebner (Eds.), *Proceedings of world conference on educational multimedia, hypermedia and telecommunications 2011* (pp. 2639–2644). Chesapeake, VA: AACE.

Wright, S., & Parchoma, G. (2011). Technologies for learning? An actor-network theory critique of 'affordances' in research on mobile learning. *Research in Learning Technology, 19,* 247–258.

Zhu, C., Valcke, M., & Schellens, T. (2010). A cross-cultural study of teacher perspectives on teacher roles and adoption of online collaborative learning in higher education. *European Journal of Teacher Education, 33,* 147–165.

PART II
APPLICATION OF MOBILE APPLICATIONS: SMARTPHONES, SKYPE AND TEXTING APPLICATIONS

FASHION DESIGN PODCAST INITIATIVE: EMERGING TECHNOLOGIES AND FASHION DESIGN TEACHING STRATEGIES

Therèsa M. Winge and Mary C. Embry

ABSTRACT

The Fashion Design Podcast Initiative educated students about podcasting by having the students share in the teaching activities as part of learning. The faculty implemented Lernen durch Lehren *(LdL) or "Learning by Teaching" pedagogy and Bloom's revised taxonomy to encourage and support creativity, independence, confidence, and soft skills (i.e., teamwork, communication, decision making, research, exploration, and presentation skills) with emerging technologies. By creating educational podcasts, students developed skills in new technologies and disseminated information to educate others about fashion design. Faculty and students discovered the benefits and drawbacks with emerging technologies as teaching strategies.*

Increasing Student Engagement and Retention using Mobile Applications:
Smartphones, Skype and Texting Technologies
Cutting-edge Technologies in Higher Education, Volume 6D, 145–174
Copyright © 2013 by Emerald Group Publishing Limited
All rights of reproduction in any form reserved
ISSN: 2044-9968/doi:10.1108/S2044-9968(2013)000006D008

INTRODUCTION

Fashion design is a highly competitive and innovative field, which requires faculty members and students to exist on the cutting-edge of emerging technologies. One such technology with the potential to be a powerful tool for fashion design (and teaching) is a podcast – digital audio and/or video media files (MP3s and MP4s) posted to the Internet as a series of downloadable broadcasts. We sought to increase student engagement and retention using mobile applications, such as podcasts, that can be watched and listened to on smartphones, tablet computers, and MP3 (and MP4) devices. Accordingly, in 2008, the Fashion Design Podcast Initiative project was developed to educate fashion design students about podcasting, and in turn, those students created podcasts to educate other students and the public about topics in the range of fashion design exhibitions.

The Fashion Design Podcast Initiative was housed within a fashion design capstone course. The focus of the course was preparing students for various types of fashion exhibitions and presentations, such as fashion portfolios, fashion shows, and showroom displays. The podcast project provided students with opportunities to explore emerging technologies in order to create fashion exhibits and presentations by posting their podcasts to the Internet and sharing this information with a broader audience beyond those in the classroom.

We, the faculty for the Fashion Design Podcast Initiative, secured a Technology Initiative Grant (TIG) from Apple Computers in 2009. Projects funded by TIG were provided educational workshops, software, and hardware. The TIG was beneficial to the success of the podcast project, in that it provided funding for training for faculty (at early stages) and students, equipment (iFlip video cameras, headsets, software, MP3 devices, etc.), and technology support.

In designing this project, we were guided primarily by two pedagogical strategies, which allowed us to incorporate emerging technologies (i.e., digital portfolios and podcasts) into the fashion design curriculum. The Lernen durch Lehren (LdL) or "Learning by Teaching" pedagogy (Gartner, Kohler, & Riessman, 1971) engaged students with the project as both learners and teachers. To shape the project, we relied on Bloom's revised taxonomy (Anderson and Krathwohl, 2001) because it most closely reflected the design process and design thinking, a common framework utilized by fashion design students.

In this chapter, we introduce the Fashion Design Podcast Initiative project and the resulting podcasts that used MP3 and MP4 media files. We implemented LdL and Bloom's revised taxonomy with the design process as teaching strategies to support students in creating educational fashion-related podcasts for the Internet. By creating educational podcasts, students not only built skills in new technologies, but also disseminated information about fashion design.

FASHION DESIGN PODCAST INITIATIVE EXHIBITION PROJECT

The purpose of the Fashion Design Podcast Initiative project was for students to create a series of podcasts about types of fashion design exhibitions/presentations to expand their knowledge and digital portfolios. We exposed students to the emerging technologies associated with creating and posting a podcast series. A podcast is a single or series of digital files containing audio and/or visual media posted to the Internet and available for listening and/or viewing (Geoghegan & Klass, 2007, pp. 1–10). Podcasts may be downloaded or streamed, usually as part of a series using portable devices (Lee, Miller & Newham, 2009). While "podcast' is an overarching term used to refer to audio, video, and audio/video broadcast, the latter two are also known as a "vodcast" because of the video component. The podcast media files are typically MP3s for audio and MP4s for audio and visual content. We use "podcast" to refer to the digital files created for the fashion design capstone course published or posted to the Internet.

EMERGING TECHNOLOGIES

The significance of emerging technologies is relevant in nearly any field of study today; however, fashion design has added pressures from its real-world industries. The fashion industry demands the fast turnarounds to meet the ever changing and materialistic culture in which fashion thrives as a multi-billion dollar industry (Jenkyn Jones, 2005). This fast paced industry is empowered by the seemingly temporary nature of fashion as a consumable product without copyright protection. Fashion designs are stolen, interpreted, shared, reframed, and recontextualized, which results in a highly innovative industry (Bollier & Racine, 2005). Subsequently, graduating students are more competitive in the fashion industry, i.e., an environment searching for constant innovation. Being comfortable with innovation includes being familiar with and easily adapting to the latest technologies, as well as recognizing the potential for emerging technologies. Alumni and students returning from internships report that a lack of computer skills or fear of technology is not acceptable in the fashion industry.

The Fashion Design Podcast Initiative project was technology intensive, requiring both faculty and students to learn and successfully utilize emerging software and hardware. The software included Microsoft Power-Point, Audacity, GarageBand, Adobe Photoshop, iTunes, and iMovie, along with hardware such as digital video cameras, headsets, microphones, and smartphones (and other MP3 and MP4 devices). Several student groups explored additional software, such as Adobe Photoshop and Final Cut Pro. In addition to learning the skills to use the new software and hardware, we became familiar with a new lexicon to effectively communicate about the technology and aspects of the project. We also learned about file types (e.g., MP3 versus MP4), uploading protocols for publishing podcasts (e.g., RSS feeds, file compression, and bandwidth), podcast supporting websites (e.g., iTunes and YouTube), and issues of copyright and intellectual property.

PODCASTS IN THE PEDAGOGICAL LITERATURE

The value of podcasts resides in its efficacy and effective communication for the creator and user (Heilesen, 2010), as well as its portability and accessibility. In academe, podcasts function as a significant resource as an alternative educational tool and vehicle for delivery of supplemental course content. Podcast use has grown in higher education as a means to reinforce class material, through review of concepts and issues once contained in lectures (Lonn & Teasley, 2009). Moreover, faculty and students can access podcasts at their convenience, listen/watch the information at a pace best for the "learner," and the content may be reviewed repeatedly on a variety of devices for deeper comprehension and insights.

The potential strength of podcasting rests in the fact that as an audio (and visual) based technology, it addresses multiple modes of learning as well as the ever-changing college student's lifestyle. The benefits include the well-documented use of supplementary audio and visual content as a teaching tool; low cost and comparatively low barriers for adoption, syndication capabilities; and the opportunities for in place or mobile learning (Lee et al., 2009). Research data, however, does not support the ways these features are fully realized as benefits for and by students (Hew, 2009). Heilsen's (2010) review of the literature of podcasting experiences in higher education demonstrate that students commonly use podcasts in a traditional manner, as supplemental learning tools within study environments in front of a computer. In contrast, the public may use the podcasts in mobile applications while multitasking (Hurst, Welte, & Jung, 2007). Lee et al. (2009) argue that podcasting in its most popular implementation exists as a supplement to in-class material and simply copies traditional behaviorist models where teachers impart knowledge. Podcasting creation and syndication, however, has the potential to follow social constructivist models where teacher, learners, and peers work to create and disseminate knowledge (Burr, 1995). Podcasts have the potential to be a creative tool in the classroom, where podcasting is used as a content-integrated pedagogical device, rather than a vehicle for documenting class lectures (McGarr, 2009). Thus, as an emerging technology, the podcast has the potential to evolve from a tool of content review to more fully fulfill the capability of the technology, in its flexibility, portability, and access.

The creation of podcasts by students emphasizes innovation in the creative creation of coursework that is shared among an increasingly mobile and smartphone-enabled population. Podcasts hold more learner value in the act of creating knowledge that is based on sound pedagogical practice (Lee, McLoughlin, & Chan, 2008). This study adds to the literature on the impact of podcasting on teaching practice and student knowledge, as demonstrating the application of two pedagogical strategies to imbed course material within the creative production of podcasts.

PEDAGOGICAL STRATEGIES FOR FASHION DESIGN PODCAST INITIATIVE PROJECT

We selected the pedagogical strategies for the Fashion Design Podcast Initiative project about a year before the course began. We sought pedagogical strategies that reflected design thinking and process, as well as teaching strategies that provided opportunities for students to engage actively in their learning experiences.

Lernen durch Lehren

LdL or "Learning by Teaching" was developed by Jean-Pol Martin, professor of didactics at the University of Eichstätt-Ingolstadt in Germany

(Gartner et al., 1971). As a teaching strategy, LdL transfers some of the teaching responsibilities to the learners, encouraging and supporting creativity, independence, confidence, and soft skills (i.e., teamwork, communication, decision making, research, exploration, and presentation skills) (Gartner et al., 1971; see Martin, 1994[1992]). Learning by teaching supports a social constructivist approach to the construction of knowledge through the employment of peer learning techniques, where in this course, peers promote understanding, students become acculturated into the community of their profession with a common construction of knowledge from multiple perspectives (Stage, Muller, & Kinzie, 1998). The method recognizes the importance of students having an active role in their education, and the value of collaboration between faculty and students for learning activities. Furthermore, students become more invested in the content when they teach it to another student.

LdL is most successful when students work in pairs or small groups, promoting communication skills necessary for shared construction of knowledge (Bonwell & Eison, 1991). The small groups create learning pods, where students teach each other through discussions, questions, and activities. Faculty members may also enter into the small groups as observers and participants to gauge the effectiveness of the LdL.

LdL is also a useful teaching strategy for understanding and utilizing diverse technologies (Martin, Klein, & Sullivan, 2007). Emergent technologies may be more fully explored with the use of LdL, because students interact with the technology firsthand and teach each other through their experiences in these intimate group settings and between student groups.

The primary limitation for LdL is the necessity for mutual adaptation from both teacher and student to be effective (Dror & Harnad, 2008, pp. 128–130). As students assume the role of teacher, the faculty member needs to step back and even at times become the student. Students are often uncomfortable with assuming a position of authority in a classroom setting, where their role is typically "learner" instead of "teacher." Subsequently, faculty members need to establish clear guidelines and boundaries for students to become "teachers" and ways to become the "student" once again. Interestingly, this course had the added dimension of public dissemination of content to the Internet, where students become teachers in a much broader sense.

Faculty considered the implications of creating Internet "artifacts" and content that exists in the public beyond the conclusion of the course. This turns some advantages of podcasting into potential disadvantages. Podcasts, for example, are always available (until removed from the Internet). This enduring impact, from an in-class vantage point, possesses the potential to be a lasting teaching and educational tool or without vetting a lasting example of inaccurate information. One of the disadvantages to podcasts is that the content may not be of the highest quality or accurate. Similar to entries on Wikipedia and videos on YouTube, podcasts are created by anyone about anything, including possible errors and the perpetuation of erroneous information.

The importance of students working in small groups is to build their communication skills; however, it also has to be monitored as a limitation for LdL. Group work is always challenging for students because it is often either over- or under-managed with members who may lack full engagement and investment. For group work to be successful it is necessary to have a strong group leader and group members who participate and meet their responsibilities according to established timelines.

LdL is a particularly useful strategy for exploring the variety of software and hardware needed to creating podcasts. Under the classroom's social constructivist mindset, students were less dependent on faculty teaching-specific technology skills and expected instead to work with peers, faculty, and outside support to find creative and efficient paths to a final product.

We utilized LdL as a pedagogical strategy to structure the Fashion Design Podcast Initiative project to support students in collaboration on research and presentations designed to educate their peers and the public about specific types of fashion design exhibitions. LdL also informed our decision for students to work in small groups rather than as individuals. In addition, we relied on Bloom's revised taxonomy to guide and evaluate the project.

Bloom's Revised Taxonomy

While Bloom's taxonomy is a common pedagogical strategy used by most teachers, it is merely a classification system for learning and teaching objectives and actions. This taxonomy and subsequent book – *Taxonomy of Educational Objectives: The Classification of Educational Goals. Handbook I: Cognitive Domain* – were the result of several education conferences focused on designing teaching activities with learning objectives in mind (Bloom, Engelhart, Furst, Hill, & Krathwohl, 1956). The original taxonomy concentrates on the cognitive domain and learning actions designated into six levels of cognitive progression: knowledge (recall), comprehension, application, analysis, synthesis (creativity, divergent thinking), and evaluation (Bloom et al., 1956). In a follow-up text – *Taxonomy of Educational*

Objectives: Volume II, The Affective Domain (1964), Benjamin Bloom, Bertram Masia, and David Krathwohl addressed the affective domain or feelings/emotions related to teaching and learning.

Lorin Anderson and David Krathwohl revised Bloom's taxonomy to address its weaknesses and more accurately represent the cognitive domain (2001). The revised taxonomy suggests that lower ordering thinking skills progress toward the higher thinking skills, beginning with REMEMBER (recall), to UNDERSTAND, APPLY, ANALYZE, EVALUATE, CREATE (Anderson & Krathwohl, 2001, pp. 5–6, 30), whereas the original taxonomy began with KNOWLEDGE, COMPREHENSION, and APPLICATION progressing through ANALYZE, SYNTHESIS, and EVALUATE (Bloom et al., 1956). While the distinction between the two taxonomies appears to be minimal, Anderson and Krathwohl changed more than terminology; they also rearranged the levels when the taxonomy is considered holistically.

For the Fashion Design Podcast Initiative project, we relied on the Blooms' revised taxonomy because of its progressive levels of cognitive learning that best reflected our learning objectives and evaluated the success of each of four phases of the project. Critiquing Bloom's revised taxonomy, Peggy Maki suggests it may not be a suitable pedagogy for multi-cognitive learning (2010, p. 91). We found Maki's criticism to be accurate. In our project, the most significant limitation for Bloom's revised taxonomy is the lack of evaluation after the CREATION step, allowing for a higher level learning without re-entering the taxonomy as at lower level. Students' experiences with the design process addressed this concern, as our initial interest in Bloom's revised taxonomy was its obvious linkages to design thinking and process.

FASHION DESIGN CAPSTONE COURSE CONTEXT

In the fashion design capstone course, faculty were interested in students understanding of types of emerging technologies as tools for communication in order to stay competitive within the fashion industry. We immersed the creation of podcasts within the capstone learning experience as the exercise of transforming and communicating knowledge for deep engagement, increased retention of the course content, and interactive discourse with faculty and their peers within the course.

The broad context of this project was inside the fashion design student's capstone course, where students synthesize their diverse fashion design experiences and knowledge into culminating projects. The capstone course provided students with opportunities to develop their portfolios and explore fashion design exhibition/presentation styles within three projects:

1. portfolio (digital and hardcopy);
2. fashion design exhibition; and
3. podcast.

We focus on the final project of the course – fashion design podcast series. Student teams created podcasts, contributing to a fashion design podcast series. This course not only synthesizes fashion design knowledge students acquire in their degree program, but also requires students to integrate the information from the capstone course with emergent technologies.

In spring 2009, thirty-two students participated in the capstone course. We divided the students into 15 groups of 2 or 3 students for the podcast project. Student groups selected fashion design-related topics for research, presentation, and development into podcasts. Students were given class time every week to meet in their groups and discuss their fashion design podcasts. While the Fashion Design Podcast Initiative project was the primary focus of the course, students also completed other assignments commonly associated with a capstone course, such as portfolios, cover letters, and resumes. A timeline is outlined in the Implementation Plan section.

The objectives for the Fashion Design Podcast Initiative project were fourfold:

1. to expose students to emerging technologies;
2. to expand students digital portfolios;
3. to explore the LdL pedagogy; and
4. to utilize Bloom's revised taxonomy as it reflects the design thinking and process.

In addition, the podcast project had four primary phases:

1. faculty members trained in the skills and technologies necessary to create podcasts;
2. students researched their specific topics and created presentations;
3. students trained in skills and technologies to create podcasts; and
4. podcasts revised according to evaluations and posted to the Internet.

The Fashion Design Podcast Initiative project gave us, the faculty members, opportunity to explore pedagogical strategies that engage and involve students in the learning process more significantly than typically allowed in a lecture course. Engagement with technology is in itself an active process, as it quickly loops the actions of learning and applying content. Coming into contact with new technology within the classroom, students naturally want to know how it empowers them to complete the assignment to get a good grade or to reach course goals. Our pedagogical strategies sought to capitalize on that process, asking students to engage in methods that produce higher order learning and retention.

DESIGN PROCESS

Part of our decision to utilize the six levels of Bloom's revised taxonomy is because it relates well to the steps of the design process, familiar to our students within their academic design major. Accordingly, the podcast learning activities were thoughtfully constructed to incorporate both the revised taxonomy and design process. This pairing of the revised taxonomy and the design process allows for "design thinking," strategic, collaborative, and creative thinking for problem-solving.

The design process as described by Don Koberg and Jim Bagnall in *The Universal Traveler* (2003) includes the following phases: accept, ideate (brainstorming), select, create, implement, and evaluate. While this list appears linear, actual process in action is rarely straightforward. Instead designers explore phases with irregularity and repetitively for some phases, such as the "evaluate" phase. The design process functions as a flexible framework from which designers explore creative problem-solving or design thinking. Design students often utilize the design process with chaotic frequency, thus faculty members need creative ways to move students to the next logical phase and ensure deep understanding of the previous phases. More specifically, we found students were content to linger in the ideate (or brainstorming) phase. While this phase is critical to recognize as a process step, students exhibited great reluctance to make a selection and move ahead. It is important to emphasize that the design process allows the flexibility for failure, and decisions need to be made but are never final, an important feature of design thinking. Consequently, when we noticed a student group had good ideas, we encouraged them to select one in order to maintain the designated schedule. Student groups were typically resistant, but addressing their fears and concerns usually allowed them to make an informed selection.

While the specific order differs between Bloom's revised taxonomy and the design process, the similarities are noteworthy and particularly beneficial for the Fashion Design Podcast Initiative project. Both function best, when students move from lower to higher order thinking only after mastering previous levels/phases and integrating past levels/phases into the current level (Table 1). Subsequently, there is the assumption that previous levels are achieved and always accessible from the higher levels, which may lead to overconfidence in students' continued progress and successes.

THE DESIGN PROCESS APPLIED TO THE PODCASTING PROJECT

At the REMEMBER and UNDERSTAND levels, students participate in the retrieval of material to summarize or interpret, which is similar to ACCEPT in the design process, where students collect research about the design problem or challenge. At this level, students in the fashion design capstone course were required to conjointly complete their research about podcasts, as well as their fashion exhibition topics in general.

There is not an easily comparable revised taxonomy level for the design process' phase of IDEATE or brainstorming. The closest level may be the APPLY level, where students explore execution and collaboration, and even play with ideas. In our project we utilized the APPLY level for students to meet in their designated small groups, share research, and discuss possible topics for their podcasts.

During the ANALYZE level, students compare, organize, and deconstruct, similar to the SELECT phase of the design process where students

Table 1. Comparison Between Bloom's Revised Taxonomy and the Design Process (Arranged from Lower Order Thinking to Higher Order Thinking).

Bloom's Revised Taxonomy Levels (Anderson & Krathwohl, 2001)	Design Process (and Thinking) Phases (Koberg & Bagnall, 2003)
REMEMBER	ACCEPT
UNDERSTAND	IDEATE
APPLY	SELECT
ANALYZE	CREATE
EVALUATE	IMPLEMENT
CREATE	EVALUATE (repeatable throughout the design process)

organize and compare ideas in order to choose the best and most achievable creative solution. At this level, student groups select topics and develop plans for execution of the presentations (and podcasts). Students may need to return to this level (and phase) if initial plans need revision. In addition, students ANALYZE their research materials and SELECT the most appropriate implementation of new technologies for their presentations and podcasts.

Both Bloom's revised taxonomy and the design process include a level or phase to EVALUATE, where students give feedback and critique for each other. Students relied on evaluation more than indicated in the revised taxonomy, similar to its use in the design process. Students gave and utilized evaluations to improve presentations and resulting podcasts.

Although occurring at different places in the sequence for the levels for the revised taxonomy and phases for the design process, CREATE is the act of designing and constructing. At the CREATE level/phase, student engaged in creative processes for their presentations, and returned again for the creation of their podcasts. Utilizing this highest level of cognitive thinking, students accessed all previous levels in the creative process.

Pedagogical Objectives

We divided the pedagogical objectives into two categories – faculty members' and students' objectives – to recognize the distinction between the two types of teaching within the Fashion Design Podcast Initiative project. We justified the students' pedagogical objectives within the LdL pedagogy, where the students occasionally functioned as the "teacher."

Faculty members' objectives include the following:

- To gain knowledge and skills for podcasting (audio and visual) with training from the university's technology support center
- To incorporate emerging technologies into the course content, a capstone design studio for fashion design students
- To instruct students in the creation of specific portfolio components, including a podcast
- To reinforce the ways projects from previous courses are incorporated into a professional portfolio within this capstone course

Students' objectives include the following:

- To understand and teach fashion design exhibition content

- To work successfully in small groups
- To develop knowledge and skills relating to emerging technologies
- To professionally design, create, critique, evaluate, and disseminate educational podcasts

IMPLEMENTATION PLAN

The Fashion Design Podcast Initiative project objectives were applied during four distinct phases of implementation, employing LdL and Bloom's revised taxonomy pedagogical strategies. These strategies are paired with a design process guided by design thinking. Similar to Bloom's revised taxonomy, each phase of implementation builds on the previous phase(s), creating a strong foundation for pedagogical strategies and learning experiences.

The timeline for the Fashion Design Podcast Initiative project began in Fall 2008 with securing the TIG grant and Phase One – faculty training. Phase Two began in Spring 2009 and lasted about three weeks, with students training on the software and hardware necessary for their podcasts as well as researching podcasts. During Phase Three, students created their podcasts, and Phase Four primarily focused on evaluations and publishing podcasts to the Internet.

Phase One

Support for the Fashion Design Podcast Initiative project came in two primary forms. First, we applied for and secured a competitive grant from Apple computers. The grant provided podcasting hardware and software, valued at $1500.00. Faculty members attended institutionally supported workshops, and conferred with each other to build skills using the software and hardware before the class began. The second form of support was access to the technology specialists who educated us in the functions of the software and hardware necessary for creating podcasts. This support was primarily available for faculty members prior to working on the project with the students; however, students were also included in two workshops focused on skill-building during the capstone course. In addition, faculty and students accessed technology support for troubleshooting and feedback, improving the final podcasts with highly specialized information and insights.

We trained in the design, creation, and development of audio and visual digital media files (MP3s and MP4s) for podcasts with the assistance of the university technology support staff and facility. This phase also included faculty members creating "rough drafts" of podcasts using software, such as Audacity, GarageBand, and iMovie, as well as organizing the project for students. The "rough draft" podcasts served as examples of good and bad practices in educational presentations, as well as an invaluable learning experience for faculty.

We began by "playing" with the software and hardware. This included videotaping the interiors of our offices, making audio recordings of our meetings, and editing family photographs, as well as attempting to pair music with video and edit video clips. We gained knowledge and experience about the software and hardware without the pressures of creating the "perfect" podcast. Most importantly we could troubleshoot, discovering the things that did not work. Podcasts, for example, with too many "bells and whistles," such as visual effects and overwhelming music, distract from the content, and worse, may make the podcast so large that it is difficult to upload and time-consuming to download for listening and watching.

We, the faculty made presentations and "rough draft" podcasts similar to those students were to create, based on weekly lectures or activities for the capstone course. While these "rough draft" podcasts were not posted to the Internet, they were useful for instructional activities. Working with podcasting software and hardware gave us insight into which processes might be more time intensive for the students, informing the development of a realistic podcast production schedule. We shared our "rough draft" podcast experiences with the students in the fashion design capstone course in order to directly address potential issues for using this emerging technology. We also used these learning experiences to shape the structure and pace of the course and our podcast-related activities for the students.

Phase Two

In this phase, students in the fashion design capstone course were arranged into groups. As is the capstone curriculum, the topics were limited to types of fashion design exhibitions, ranging from runway fashion shows to visual merchandising. Future podcast projects could explore any number of topics that would expand students' understanding of fashion design.

In implementing LdL, students were divided into small groups of two or three. Each group was responsible for researching and creating a presentation about a fashion design exhibition style. After giving the presentation in the classroom, groups adjusted presentations based on faculty and peer feedback, and then turned these revised presentations into podcasts. Faculty members and group peers evaluated members of each group for their contributions and participation.

The role of the teacher was to prepare, guide, and support students in research, presentation, and evaluation. Students assumed the role of "teacher" when giving the presentations to faculty members and peers. To ensure that students were providing correct information, they were given research assignments and assessed on their understanding of the information.

This was a dynamic phase where students explored ways to create digital presentations for classroom environments, which closely reflected the CREATE level of the Bloom's revised taxonomy. Each student group researched a chosen type of fashion exhibition or presentation, such as runway fashion shows, gallery exhibitions, trunk shows, showroom displays, and digital portfolios. Students were given 4 weeks to complete their research and presentations. Also, during this phase of the project, groups were given time in-class for meetings allowing faculty to guide and assist students in their activities. These in-class meetings also supplement the limited times available for students to meet outside of class.

Student groups were taught how to use the software and hardware, and were able to borrow the hardware from faculty for the creation of their presentations and subsequent podcasts. In all, there were 15 student groups who gave presentations in the classroom environment. Most of the groups utilized Microsoft PowerPoint for their presentations, but a few used iMovie or other video editing/production software.

Directly following presentations, students attended workshops led by university technology experts primarily focusing on skill-building activities for podcast-related software. The first workshop reviewed software (e.g., GarageBand, Audacity, and iMovie) for creating MP3s and MP4s for podcasts. The second workshop took place near the end of the project and focused on ways to save and post podcasts successfully to the Internet. We the instructors also hosted a technology workshop for Adobe Photoshop.

The workshops hosted by the technology support staff members were fast-paced, introducing a variety of new topics and platforms all at once. Several students required additional tutorials to master the skills and apply them to their particular creative work. In navigating and acquiring technology skills, the LdL small group strategy was extremely beneficial; students were able to assist each other in the learning process as well as functioning as teachers between groups. After the workshops and a few tutorial and practice sessions, students were able to demonstrate the skills necessary to utilize the software used to create podcasts; the proper ways to save audio and video digital media files; and methods for uploading podcasts to the Internet.

Data on student preferences of the optimal length of time for a podcast are mixed, with some suggesting it should be the length of a song (2–4 minutes long; Clark & Walsh, 2004; Hew, 2009). Others argue that as podcasts are used to deliver instructional content, the length of time is a more complicated negotiation, with much based on the context of how it is used in the course (Hew, 2009). Based on previous exposure to the technology, we decided to limit presentations to 5 minutes for three reasons: (1) the time limit made presentations more manageable and consistent from one group to another; (2) podcasts with audio and video become large files and it was necessary to limit the length of the resulting podcast; and (3) since the final podcasts' audience were primarily students selecting content through iTunesU, length may impact viewers' interest level.

Time limitations also required students to distill and prioritize their research according to their content and audience. Students needed to determine the most important information to convey, as well as how to appropriately communicate the chosen content. Accordingly, we assisted and guided students in their efforts to create a hierarchy of information, as well as providing guideposts for students to assume roles as teachers.

Because presentations were to be turned into podcasts, student groups also needed to consider how the content transferred to the podcast's audience (peers vs. public), and how others outside the classroom might interpret and value the content. As anticipated, students were able to address their peers' expectations for the podcasts more successfully than the general viewer. In fact, student groups had difficulty determining the specific audience for individual podcast topics. Students were encouraged to reflect on their hierarchy of information in order to predict their audience.

Faculty members and peers in attendance gave both written and verbal feedback to each presenting group, reflecting the EVALUATE level of Bloom's revised taxonomy. A major issue with evaluation work was how students were reluctant to "criticize" peers. To address this issue, the faculty asked that written evaluations be anonymous. In addition, the written evaluations were collected by the faculty and reviewed before returning the feedback to student groups. (If we revisited this project, we would compile the feedback both written and verbal to share with each student group.) Keeping to the time limit proved a challenge for all but one student group for the presentations. Fortunately, most of the groups were able to address this issue in their final podcast.

During the research process, we requested each student group to ANALYZE and EVALUATE a podcast from the Internet. The student groups reported on their findings to the class. Most notably students expressed concerns about the length of time it took to download a podcast and the length of the podcast. These two time issues were related because the longer the podcast the longer it takes to download it, and the less likely a listener/viewer is to finish it. Also, student groups did not find many podcasts including visuals or video, and gave positive feedback when they learned that they would be including some type of visual component. Accordingly, students gained KNOWLEDGE about existing podcasts and how they may be able to implement this information when they CREATE podcasts of their own. The student feedback also provided the faculty with justifications for decisions regarding the length of time for the podcast and including visuals, which would prove to be the most problematic portions of the project.

Phase Three

In Phase Three of the project, student groups further implemented the ANALYZE and APPLY levels of Bloom's revised taxonomy when they attempted to cope with and utilize the evaluations of their presentations. The evaluations were meant to be an efficient way to improve the presentations and the subsequent podcasts; however, the faculty found this phase to be extremely challenging due to students' difficulty accepting and using the evaluations. Many of the students perceived the evaluations as criticisms, and often interpreted the feedback as personal attacks.

In interpretation of the feedback from their evaluations, we discovered students were having difficulty distinguishing between beneficial critiques and arbitrary comments. This is a common issue with design critiques, so both faculty and students had dealt with it before. With this project, however, students struggled significantly with ways to use the feedback addressing presentation style and how this information could benefit their final podcast. Several groups, for example, were given critiques about talking too fast during their class presentations. These groups dismissed the feedback because they did not predict that their rate of speech would impact the podcast and they needed to squeeze all of their information into the 5-minute time limit. In all cases, the faculty needed to clarify that the time limit did not justify "rushing" through complex information. Consequently, the class explored ways to focus tightly on a topic and streamline information into understandable components. In the evaluative phase, it was necessary for faculty to meet with each group and provide guidance for understanding the evaluations in the context of improving their presentations and ultimately their podcasts.

All groups received feedback about copyright issues from the faculty. As these podcasts were posted to the Internet, Fair Use policies did not apply. Students resisted our cautions about using copyrighted materials in their podcasts, especially regarding the use of music. Students cited numerous examples of copyrighted music used for YouTube videos and podcast series. All students were required to review the university's posted copyright material policies. The issue led to rich discussions about intellectual property limitations, which have wide-reaching implications to relevant fashion industry debates. Still, the students perceived this as very limiting, and so in addressing this issue, we suggested that each student group create a music track (MP3) on GarageBand, Audacity, or other software allowing for the creation of original musical scores. Most groups created original music or used copyright-free music for their podcasts. Despite cautions, one group continued to use copyrighted music, and this resulted in their podcast not being posted to the Internet.

The students then applied what they learned from the evaluations of the presentations to translate the content into shorter, distilled segments using video and audio technologies. This again put students through a design process, where they moved out of evaluative work to ideate and CREATE their fashion design exhibition podcasts. In addition, students attended problem-solving sessions where various software and platforms were explored to create the first version of their podcasts.

Phase Four

During Phase Four of the Fashion Design Podcast Initiative project, student groups shared their podcasts with the class and again received evaluations, from which they created and posted the final podcasts. This was the most technology-intensive phase of the project, as content was mostly determined, and the focus was on execution of the final project. Accordingly, evaluation feedback primarily focused on technical issues, with occasional comments about presentation style or depth of research.

The student groups also showed their first and second versions of podcasts to technology support staff for immediate feedback; specifically they sought feedback on technology issues and file compression. Regarding the latter, students were ever mindful about file size for successful publishing to the Internet. In addition to peer and faculty evaluations, students made changes based on the support staff members' evaluations and critiques of their podcasts.

The student podcasts were redesigned based on evaluations before receiving approval to be posted to the Internet. Eight of the podcasts had technical or copyright issues and were not posted to the Internet. Subsequently, seven podcasts were posted to iTunesU, a subsection of iTunes, and made available on the Internet.

OUTCOMES

After reviewing the Fashion Design Podcast Initiative project, we were pleased with the successes and learned how to improve the project when repeated in the future. Students began with limited knowledge of emerging technologies used for creating podcasts; in fact, only a few students subscribed or even heard/watched a podcast series when the project began. We encouraged the students to research existing podcasts, and even subscribe to podcast series that they might enjoy. (Podcast subscriptions do not commonly cost money.)

The 15 student groups gave presentations, which were revised into individual audio and visual podcasts. All groups included music as part of the podcast; 10 groups created original soundtracks on GarageBand or similar music production software, 4 groups used copyright-free music, and 1 group used copyrighted music without permission of the artists. All student groups utilized visuals as part of their podcasts, and some groups even created movies. The use of both audio and visual files creates large digital media files to be incorporated into the podcast files (MP4s). Consequently, even with file compression, four podcasts exceeded the available bandwidth for uploading and publishing the digital files of each podcast to the Internet.

Table 2 illustrates the topics and types of technologies used (i.e., hardware and software) by students in the creation of their podcasts.

Table 2. Fashion Design Podcasts.

Podcast	Description	Technology(ies)
Trade Show (not published to Internet)	Merchandise, kiosk, signage, and marketing	Digital photographs (SLR camera)
Fashion Illustration (not published to Internet)	Explores illustration techniques and media	Digital scans of illustrations (Adobe Photoshop)
Website (not published to Internet)	Creating graphic designs, posting images, and publishing a website	Screenshots Graphics (Adobe Photoshop) music (GarageBand)
Showroom (not published to Internet)	Details of activities and outcomes for fashion showroom displays	Digital photographs (SLR camera)
Fashion Magazine (not published to Internet)	Components of creating a fashion magazine	Digital photographs (SLR camera)
Gallery Exhibit (not published to Internet)	Secure fashion designs for gallery display	Digital photographs (SLR camera)
Boutique (published to Internet)	Instructions for creating visual displays of merchandise	Digital photographs (SLR camera)
Photography Session (published to Internet)	Securing fashion designs, models, and staging photoshoots	Digital photographs (SLR camera) video (imovie)
Fashion Design Promotional Package (published to Internet)	Business card, letterhead, gift bag, and "leave behind"	Digital photographs (SLR camera) Microsoft PowerPoint
Flash Mob (published to Internet)	Students and faculty participated in a flash mob promoting a fashion design gallery exhibit	Video (iflip video recorder) imovie music (Audacity)
Digital Portfolio (published to Internet)	Instructions for converting hardcopy illustrations and photographs into digital files, and creating a digital portfolio	Video (iflip video recorder) movie (Microsoft PowerPoint) music (GarageBand)
Trunk Show (published to Internet)	Videotaped a recreation of a fashion trunk show	Video (iflip video recorder) music (GarageBand)
Visual Display (not published to Internet)	Videotaped the creation of various fashion displays, such as window displays and in-store displays	Digital photographs (SLR camera) music (GarageBand)
Lookbook (not published to Internet)	Documentation of the process of creating a lookbook	Digital photographs (SLR camera) graphics (Adobe Photoshop) music (GarageBand)
Fashion Show (published to Internet)	Stop animation-style detailing the behind-the-scenes activities for a fashion show	imovie music (GarageBand)

Student groups' fashion design podcasts are detailed in Table 1: Fashion Design Exhibition Podcasts. The trade show, fashion illustration, website, showroom, magazine, gallery, and boutique were not posted to the Internet, while the seven podcasts posted to the Internet included the following: (1) runway fashion show, (2) digital portfolio, (3) boutique visual display, (4) fashion photography session, (5) fashion flash mob, (6) fashion design promotional package, and (7) trunk show. Each of the seven podcasts from the Fashion Design Podcast Initiative series is accessible at the following URL: http://podcast.iu.edu/Portal/PodcastPage.aspx?podid=9b7268d0-c0a5-4973-ad0b-5bfd0c013d58 (Winge & Embry, 2009).

We the faculty were ultimately responsible for the posted podcasts, and, therefore, made final reviews on the level of achievement of project goals and appropriateness of content. Only seven of the 15 podcasts were posted to the Internet. The remainder of the podcasts were not posted because of technical or copyright issues. Four of the podcasts were too excessive in size to post successfully; three more had significant and irresolvable technical issues; and one podcast contained copyrighted music and was deemed unethical to post. All student presentations were recorded with digital video recorders. Digital recordings were available for students to use in their podcasts. While groups did not use the footage in their final podcasts, several groups viewed the videos for ways to improve the execution of the presentation.

By participating in the Fashion Design Podcast Initiative project, students gained experience with teamwork, presentations, teaching, and emerging technologies. Students also added to their digital portfolios with either a presentation or podcast demonstrating their research of a type of fashion design exhibition.

The final posted podcasts function in four primary ways: (1) the podcasts serve as archival evidence of the Fashion Design Podcast Initiative project and support from Apple Computers; (2) the podcasts inform and educate the general public to fashion design students about types of fashion design exhibitions; (3) the podcasts improved students' digital portfolios, demonstrating their knowledge and usage of emergent technologies; and (4) the podcasts function as promotional tools for both the university and the fashion design program.

PEDAGOGICAL IMPLICATIONS AND FINDINGS

After the completion of the Fashion Design Podcast Initiative project, we reviewed the capstone course, evaluations from each phase, student course evaluations, our notes, and resulting podcasts. This review revealed that utilizing emerging technologies in the university classroom is a complex and challenging process. Our findings revealed student and faculty members' issues with emergent technologies, understanding of pedagogical strategies for teaching and learning emergent technologies, course workload, and quality of discourse.

Student Issues with Emergent Technologies

Despite the "connected" generation of students obsessed with cell phones and Facebook, we noted more than half of the students were intimidated by the software and hardware introduced in the capstone course. We concluded that students' fears manifested from primarily two issues: (1) perceived fears of technologies and (2) lack of confidence. These fears manifested as combative verbal exchanges, missing classes (especially during technology-intensive days), and procrastination. We had not anticipated dealing with student issues related to technology, but we dealt with it directly and continued to progress with the project.

Perceived Fears of Technologies

Students perceived the emergent technologies and the podcast project introduced in the capstone beyond their capabilities. Students made random and unfounded distinctions between their use of smartphones, ipods, tablets, and laptops from the emergent technologies we introduced in the capstone course. Subsequently, we adjusted our teaching strategies to assist students in seeing the similarities between the technologies they know and the technologies we were teaching. Classroom discussions often revealed these similarities, which provided opportunities for further discourse regarding evolution of technology as it connects new to old, as well as its relationship to the emergent technologies.

New technology frequently presents a steep learning curve and is time intensive, similar to the design process. We considered the fashion presentations' and podcasts' content equally to reinforcing the skills that students secured to design and create podcasts. Consequently, the content of a given podcast became a secondary consideration. We found it important to emphasize relevancy of the process of learning to students.

Still, we had a few students with significant phobias about technology. To complicate matters, the most technology-phobic students chose to be in groups together. Consequently, there were two student groups who expressed great concern about participating in the project and requested an alternate project. We addressed their concerns with our experiences using the new technologies. In the end, both groups successfully created their podcasts, but unfortunately only one was posted to the Internet, while the other podcast was too excessive in size to be published.

Lack of Confidence

Students lacked confidence in being able to use emerging technologies because the software and hardware did not reflect the types with which they were already familiar. They also lacked confidence in their own abilities to learn new materials, teach others, and use "technology." Accordingly, we positively acknowledged students' minor accomplishments, and reassured and encouraged risk-taking efforts especially in connection to the new software and hardware. The students responded well to the positive feedback and encouragement, and after a few successful achievements with the new technology, most students showed marked improvement in classroom behaviors and attendance. We faced occasional setbacks when students interpreted design critiques and evaluations as personal affronts and allowed them to negatively impact their confidence.

Student fears manifest into issues in classrooms that faculty are ill-prepared to handle. Worse, it is often difficult to determine the root cause of the disruptive behavior. Fortunately, many student fears are manageable if instructors practice active engagement with students. Accordingly, we interacted with students in small groups during the fashion design capstone course with a student to teacher ratio of 16 to 1. Obviously, this type of interaction is not possible in all classrooms where the faculty to student ratio is higher, which suggests a significant reason to teach emerging technologies with small student populations.

Faculty Issues with Emergent Technologies

Students were not the only ones with concerns about the new technologies; faculty also had moments of doubt and despair. Specifically, we the faculty were initially concerned about our abilities to secure the needed skills to use the new software and hardware. Moreover, we underestimated our skills and overestimated those needed to create and teach about podcasts. After classes, training, and using the new technologies, we gained the confidence necessary to use and teach the technology most closely associated with creating and publishing podcasts. Still, we were humble in the face of questions and issues that arose beyond our skills. We quickly sought advice and instruction from online sources and technology support staff. Support staff responsiveness was critical to keeping the project moving and avoiding entrenched student frustration.

Access to technology was a challenge we had not fully anticipated. We were able to loan video cameras, headsets, and microphones to students supplied to faculty through the grant, and most students had their own computers. Still it was necessary for two student groups to use university computer labs to access the needed technology. The real challenge proved to be access to the necessary software to complete the podcasts, specifically the video/visual and audio editing. Consequently, we worked with the university's technology support staff and negotiated dedicated time at a computer lab with the necessary software.

We also had concerns about the amount and quality of podcasts produced by student groups. Subsequently, we were rigorous with critiques and evaluations, and expressed the need for "professional" podcasts from each student group. Fortunately, this was not an issue as students were motivated to create innovative and professional podcasts because of the public venue via the Internet.

Finding comparable and relevant podcasts was a challenge, especially since few published podcasts included similar emergent technology files (e.g., combination audio and video digital files – MP3s and MP4s). Consequently, it was difficult to critique and evaluate the significance of the fashion design exhibition podcasts. We subsequently relied on feedback to the podcasts to determine their overall outcomes and impact.

Strategies for Teaching and Learning Emergent Technologies

Our findings show that LdL and Bloom's revised taxonomy were effective strategies to combine to explore teaching and learning with emergent technologies. We outline the ways our teaching strategies, balance, and workload contributed to the successful use and purpose of emergent technologies.

LdL and Bloom's revised taxonomy aided us in preparing the students to teach one another from their presentations and podcasts. Specifically, these pedagogical strategies provided an articulated framework and therefore functioned as touchstones when facing challenges that arose during the podcast project. Most significantly these strategies assisted us to move students from lower to higher order thinking skills.

There were some notable drawbacks to LdL and Bloom's revised taxonomy. Most notably students had difficulties working in small groups. While the small group divisions made the projects more manageable for faculty, students encountered expected group challenges. Some student groups reported lack of participation and poor meeting attendance from one or more members in a given group. Most of the student groups discussed concern over (un)even distribution of workload between team members. In an attempt to manage the small group issues, we provided each student group with evaluation forms to be completed for each member of the group. We also appointed group leaders to manage workloads. While these efforts did not solve all of these common group work challenges, it provided students with a way for their concerns and struggles to be heard and addressed in a timely manner.

Also, we found it necessary to be flexible about the specific sequence of Bloom's revised taxonomy in practical use within the context of the classroom and project. Student groups progressed through the levels of the revised taxonomy (and the design process) at individual paces. Still, all levels of the revised taxonomy were achieved eventually.

Balance Course Workload

Critics of podcasting technology use in the classroom reference concern over the increase in workload for instructors, including the lack of technical support (Blaisdell, 2006). These issues were apparent as potential challenges but were mollified through the institutional support of the project and the collaboration of faculty.

In our effort to focus on content and knowledge building, our greatest challenge, next to helping students overcome their fears of using new technologies, was finding balance between teaching strategies and technical skill-building. While easy and convenient to focus solely on skill-building for students, we continually returned to Bloom's revised taxonomy to guide our continued progression through the project.

In reflection, students' workload was excessive for a three-credit course. While the course requirements initially reflected three credits, as the course progressed we realized that students were spending more time than anticipated on creating the content for their podcasts. Specifically, they spent excessive amounts of time producing music (MP3s) and videotaping footage for the podcasts. Once students secured the necessary skills to use the new technologies, they enjoyed spending time creating content for their presentations and podcasts. We had rigid deadlines and checkpoints that discouraged students from lingering too long in any one phase of the podcast project.

Faculty members' workload was primarily divided between two faculty members; however, we, at times, relied heavily on four university technology support staff members. Using the small group strategies discussed with LdL pedagogy assisted faculty workload because it meant fewer projects to manage overall. This project was only possible because of the extensive support and strategic pedagogies.

Typically, only one faculty member is assigned to the fashion design capstone course (30–40 students), which means a project of this type may not be repeatable. It is not advisable that new technologies be taught to student numbers over 15 without additional faculty. We found that a robust learning environment focusing on emergent technologies depends on the reliability and knowledge of the technology support staff. At several points during the project, the technology support staff was needed to address issues and questions in addition to training and skill-building activities that they led.

Quality of Discourse

The Fashion Design Podcast Initiative project elevated the classroom discussions to a higher level of discourse regarding emergent technologies and their potential in education and the fashion industry. The classroom discourse revealed student issues and achievements, as well as insights and complaints about using emerging technologies. The high quality of this discourse was due in part to social constructivist loose structure (see Burr, 1995) we promoted for classroom discussions. Such discussions provided students with occasions to address issues and concerns, and introduce new knowledge in a timely and efficient manner. It also created unique opportunities for faculty to engage with student groups and individual students in informal and cooperative ways.

EVALUATIONS AND REFLECTIONS

The impact for the Fashion Design Podcast Initiative project is evaluated in two ways: (1) feedback and (2) podcasts. Students and faculty members qualitatively evaluated the projects at all phases. All podcasts were available for enrolled students via a campus-based dissemination tool connected to iTunes. The student podcasts function as a portion of the student's digital portfolio and were accessible to the public beyond the university community.

Students developed digital presentations of their chosen type of fashion design exhibition. The resulting podcasts were then evaluated by peers and faculty members for design, content, and educational value, as well as considered for its accessibility, usefulness, user-responsiveness, and enhancement of learning. Based on the feedback provided in the evaluations, students edited the podcasts and sought faculty member support for final posting to the Internet.

Student Evaluations

Students completed evaluations for the course and the Fashion Design Podcast Initiative project. Evaluations of the overall project revealed the need for more exposure to emerging technologies and skill-based workshops. In addition, we received positive feedback on the posted podcasts for the outcome from the project and the educational value of the podcasts.

From the student evaluations for the course, we discovered that students (96%) felt they learned a large amount of new information from the course. In agreement with many studies that find students respond favorably to podcasting experiences, we also learned that students (93%) positively responded to the types of emergent technologies that were taught (Heilesen, 2010).

Conversely, the evaluations also suggested that students (46%) did not find the workshops overall useful. This statistic is interesting because students needed the skill-building workshops in order to execute their podcasts. It is our hypothesis that the negative evaluations of the workshops relate to the presentation style (which was often highly technical and detailed in ways that were not connected to the use of the technology) or poor reflections on their actual need for skill-building workshops. Students often over-estimated their skill set and underestimated the skills necessary to achieve their desired outcomes, which was established by student evaluations and faculty observations.

Faculty Evaluations

The faculty evaluations were informal and based on observations in the workshops and classroom sessions, as well as interactions during class activities and individual meetings with students. We were less concerned about the podcasts as outcomes, as we were interested in the process of learning an emerging technology. We anticipated a certain amount of discomfort from students working with new hardware and software; however, we were impressed with the student's adaptability and efficiency with complex technologies. While the Fashion Design Podcast Initiative project was a challenge for students and faculty, it was also beneficial and educational for both. Students with these skills are more competitive in the fashion industry for having experienced the process for learning new technologies; these experiences will transfer to future technologies.

SUMMARY

Addressing the need for fashion design students to be competitive in an increasingly innovative and technology-driven industry, the Fashion Design Podcast Initiative project exposed students to emerging technologies with the potential to positively impact the fashion industry. This project provided students with the opportunity to add to their digital portfolios by creating an educational podcast focusing on a type of fashion design exhibition. Students gained experience with teamwork, presentations, teaching, and emergent technologies.

The Fashion Design Podcast Initiative project and resulting podcasts reflected the pedagogical strategies of LdL, Bloom's revised taxonomy, and the design process. Students utilized skills in emerging technologies to create podcasts about types of fashion design exhibitions. Despite the successful use of emergent technologies in the capstone course, our findings suggest that both faculty members and students were confronted with challenging issues with new technologies. Overcoming these challenges proved beneficial in future work with technology, as well as deeper comprehension and insights. In addition, the Fashion Design Podcast Initiative project demonstrated that podcasts function as powerful pedagogical tools that move beyond the transfer of information to students, and engage students in technology, collaboration, creative problem solving, and dissemination of ideas.

REFERENCES

Anderson, L. W., & Krathwohl, D. R. (Eds.). (2001). *A taxonomy for learning, teaching, and assessing: A revision of Bloom's taxonomy of educational objectives.* New York, NY: Longman.

Blaisdell, M. (2006). *Academic MP3s: Is it iTime yet? Campus Technology.* Retrieved from http://campustechnology.com/articles/40744/. Accessed on January 15, 2012.

Bloom, B., Engelhart, M., Furst, E., Hill, W., & Krathwohl, D. (1956). *Taxonomy of educational objectives: the classification of educational goals. Handbook I: Cognitive domain.* New York, NY: Longmans, Green.

Bollier, D., & Racine, L. (2005). *Ready to share: Creativity in fashion and digital culture.* Paper presented at Ready to Share: Fashion & the Ownership of Creativity. USC Annenberg School for Communications, Los Angeles. Retrieved from http://www.learcenter.org/pdf/RTSBollierRacine.pdf. Accessed on January 15, 2012.

Bonwell, C., & Eison, J. (1991). *Active learning: Creating excitement in the classroom AEHE-ERIC higher education report no.1.* Washington, DC: Jossey-Bass.

Burr, V. (1995). *An introduction to social constructionism.* London: Routledge.

Clark, D., & Walsh, S. (2004). *iPod-Learning [White Paper].* Brighton: Epic Group.

Dror, I. E., & Harnad, S. R. (2008). *Cognition distributed: How cognitive technology extends our minds.* Philadelphia, PA: John Benjamins Publishing.

Gartner, A. M., Kohler, C., & Riessman, F. (1971). *Children teach children. Learning by teaching;* New York, NY: Harper & Row.

Geoghegan, M. W., & Klass, D. (2007). *Podcast solutions: The complete guide to audio and video podcasting, second edition.* New York, NY: friendsofED.

Heilesen, S. B. (2010). What is the academic efficacy of podcasting? *Computers & Education, 55*(3), 1063–1068.

Hew, K. F. (2009). Use of audio podcast in K-12 and higher education: A review of research topics and methodologies. *Education Technology Research and Development, 57,* 333–357.

Hurst, W., Welte, M., & Jung, S. (2007). An evaluation of the mobile usage of e-lecture podcasts. In *Proceedings of the 4th international conference on mobile technology, applications, and systems and the 1st international symposium on computer human interaction in mobile technology.* ACM, Singapore (pp. 16–23).

Jenkyn Jones, S. (2005). *Fashion design.* London: Laurence King Publishing.

Lee,, M. J. W., McLoughlin, C., & Chan, A. (2008). Talk the talk: Learner-generated podcasts as catalysts for knowledge creation. *British Journal of Educational Technology, 39*(3), 501–521.

Lee, M. J. W., Miller, C., & Newham, L. (2009). Podcasting syndication services and univeristy students: Why don't they subscribe? *Internet and Higher Education, 12*(1), 53–59.

Lonn, S., & Teasley, S. D. (2009). Podcasting in higher education: What are the implications for teaching and learning? *Internet and Higher Education, 12*(2), 88–92.

Koberg, D., & Bagnall, J. (2003). *The universal traveler: A soft-systems guide to creativity, problem-solving, and the process of reaching goals, hird edition.* Menlo Park, CA: Crisp Learning.

Maki, P. L. (2010). *Assessing for learning: Building a sustainable commitment across the institution, second edition.* Sterling, VA: Stylus.

Martin, J. (1994[1992]). *Vorschlag eines anthropologisch begründeten Curriculums für den Fremdsprachenunterricht [Proposal of an anthropologically founded curriculum for the teaching of foreign languages*]. Tübingen: Narr Verlag. (zugl. Habilitations-Schrift, Universität Eichstätt).

Martin, F., Klein, J. D., & Sullivan, H. (2007). The impact of instructional elements in computer-based instruction. *British Journal of Educational Technology, 38*(4), 623–636.

McGarr, O. (2009). A review of podcasting in higher education: Its influence on the traditional lecture. *Australasian Journal of Educational Technology, 25*(3), 309–321.

Stage, F. K., Muller, P. A., & Kinzie, J. (1998). Creating learning centered classrooms: What does learning theory have to say? *ASHE-ERIC Higher Education Report, 26*(4), 1–121.

Winge, T. M., & Embry, M. C. (2009). *Fashion design exhibition podcast series*. Retrieved from http://podcast.iu.edu/Portal/PodcastPage.aspx?podid = 9b7268d0-c0a5-4973-ad0b-5bfd0c013d58. Accessed on January 10, 2012.

THE INNOVATIVE USE OF PERSONAL SMART DEVICES BY STUDENTS TO SUPPORT THEIR LEARNING

Anne Nortcliffe and Andrew Middleton

ABSTRACT

Research into the autonomous use of MP3 audio recorders by students in UK higher education demonstrated that students were innovative in their autonomous use of the devices. They used them to capture learning conversations from formal and informal situations to personalise and enhance their learning. However, today smartphones and other smart devices have replaced the necessity for students to carry multiple mobile devices including MP3 recorders. This chapter builds upon the earlier work and presents a small qualitative study into how students are autonomously using their smart devices to support their learning. The research explores the hypothesis that students are being innovative in the ways in which they are using their smart devices to support their formal and informal learning. The study involved five students who own smart devices who were invited to discuss their ownership of smartphone and tablet technologies and the ways they used them in their studies. The students first completed a short questionnaire and were then interviewed in small groups. The results agree

Increasing Student Engagement and Retention using Mobile Applications:
Smartphones, Skype and Texting Technologies
Cutting-edge Technologies in Higher Education, Volume 6D, 175–208
ISSN: 2044-9968/doi:10.1108/S2044-9968(2013)000006D009

*with previous research into student use of smart devices and describe
autonomous engagement facilitated by personally owned smart technologies. The study identifies continuous patterns of pervasive engagement by
students and concludes that more thought should be given to disruptive
innovation, digital literacy and employability.*

INTRODUCTION

Earlier work conducted by the authors investigated the autonomous use of
MP3 audio recorders by students in UK higher education to enhance their
learning. It showed that students used the recorders they had been given in
many ways, but it was the disruptive, innovative and autonomous use of the
recorders to support their peripheral engagement with the formal
curriculum that was most significant.

Two years after the MP3 recorder research, this chapter reports on a small
qualitative study into the autonomous use of personally owned smart
devices by students and considers how these devices are changing the way
students engage with their studies. The issue of student ownership of
technology has changed: not only do the smart technologies that many
students bring to university have recording functionality, but they can also
run diverse free or cheap applications ("apps") that are potentially useful to
student productivity.

The chapter begins by introducing key ideas that situate the research and
by describing the inherent potential of smart devices and the barriers to
innovation. This is followed by a review of literature and findings from our
earlier study into the use of MP3 recorders by students.

In moving our attention to smartphones and tablet PCs, we were not
expecting to find evidence of widespread autonomous innovation. Instead
we expected to discover diverse and rich accounts of personal innovation addressing priorities determined by individual students. As a study of
emerging innovation, the scale of ownership at this stage was not important.
The main drivers for us were student interest, imagination and the attitudes
towards using personal technology for academic work as indicators of a
shift towards learner independence in the use of learning technology, even
where the devices and apps were not primarily bought for academic
purposes. The research therefore adopted a qualitative approach capable
of drawing out student attitudes as well as examples of what students
have done.

BACKGROUND

Bring Your Own Device (BYOD)

Investment in smart devices is significant for most students, especially at a UK 'post '92' university like Sheffield Hallam where the majority of students do not come from affluent backgrounds (Bowers-Brown, 2006). While all students these days might be expected to bring their own mobile device to university, the decision to purchase multifunctional, smart technology is of a different order. The rapid growth in the range of alternative multifunctional connected technologies means our students and their families have to make a difficult purchasing decision: Mobile phone? Smartphone? Tablet PC? Laptop? Notepad? PDA (Personal Digital Assistant)? or Desktop PC? How do students decide and what advice is available to them?

At the same time universities are finding their investment decisions are changing too, with planners recognising student expectations for widespread digital connectivity whether on or off campus (JISC, 2006; Oblinger, 2006). University investment in physical formal and informal learning spaces needs to reflect different expectations and behaviours, especially where technology is concerned and as the JISC study into designing effective learning spaces highlights 'spaces are themselves agents for change' (JISC, 2006, p. 30).

Disruption, Autonomy and Innovation

Research and Development into learning technology is often concerned with how it can bolster existing formal pedagogic philosophies and methods, rather than in how technology becomes a 'game changer', positively disrupting the existing paradigms. However, pedagogy has largely been determined by historic constraints. The lecture theatre, e.g., was invented in medieval times as a technical solution in response to the difficulties scholars had in communicating their knowledge. Bligh (2000) and others have highlighted how ingrained some ideas about teaching and teaching environments are, even after constraints have been removed. If technology, and specifically personally owned smart technology, removes many constraints relating to communications, educators need to reassess learner engagement, access to and expectations of formal and informal learning spaces and resources, and independent and social learner productivity.

It is suggested that the learner's ready access to intuitive, familiar and highly usable smart device technologies exemplified by Apple's iPad, but found in myriad smartphones and tablet PCs, will result in the phenomenon of what Bower and Christensen (1995) initially termed *disruptive technologies* and what Christensen subsequently reconceptualised as *disruptive innovation* (1997). It is the behaviour associated with such technology, rather than the technology intrinsically, that is significant.

The idea of disruptive innovation is useful in the context of Education where the changing relationship between the teacher and the learner has been central to ongoing research, a debate heightened by the widespread adoption of digital technologies (Mayes, Morrison, Mellar, Bullen, & Oliver, 2009).

Traxler (2010, p. 156) discusses the notion of the 'strong' disruption that results from the advent of ubiquitous, personally owned mobile technologies and how the 'long-term consequences must be to challenge the authority of the curriculum' and dominant thinking about the nature of formal learning. Kukulska-Hulme and Traxler (2005) and many others have developed the concept of mobile learning. This has been framed variously; however, Kukulska-Hulme and Traxler (2005, p. 42) set out the attributes of mobile learning as being 'spontaneous, portable, personal, situated; it can be informal, unobtrusive, ubiquitous and disruptive'.

Among those who plan and deliver teaching at scale, it is a lack of ubiquitous technical interoperability that has held back the widespread reappraisal of the learning environment, although specialist and exceptional mobile learning interventions have been numerous. Technological ubiquity supposes that a technology is familiar, commonplace and widely accessible, characteristics evident in smart devices. Growth in the personal ownership of smart devices suggests education should prepare itself for changes to student behaviour and their expectations for the use of engaging technologies.

Creativity, Autonomy and Self-Regulation

Learner creativity and critical thinking coupled with confident, self-regulated autonomy may be the prerequisite learner attributes to the widespread adoption of disruptive technologies. However, a lack of digital literacy may create a barrier to innovation in this emerging area of using smart devices for learning. Theory about the ways groups think (Janis, 1972) explains why creative, independent thinking may be quashed and become a barrier to disruptive innovation. Groupthink theory suggests that group members display a tendency to value cohesive behaviour and group unanimity above their individual motivation to pursue even realistically appraised courses of action.

The importance of self-regulation and self-directed learning to independent academic innovation is discussed by Song and Hill (2007). They conclude that the learning context, especially where this involves technology, influences the level of learner autonomy, the efficacy of learner strategies and their use of resources.

Autonomy and self-regulation can be framed in ways that suppose a formal and conscious path is being strategically followed by the learner; however, it is useful to consider a less formulated idea of autonomy and self-regulation in understanding the relationship of disruptive innovation to the student use of smart devices. The idea of pervasion is also relevant in considering this (Kukulska-Hulme & Traxler, 2005). In reflecting on the diverse ways that students had used audio recorders in our study of MP3 recorders (Middleton & Nortcliffe, 2011), the richest experiences happened in a space between students' formal engagement with the delivered curriculum and their informal engagement as students; the degree of intention being another way of expressing this. It is often the impromptu or spontaneous moment that offers the richest engagement.

While a weakness of smart devices is their inability to technically perform multi-tasking operations, one of their apparent strengths is that they enable and promote multi-tasking user behaviour by being pervasive and available to use in diverse contexts. Multi-tasking behaviour has been identified as a feature of the NetGen learner, whereby students optimise the use of their time and take from each learning situation what they need (Lohnes & Kinzer, 2007). In informal situations, as our ongoing work is suggesting, the relationship of being at university to family life alters when a student plays a piece of audio feedback on an assignment to a sibling or parent, for example. Delineation between study, life and work is fading and the pervasive, persistent nature of smart technology is part of that change.

The multiple technologies used by the NetGen learner are not the cause of a 'multi-processing' phenomenon (Brown, 2000); previous generations have always attempted to do more than one thing at a time. However, smart devices do create opportunities for students to respond to ideas immediately and engage in discourse differently because of the new access they provide for recording and distributing data. Though it is questionable whether the level of discourse (Burgess, 2000) and learning is of any quality when students engage in multi-tasking (Edwards & Gronlund, 1998; Fischer, Morris, & Joslyn, 2003; Hembrooke & Gay, 2003; Ophir, Nass, & Wagner,

2009). Therefore, we need to know more about student interest and behaviour before deciding about the prudence of smart technologies and multi-tasking.

Connectivity

Unlike our previous interest in the disruptive possibilities of portable audio recorders and the ways in which the recorded voice can enhance educational discourse, the smart devices under consideration here now incorporate connectivity. If change in access to learning environments is an important factor in understanding disruption and innovation, then the connectivity of devices introduces an important consideration.

The value of a formal, higher education is very much about interactivity and social engagement. The benefits of a university education would be considerably less if education was only concerned with the process of accessing and absorbing knowledge and skills: it is how we assimilate knowledge together and how this develops understanding that is important. Pursuing the app and further development of knowledge is fundamentally a socially mediated activity. A challenge in our initial audio work, therefore, was the lack of technical connectivity between the MP3 recorder and the situation in which the recording was to be used. Although it is a minor inconvenience to download content from a portable device in order to make it available on a network, it is an important inconvenience nevertheless. It requires technical skills and confidence that many academic users do not have.

Device connectivity enabling integrated user behaviour, a characteristic of smart devices, supports the immediacy and fluency that is so important to socially mediated learning.

MOBILE LEARNING

Mobile Learning Pedagogy

Smart mobile devices establish a potential for ubiquitous learner engagement that is often referred to as 'learn anything at anytime and anywhere' (Sakamura & Koshizuka, 2005). This is complemented by the notion of 'learn any how' in our work. Anytime and anywhere learning suggests the potential for developing learner autonomy, but autonomy is epitomised by the learner's own decision about *how* they will engage so that it meets their needs and addresses their situation optimally. This highlights the importance of conceptualising behaviour in terms of disruptive innovation and personalisation when considering the potential of smart technologies for learning.

Mobile learning affects traditional student learning strategies, both in and out of the classroom, by extending the environment and the opportunity for engagement (Jeng, Wu, Huang, Tan, & Yang, 2010), learning opportunities that can be autonomously driven by curiosity using smart devices (Camargo, Bary, Boly, Rees, & Smith, 2011).

Sharples, Taylor and Vavoula (2007) highlight mobility as an important factor in understanding the disruptive significance of mobile learning. While the use of different locations for learning is of interest, they identify the act of moving through and between spaces, people and contexts as one which creates new opportunities. The portability of devices offers new opportunities as to who, when, where, what and how students and academics engage with one another for learning purposes (Sharples, Arnedillo-Sanchez, Milrad, & Vavoula, 2009; Traxler, 2009). Therefore, for the educational provider, smartphones and smart devices can be used to create new personalised learning experiences incorporating methods that have not been previously conceived.

Disruptive innovation is best viewed in terms of changes to engagement rather than changes to technology per se. Ruth (2012) refers to this using the metaphor of the screenface: It is more useful to think about the act of learners engaging than the specific tools that facilitate their learning. However, mobile learning presents a complex shift in socially mediated learning and is ethically, technologically, and socially problematic (Vavoula & Sharples, 2008).

While its potential is palpable, the reality is that interoperable mobile technology is not yet universally available across the student population. For those who do have access, there are indications of widespread adoption by students (Jones, Ramanau, Cross, & Healing, 2010) and where academics and students already use mobile technology extensively for personal and work purposes, they are more likely to use it in their academic practice (Corbeil & Valdez-Corbeil, 2007).

Existing studies clearly indicate that ubiquitous learning can be powerful in facilitating meaningful learner immersion, learning that is likely to be enhanced by active, authentic, constructive, cooperative and personalised engagement (Huang, Chiu, Liu, & Chen, 2011). Nevertheless, some of the many areas that need further investigation at the institutional level include the benefits of mobile learning to all and how this will impact investment plans, useful and acceptable behaviours and attitudes, managing consistent and widespread adoption, and encouraging learning autonomy in using personal devices.

The Potential of Mobile Technology for Learning

The potential of mobile technology for learning can only be realised by users adopting the technology. Hwang, Chen, Chu and Cheng (2012) propose the Technology Acceptance Model (TAM) framework to explain how the adoption of technology is influenced by several factors: perceived ease of use (PEU), perceived usefulness (PU), attitudes towards technology usage (ATT) and behavioural intentions (BI) towards the new technology.

Chen, Park and Putzer (2010) also note how the perceived usefulness and ease of use were key factors in the adoption of smart devices by medical professionals. Shin, Shin, Choo and Beom (2011) also identified the importance of usability to user adoption, specifically high-quality screen resolution, interoperability, and network accessibility, reliability and security.

Converging Phone Technologies

Mobile phone design has changed markedly since they were first introduced. Integrated cameras, audio recorders, and PDA functionality are now commonplace. However, there is little known about consumer preferences or about how they actually use the functionality available to them (Han, Chung, & Sohn, 2009).

There are many small scale studies of how mobile phones with converged functionality have been used to support pedagogic innovation. However, much of the literature has talked about the potential for this converged technology to be widely adopted, rather than actual general changes in user behaviour (Lee, 2006; Oliver & Goerke, 2007). Tucker and Winchester (2009) also consider potential in their examination of converged phone and video technology to support the just-in-time learning needs of professionals, an area also investigated by Vozenilek, Huff, Reznek and Gordon (2004) who considered the transfer of medical learning pedagogy ('see one, do one and teach one') to the mobile realm and found the technology difficult to apply and inappropriate.

Wu, Yang, Hwang and Chu (2008) used mobile phones to guide their learners and to increase their contextual awareness of their in situ learning experience. Mitchell, Race, and Clarke (2005) used QR codes to provide access to additional learning material that could be accessed via smartphones through a graphical 'quick response' link to web-based media, an approach that was found to inspire young learners to engage more. Chen, Chang and Wang (2008) found that mobile PDA and phone technology can provide tutors with mechanisms to scaffold, organise and communicate with learners, e.g. through calendar alerts of timetabled sessions and assessment submissions.

These examples highlight the importance of asking the question: who should be taking responsibility for organising the students' learning – the student or academic? How might this change now?

SMART TECHNOLOGIES

The Potential of Smartphones for Learning

Technological innovation has continued to merge the functionalities associated with the mobile technologies of PDAs, MP3 recorders, video cameras and phones. This means it is no longer necessary for students to purchase or choose between separate devices unless they have specialised high-quality requirements (Han et al., 2009).

Hardware convergence has been complemented by the emergence of smart device apps. There are, e.g., numerous smartphone audio apps available, each of which has the potential to support students and academics in capturing different conversational learning experiences (Nortcliffe, Middleton, & Woodcock, 2011). Audio recording apps are only one type of app, of course, and there are innumerable other apps available to smart device users for supporting student engagement with learning (Woodcock, Middleton, & Nortcliffe, 2012a).

In 2009, Hendery forecasted that smartphone ownership was expected to exceed the number of PC users in 2014. In 2009 that already represented 29% of the mobile phone market. There are over 600,000 iPhone apps (Costello, 2012) and 450,000 Android apps available to users (Paul, 2012). In terms of what end users are actually doing, Murphy (2012) claims that over 25 billion iPhone apps have been downloaded and Whitney (2012) estimates that 10 billion apps have been downloaded by Android users.

This level of adoption, therefore, suggests that education needs to look at the potential of smart device apps and how they are being used by students autonomously to support their learning.

The Smartphone Learner

Clough, Jones, McAndrew, and Scanlon (2008) identified how enthusiastic student smartphone users deployed their devices to support their personal organisation, indirectly improving their approach to study. Some of these students adapted the use of apps they already had installed to meet their learning needs rather than look for bespoke learning apps. The enthusiasts later recruited by Clough, Jones, McAndrew and Scanlon (2009) adapted their devices and a variety of mobile apps to support their need for: written, visual and aural data gathering; information retrieval, sharing and construction; collaborative learning activities; and contextual and constructivist learning.

Woodock, Middleton and Nortcliffe (2012a) identified smartphone learners using a diverse range of apps to support their learning, though mainly for productivity, web browsing, and organising themselves. However, the following year subsequent research indicated an increase in the number of smartphone learners and the use of the smart devices for learning was found to be more focused, with web browsing becoming an important feature of student accounts (Woodock, Middleton, & Nortcliffe, 2012b). These results are consistent with Boticki and So's (2010) research of the student usage of the HTC smartphone for learning which found that students who used their phones for study in personal spaces were primarily browsing the Internet and for creating interactive digital pieces of work.

There are innumerable apps available to smart device users for supporting student engagement with learning (Woodcock, Middleton, & Nortcliffe, 2012a). There are, e.g., many smartphone audio apps available, each of which has the potential to support students and academics in capturing different conversational learning experiences (Nortcliffe et al., 2011).

Smart Device Learning Mediated by Educators

In higher education, students and staff are also beginning to use personal technology to support their academic practice in situations that cross physical and temporal boundaries (JISC, 2009) and educators are developing many specific ways in which smart devices can be used to support learning.

Yan (2009) considered how collaborative engagement with learning through smartphones could be developed by the academic and suggested this could be promoted by the provision of online learning suites and social tagging activities. Cochrane (2006) looked at the design of Web 2.0 social media in ways that supported social constructivist engagement and issues of accessibility to smartphones by users. Hwang et al. (2012) have developed Web 2.0 learning technology so that it is readily accessible to smart devices to open up the potential for learning out of doors, e.g. for plant identification in the schoolyard. Huang, Jeng and Huang (2009) provided a micro-blogging facility so that it was accessible to smart devices in order to support peer supplementary teaching and collaborative learning. Boticki and So (2010) found that mobile devices can help the educator to redirect informal student enquiry-based learning into a more formally structured learning design.

However, Cochrane and Bateman (2010) found that much of the mobile learning initiated by students was serendipitous rather than being framed and planned by the academic and that students were not demonstrating the digital fluency that was initially expected of them. This recognition has emerged in several other studies of academic innovation, for example a study conducted by Röpke and Schneider (2012) looking at the embedding of QR codes in course texts and in a study by Santos, Valdeni de Lima, and Krug Wives (2012) where QR codes were embedded in lecture slides to provide additional dynamic learning material.

Again the question needs to be asked, is it appropriate for the educator to assume responsibility for the development of smart device content and, if so, are such approaches signalling an unnecessary, anachronistic student dependence on the academic?

Franklin (2011) suggests that smart devices create a new paradigm for educators to re-establish new learning communities and pedagogy to develop students' digital literacy skills and this, as Jewell (2011) notes, is particularly important because smart devices are becoming integral to professional practice. Smartphones, e.g., are becoming more common and making a positive impact in the medical professions (Boulos, 2011; Chen et al., 2010).

Smart Device Apps Developed by the Educator for Learning

The University of Leeds Medical School has developed an iPhone e-portfolio app to support the reflective practice of medical students on placement (JISC, 2011a); however, the app also has the potential to support the reflective practice of any student on placement. At the University of Bradford, the UoB smartphone app provides mobile accessibility to learning service resources for students, including information about the location of nearest IT room as well as access to the library search engine (JISC, 2011b). At Sheffield Hallam University, the CrystalViewer iPhone app has been commissioned by a member of staff as a free educational learning tool to supplement lectures on Metallurgy (Disobedient Media, 2010). The University of Southampton has adopted an alternative approach to developing or commissioning smart device learning apps by engaging computing students who are able to tap into open data sets provided by the institution (Davis & White, 2012).

From Digital Voice to Smart Learners

Our research into the use of smart apps in higher education continues our enquiry into how technology can be used to enrich the personal academic experiences of students and staff.

The advent of small mobile high quality audio recording devices created an opportunity for academics to audio record their own lectures and tutorials and to distribute these recordings to students via podcast channels without the need for costly institutional infrastructure and support (Nortcliffe & Middleton, 2006). However, lectures offer only one element of a blended learning experience in which the spoken word plays a central role. For example, formal and informal discussions between tutor and student are highly valued as a way of providing feedback on student work, albeit ephemeral in nature (Nortcliffe & Middleton, 2007, 2009a, 2009b). Making audio recordings of feedback conversations extends the life and value of important conversations by creating new opportunities for the conversation to be revisited later, as determined by the student. This disrupts patterns of learning potentially: students may now expect, or be expected, to reconnect with earlier conversations to examine or reflect on their growth or discover new meanings in the conversation that may have been missed before (Nortcliffe & Middleton, 2008).

The introduction of smartphone audio apps, email communication apps and the integration of app functionality has enabled the academic to simplify and increase the efficiency of producing feedback on students' coursework leading to benefits for the academic and student (Nortcliffe &

Middleton, 2011). Smartphones have also been shown to have a role in improving engagement with otherwise ephemeral project supervision (Nortcliffe, 2010). It is the portability and connectivity of the device that simplifies the process of capturing and distributing academic learning conversations, whether these are intrinsic (e.g. an intended part of project supervision or coursework feedback) or extrinsic and opportunistic (Middleton & Nortcliffe, 2011).

In our work it was felt that the extrinsic potential of the digital voice to enhance learner engagement, especially in relation to learner autonomy, needed to be explored further and, in pursuing this, it became evident that it is important to consider who should have responsibility for recording and distributing recordings. In 2009 we asked whether this should be the academic or the student; the question of whether an institutional audio-visual service might have a role was no longer central in our work. We concluded that if the main benefactors are the students, it was inappropriate for the responsibility to be assumed by the tutor (Nortcliffe, Rossiter, & Middleton, 2009), a conclusion that was at odds with the growing literature on audio feedback where giving feedback on student work is usually understood as a duty of the academic, but in agreement with the idea of the student as self-regulating learner (Nicol & MacFarlane-Dick, 2006). A shift in responsibility, it was felt, promoted digital literacy and employability.

Student Audio Autonomy

Several associated studies were generated from a year-long project which involved 100 student volunteers at two Sheffield universities. The students were each presented with a mobile audio recording device and, over a year, they were asked to report on how this helped them with their learning. They demonstrated diverse imaginative approaches to using the devices by making audio recordings of conversations with tutors, peers and others and by recording their own ideas as they occurred to them to support their coursework (Rossiter, Nortcliffe, Griffin, & Middleton, 2009).

The project induction for the students advocated creativity and autonomy and consequently the many and diverse approaches developed by the students ranged from the management of learning data to examination preparation (Middleton & Nortcliffe, 2009). A project focus group identified how students had used their devices to support multifarious learning activities with many using their devices flexibly to address their changing needs and opportunities with recordings being made for independent and group study. Students explained:

> I try to carry it around with me all the time just for anything that crops up. (Student A)

> I've used it for seminars, group work and lectures as well. And I used it on my placement as a kind of diary record. (Student B)
> I use it for little groups when we're doing group work seminars, meetings with my supervisor. I find it really useful for revising. I record my [written] notes and then listen back to it again and again and again. (Student C)

From the student perspective the common themes identified through the related studies confirmed how the device removed constraints in terms of time, access to people and the physical space they used for learning (Middleton et al., 2009). The mobile audio device enabled them to blend the formal, semi-formal and informal learning opportunities available to them.

Middleton et al. (2009) considered the mobile audio devices to be discrete, highly mobile and simple to use for capturing otherwise ephemeral events.

In summary, the devices promoted learner autonomy by supporting their transition from formal provision into wider, self-determined contexts – the technology followed the learner whatever the their learning status, a shift from the need for the learner to engage through predetermined facilities in a premeditated way (Nortcliffe & Middleton, 2010).

METHODOLOGY

Research Focus

Research into how students are using smart devices for learning conducted during the last two years at Sheffield Hallam University in the Faculty of Arts, Computing, Engineering and Science has identified that smart device ownership in the student population of 5300 is increasing from 69% (with a confidence interval of 7 for a 99% confidence level) in 2010–2012 to 87% (with a confidence interval of 3.8 for a 99% confidence level) in 2011–2012. The later 2012 study (Woodock et al., 2012b) put smart pad ownership at 1% (with a confidence interval of 1.13 for a 99% confidence level). This analysis led to the qualitative study presented in this chapter. The research asked the following question:

> How are students using smart devices, including smartphones and tablet PCs, to support their learning and why?

Participant Selection

Sheffield Hallam University students known to own smart devices from the Computing and Engineering departments were invited to attend one of two workshops offered on consecutive days. Twenty three were invited by a fellow student in the Computing department and a further 12 students from Engineering and Computing departments were invited by the faculty researcher to attend the workshop.

The invitation explained the research was interested in the apps used by students to support their studies. The invited students were demographically diverse in terms of age, gender and background.

However, only five students took part: three at the first workshop and two at the second workshop. Four were final year students, the other was in his second year of study. All were studying a Computing-related course, and all were male and in their early 20s.

Participation was affected by the scheduling of the research which sought to ensure the activity was seen as being separate from teaching and that it did not conflict with scheduled assessments. Further, many of the students have part-time jobs and were involved in exam revision.

Represented Technologies

Four of the students owned Android phones and tablets (pads) and the other student owned an iPad2 tablet and an Android phone. The preference for Android devices is likely to be affected by the sample's inherent computing interest and the relatively open architecture the Android affords programmers. Students on Computing courses are more inclined or required to use a wider variety of technology to support their studies than arts-based students (e.g., Kennedy, Krause, Judd, Churchward, & Gray, 2006). In debates about the propensity of younger students to more readily take to digital technology, Bennett, Maton, and Kervin (2008) noted how students in some disciplines displayed different levels of engagement.

Approach

The approach took the form of a Show'n'Tell workshop: It was important that the students were not only research subjects, but that they were likely to be interested in and responsive to the ideas presented by their peers, being self-motivated, curious and already engaged in the subject. The workshop was scheduled during non-teaching time and it was made clear that student involvement would have no direct bearing on any assessment of their academic work.

The students were invited to give a 5 minute presentation on each of a number of apps installed on their smart device, selecting those that they regularly use to support their learning. In particular they were asked to set out the benefits they had identified in using the app in their studies. The workshops were therefore run as a semi-structured focus group using a media elicitation method. The demonstrations were video recorded with the students' permission and, following the presentations, a discussion about the apps involving all presenters and the researcher was conducted and audio recorded (Cohen, Manion, & Morrison, 2000). Finally, the students were asked to complete a short paper-based survey composed of 10 questions presented as Likert scale fields with accompanying open comment fields. The survey, therefore, provided a more detailed and structured qualitative evidence base with respondents informed by both the presentations and the ensuing discussion.

RESEARCH RESULTS

A concurrent survey conducted by a student studying Computing (Armstong, 2012) revealed that 87% of 474 respondents from Sheffield Hallam University, Faculty of Arts, Computing, Engineering and Science (student population 5300) stated they owned a smartphone. Android phones were most common among the students (41%). Ownership of other smartphones was as follows: iPhone 29%; Blackberry 16%; and other/ unknown 12%.

Show'n'Tell Smart Device Apps for Learning

The students identified a number of useful smart device apps that they used to support their learning. Following an analysis of the Show'n'Tell focus group transcriptions, the common theme was how the devices could be applied to enhance student engagement through providing ubiquitous access to their study, as shown by the following student comments:

Student A: [Google Drive] Crack it open on tablet, mobile, wherever.

Student D: My main thing is I don't connect my iPad to a PC regularly. What I want is the means ... to access my files without connecting a cable or connect to my home network. A major selling point is to access my files wherever I go.

Student B: [It's] handy, portable. You pick up your phone, see you've got work to do.

Student E: [I work on my dissertation] when I am on the bus.

The apps used by students to support their studies can be further categorised into four types of study behaviour:

1. Productivity;
2. Organisation;
3. Communication;
4. Multi-tasking.

The rationale given by students for their use of an app typically fulfils one or two of these themes. For example, students explained how the Facebook and DropBox apps were useful for supporting their organisation and communication, especially with group-work:

Everyone is on Facebook .... It's an easy and simple way of keeping in contact and discussing what is going on ... Good for organising, like events ... group-area, setting up a meeting. It shows on the Calendar. (Student A)

I use DropBox. I need to use files use for groupwork. The best things is you can share folders and if one person makes changes that are inappropriate or deletes [files] ... you have access for free to previous versions. (Student D)

[DropBox is] very useful. [You can] look at documents ...save them and upload them ... can't edit on the smart device live ... you have to download .... [It] keeps a history of all the versions of documents, so if you delete something accidentally you can easily reload the document. (Student C)

Student B highlighted Evernote as an alternative to DropBox for aiding production, organisation, and capturing learning materials, as provides the functionality to capture and insert images and audio recordings into Evernote notes.

Evernote ... you can create notes, ... you can take snapshots of lecture materials ... slides or anything that is written down in seminar on blackboard ... tag in your notes and tag them together and share your notes ... share them [by emails]. (Student B)

It was also reassuring to note that a couple of the students were using audio recording apps to gather formal learned conversations, which is consistent with previous research (Middleton & Nortcliffe, 2009a).

Voice Recorder ... I found pretty useful ... to take notes in lectures, I find I nod off and go into my own littlezone, I can take recording and listen to key parts of the lecture.

(Student B)

[Phone voice recorder] record in lessons and lectures, when they are talking about a very important subject ... transfer them across to laptop listen to them again ... [when re-listen] to gather notes especially if you miss the crucial points in the lesson. (Student C)

Student E explained how he used the Final Countdown timer app for the iPhone to help him manage his work. 'It shows you in the app and on the home screen [of the phone], how long you have got left'.

Student B talked about how he used Google Calendar. 'It syncs to my Gmail. If [the tutor] adds updates, it notifies me'.

Student C also valued Google Calendar. 'It helps you organise your life so much more easily, especially as I have got a terribly short memory'.

The students particularly valued the apps that helped them to organise their study time and apps that supported their multi-tasking. Student E, e.g., discussed how useful he found OverSkreen, an app designed to make the tablet's web browser float over above other apps. This functionality helped him work in the other app while viewing learning resources on the web, thereby removing the disjointedness of toggling between apps.

Many of the apps demonstrated in the Show'n'Tell session, however, are dependent upon wireless connectivity; Student E highlighted the importance of identifying Wi-Fi hotspots using Wi-Fi Analyzer app, 'You can see where are the best Wi-Fi signal nodes'.

Some of the apps noted as being particularly useful by students in the Show'n'Tell workshops and recommended as being useful for any student are shown in Table 1 alongside some notes on their benefits and limitations.

Smart Devices for Learning Questionnaire Results

The student workshop participants completed a short survey after the Show'n'Tell demonstrations. This was to gather additional qualitative results on how smart devices are supporting their studies (Table 2). Though a small-scale study, the Likert and open question responses indicate a student consensus that the smart devices have changed every aspect of their studies for the better. It has changed how they engage in and outside of the classroom with their studies and their peers in group-work assessment. The smart devices and apps have made their learning more ubiquitous, personalised and assisting them to define when they learn, in and outside the formal curriculum. The students also agreed that using smart devices is aiding their personal professional development for employment through the

Table 1. Smart Device Apps for Learning – Examples of Apps Discussed by Focus Group Participants, May 2012.

App	Study Behaviour	Functionality and Benefits	Limitations
Any.do*Android*	Organisation	Create a task list by typing or voice input that can sync with Google tasks. Set priorities, lists into folders and tick off of tasks when complete. Create collaborative to-do lists and share via Any.do members, Facebook or email. Requires less information to create than a Google task entry. Presents an easy to use view of all pending tasks	Further editing and the edition of more information is required when synced with Google tasks
DropBox*Android and Apple*	Productivity Communication	Synchronise, upload and download files. Create DropBox shared folders for groupwork. Limited free storage space supports version control. For groupwork purposes, it shows where edits have been made to documents. DropBox enables the user to easily access and read or view files and returns the user to the same location in a previously viewed file upon exiting the app	Poor rendering of PowerPoint slides perfectly. It does not play any animation in files Files have to be downloaded and opened in another app to edit them, which results in the concurrent editing of files by group members and loss of data Registration is required. Though the first 2 GB are free, costs escalate after that Shared folders use memory from each member's storage quota

Table 1. (*Continued*)

App	Study Behaviour	Functionality and Benefits	Limitations
Evernote *Android and Apple*	Productivity	Enables the user to type, capture images, and manage audio recordings. The notes can be uploaded for backup and stored online with Evernote. Documents and images can be shared with other Evernote users. Enables users to upload the output of other sources to the Evernote cloud, e.g. notebooks made in the iPad Penultimate	Sharing limited to other registered Evernote users
Facebook *Android and Apple*	Communication Organisation	Enables students to live chat, particularly helpful if working in a group away from one another. Facebook and the calendar entry synchronise with Google Calendar	Facebook can be a distraction to the learning in a classroom/formal learning environment and independent study time
Final Countdown *Android*	Organisation	Users enter important deadlines which are shown on the home page of the smart device. Items can be configured to illustrate a regular visual notification of the countdown in time for assessments submission deadlines, functionality not provided by most calendar apps. This is particularly beneficial for assessments with distant deadline dates that can be easily forgotten	Once a countdown has been initiated, the app is always running and has been known to contribute to the freezing of some Android devices

App	Category	Description	Issues
Gmail *Android and Apple*	Communication	Gmail synchronises with the university student Gmail. All the functionality of Gmail on the smart device is more effective than the university's own mail app, which doesn't support the attachment functionality	None were identified.
GoDocs *Apple* and **Google Drive** *Android*	Productivity Communication Multi-tasking	Provides access to a user's Google cloud app account, e.g. Google Docs. The user can share documents with other users and edit files live on the smart device. Changes made by other group members are easy to identify and therefore whether they are contributing to the groupwork	The only Google app not supported is Google Chat though it also does not support viewing presentation slides The device needs to be connected to the Internet to view and edit files
Google Calendar *Android and Apple*	Organisation	Create, send and accept invitations for meetings and set up alerts. Supports synchronisation of multiple calendars (i.e. desktop, smart device, Facebook etc.). Data includes time, location and subject, of event, notes or message, and participants' availability. Enables students to organise their time for timetabled sessions and study management including groupwork meetings and assessment planning	None were identified
OverSkreen *Android*	Multi-tasking	The web browser app is able to work as a window above other apps or the device's home page. Enables the user to breakout from the full-screen display	None were identified

Table 1. (*Continued*)

App	Study Behaviour	Functionality and Benefits	Limitations
		of other apps and multi-tasking. For example, making notes in Evernote while reading articles found through Google Scholar	
SmartOffice *Andriod and Apple*	Productivity	Office tool that enables the user to create and edit MS Office documents, spreadsheets and presentations off-line. Files can be downloaded from Google Drive and DropBox and edited off-line. Images can be inserted into documents from smart device camera or photo library. Files can be shared via email in MS Office file extension format or PDF	Users cannot save files to Google Drive or DropBox, therefore the user cannot move from device to device to edit files when the power on the devices fails
SmartOffice *Andriod and Apple*	Productivity	Office tool that enables the user to create and edit MS Office documents, spreadsheets and presentations off-line. Files can be downloaded from Google Drive and DropBox and edited off-line. Images can be inserted into documents from smart device camera or photo library. Files can be shared via email in MS Office file extension format or PDF	Users cannot save files to Google Drive or DropBox, therefore the user cannot move from device to device to edit files when the power on the devices fails

Voice Recorder *Andriod* *(except on Samsung Galaxy Nexus)*. Nortcliffe, Middleton, and Woodcock (2011) provided a comprehensive review of iPhone and iPad audio recorders for learning	Productivity	Saves files in 3GA format, file type, but can be changed on a PC by changing the file extension to MP4. Effective voice recorder for collecting learning conversations whether in groupwork, class or lecture. Users can search by title of files or date. Audio files can be shared by email or transferred to Google Drive or other file sharing apps	The files are 3 GA, therefore 25 minutes recording is 11 MB, so they soon become too large for an email attachment
Wi-Fi Analyzer *Andriod and Apple*	Productivity Communication	Enables the user to identify the optimal Wi-Fi hotspot for online productivity and communication activities. The app clearly displays signal strength as the user roams between Wi-Fi hubs or plays increasingly intense audio alerts as the user approaches the optimal Wi-Fi signal strength	None were identified

Table 2. Smart Devices for Learning Questionnaire Results.

	Strongly Agree	Agree	Neutral	Disagree	Strongly Disagree	Does Not Apply to Me
Using your device to support your learning was a factor in your decision to purchase your device (or ask for it as a gift)	2	2			1	
My smart device has changed how I study	1	4				
My device has changed how I access information, resources, activities and/or people relating to studying on my course	2	3				
Using my device has changed the way I think about how I study	1	3	1			
My device has changed how I contribute to or engage with groupwork		3	1			1
My device has changed how I engage in or contribute to lectures, seminars and other taught situations, e.g. Google Searching, note making etc.	1	3	1			
My device has changed when I engage in my studies	1	2	2			

How?
Agree: 'The use of apps was very appealing', 'Use all the apps to complete work', 'For my touchpad, I could see the benefit of an instant access to the timetable'.
Disagree: 'Price and function only'.

Why?
'I don't need to use my laptop all the time', 'makes it easier to get important notes from lectures by voice recording or making digital notes', 'content consumption', 'It records my lectures and I use my phone to keep connected remotely', 'Being able to communicate in real time is very useful'.

In what ways?
'Don't need to get my laptop out of my bag to look for information', 'I am to access my work from anywhere', 'I have found it useful to be able to pull documents from web to view them instantly anywhere', 'Facebook and group-work', 'Editing docs on the go'.

How?
Agree: 'I am able to have a more flexible work time', 'I can use my tablet wherever I can', 'Locations, I can work everywhere'.

How?
Agree: 'Being able to edit documents as a group is useful', 'Calendar and Facebook', 'It is very useful for making notes and recording meetings'.
Disagree: 'Not use for groupwork'

How?
Agree: 'Search terms is useful', 'I record lectures and discuss what I don't understand via Facebook', 'Making notes easier'.
Neither: 'Note taking, but limited'.

What change in times have you noticed?

  Agree: 'Contact consumption', 'Gave me the ability to work away from desk', 'I can access everything everywhere including in bed'.

  Neither: 'I still do my studies when it suits me'. — 1 2 2

My device has changed where I engage in my studies

What change in locations have you noticed?

  Agree: 'Yes it means that I can complete assignments on the bus', 'I am able to engage more in lectures'.

  Neither: 'Locations, I can work everywhere'. — 1 2 1 ... 1

I am selective in how I use my device to support my studies

In what ways are you selective?

  Strongly disagree: 'Use it for everything, all assignments, revision, note-taking'.

  Agree: 'Avoid content creation', 'Sometimes I use my phone for more of an entertainment system'. — 2 1 1 ... 1

I regularly look for apps that may help me informally and formally engage with my studies

How methodical are you?

  'If I know what I want I will search for it and I also look through the top apps', 'I use *whatsapp* to communicate with people and I also use Facebook chat to talk'.

  Strongly disagree: 'I use web mostly, avoid apps'.

My personal smart device complements or is replacing existing ways of studying (including with other technology)) at university or outside the university. — 1 1 2 ... 1

Explain more about this change

  Agree: 'I hardly use my laptop anymore'. 'Notepad and organisers have been replaced with Calendar and Google Drive'.

  Neither: 'I believe that smart devices could, but [have] not replace[d existing ways of working]'.

Using a smart device makes me a better student — 1 2 2

Comment

  'I can be more efficient doing my work', 'It means I can spend more time on my assignments'.

Using a smart device enhances my employability — 1 4

What connections do smart devices have with employability do you think?

  'Various contacts via LinkedIn', 'I can use app to look for jobs, etc.', 'Because they may want to implement mobile devices into their workplace'.

My device helps me learn with other students — 3 1

Why?

  Agree: 'I can connect to my group using Facebook', 'using Facebook and Google Drive to share documents and thoughts'.

  Does not apply to me: 'I don't work with others'. — 1

development of their mobile digital fluency and commercial networking via using the LinkedIn app.

DISCUSSION

App Typology for Analysing Study Behaviours

This small study explored the hypothesis that students are being innovative in their use of smart devices to support their formal and informal engagement as learners. It found that students valued the flexible access to learning that their devices and installed apps offered them and they appreciated how this helped them to be more organised and productive, whether they were working independently or with others.

The respondent group was very small and of a similar demographic: all male, early 20s and from similar disciplines. This affected the nature of the apps that were discussed in the focus groups. The development of a typology is useful as it begins to highlight the informal and formal study behaviours that students associate with smart, personally owned technology. We have used Productivity, Communication, Multi-tasking, and Organisation as categories based upon the descriptions by students for how apps are used and valued. More work involving other disciplines is needed in this area to develop this analytical typology.

Some references to apps were made in passing that were not addressed in detail during the focus groups. References to communication apps, e.g., indicate how some students who are not co-located appreciate the means to easily communicate with each other.

Students Changing the Nature of their Engagement

The students highlighted how the devices helped them to multi-task: They used the smart technology to remain actively engaged in their work across the nominally demarcated boundaries of life, work and study. For example, Student A reported how, with an imminent deadline, he edited his Google Doc on Google Drive while he was cooking his evening meal.

A recurring theme in the focus group discussions was how personal smart devices promote persistent 'always on' behaviour. Student D observed, 'It is really interesting the way people expect people to use technology is to be focusing on one or two things at once. The way people really use technology, it is more chaotic than that'. The appearance may be of chaos, but clearly there is purpose and personal motivation underpinning the use of smart devices in informal situations.

The nature and purpose of student engagement has changed therefore and is quite different to what might be expected in an account of a formal taught situation. The technology has changed the learning environment and, arguably, can be described as the learning environment. The student has control of this technological environment as we concluded in earlier work on the use of personal audio recorders (Middleton & Nortcliffe, 2011). This affects their motivation, sense of their own responsibility as learners, sense of ownership over their learning and their perception of their learning efficacy and autonomy. The idea of persistent autonomous engagement appears to be valued by the students. It is not suggested that prior to smart technologies a student would only ever engage in their studies in a formal way and on campus, rather that access to powerful, connected computing from anywhere and at any time encourages the student to use the tools in ways that they believe are productive and generally helpful.

This persistent use of personal smart technology also suggests a change in the role of technology in education: it is perhaps less instrumental and more pervasive, being less task orientated and more environmental. Taking an environmental view helps us understand how smart technologies promote productive learner engagement in terms of interactivity and organisation as much as how they are used to access substantive content.

The results illustrate how communication and interactivity are behaviours valued by the students. Their descriptions of groupwork show how smart apps enabled group members to work together even when they were not co-located. Respondents described how they used Google Docs, DropBox and other file sharing tools to produce group reports and noted how support for version control was helpful. Version control functionality, according to the student testimony and accounts from other studies (Dearman & Pierce, 2008), was not only useful, but it enabled them to manage their documentation professionally and this demonstrates how behaviours developed at university have implications for digital literacy and employability. These are seen to be further enhanced when considering the management of personal technology, how students take responsibility for identifying and evaluating their personal technologies. The self-selection of online services, e.g., added authenticity to their project work.

There are cognitive and psychological implications that need to be considered too: how does an 'always on' state of mind affect the learning, the study-life balance and the well-being of the student? Persistent autonomous engagement with learning raises questions about the intensity and the quality of the students' engagement with their learning and their course in general. Again, there are potential implications here for digital literacy and employability, as well as for learning and teaching, and further work is needed to look at the cognitive and psychological dimensions of this area of disruptive innovation.

This study has allowed us to begin to explore the potential of positive, disruptive innovation underpinned by the autonomous adoption of smart device technology by students. At this stage change is happening *around* engagement with existing forms of formal provision; however, the nature of the formal provision itself has not been disrupted to any great degree. In the future we would expect the design of formal provision to take account of the flexibility afforded by smart devices and to be cognisant of the possible shift towards greater learner autonomy. Before this shift is possible, however, curriculum designers will need to see greater student ownership of interoperable smart devices and a shared expectation of the value of such technologies to learning.

Creativity and Academic Influence

The examples referred to in this study, unlike our previous work, do not provide evidence of students' intentional creative engagement with the technologies; however, as the benefits of using smart devices gain wider recognition we would expect more creative engagement with the possibilities. The essential learning task had not changed in this study, it was the learner's behaviour. This suggests that academics need to reconsider the formal pedagogy in order to appreciate the full potential of disruptive innovation. At the same time, as noted earlier, learner creativity and critical thinking coupled with confident, self-regulated learner autonomy need to be developed before widespread adoption of smart technologies and behaviour can happen. Furthermore, greater understanding of the potential needs to be developed to influence the purchasing behaviours of students as they evaluate personal technologies on entry to university or while studying. It is not clear how, or if, influence over such decisions can happen, or if it is a question of students gaining familiarity and confidence with their smart devices. For example, 2 weeks after the Show'n'Tell event, the researcher (as an academic) observed Student C initiate a creative innovative use of their smart device in a group assessment feedback session. The activity involved Skype app on the Student C's HTC smartphone connected to the

University Wi-Fi, and a PC connected to the Internet belonging to a fellow group member at home for medical reasons. The use of Skype enabled the physically non-attending student to actively participate, contribute, reflect and receive the group feedback with his fellow group peers from the academic (researcher). The smart technology experience was seamless, nonintrusive and enabled all parties to benefit from the feedback learning experience.

Therefore, from our own point of view, as academics and educational developers, there remains a question of what we can or should do about developing innovation in the use of smart technology. Especially when considering the way academics practice is changing through use of their own personal smart devices to support student learning (Nortcliffe and Middleton, 2011). The answer is possibly just to observe the change as an organic phenomenon. However, the emerging evidence suggests it is useful to challenge assumptions about the long-standing behaviours and expectations of both students and staff about accepted practice. We suggest it is timely to pay more attention to the rich and meaningful ways that students are developing themselves for their engagement with the curriculum by using their own smart devices.

The idea of Bring Your Own Device (BYOD) is an expression of disruptive innovation. There are clearly perceived benefits to this changed state of engagement, whether considering study, work or a mix of the two. However, further work is needed to look at the quality of engagement and the opportunities that exist for changing learner and academic expectations.

REFERENCES

Armstong, M. (2012). *An investigation into how e-learning applications can effectively be seeded to students with smartphones.* Undergraduate computing programme project report as part of BSc Computing. Department of Computing, Sheffield Hallam University.

Bennett, S., Maton, K., & Kervin, L. (2008). The "Digital Natives" debate: A critical review of evidence. *British Journal of Educational Technology, 39,* 775–786.

Bligh, D. (2000). *What's the use of lectures?* San Francisco, CA: Jossey-Bass.

Boticki, I., & So, H. (2010). Quiet captures: A tool for capturing the evidence of seamless learning with mobile devices. In K. Gomez, L. Lyons & J. Radinsky (Eds.), *Proceedings of the 9th international conference of the learning sciences* (pp. 500–507), 29 June–2 July 2010. Chicago, IL, USA.

Boulos, M. N., Wheeler, S., Tavares, C., & Jones, R. (2011). How smartphones are changing the face of mobile and participatory healthcare: An overview, with example from eCAALYX. *Biomedical Engineering Online, 10,* 24.

Bower, J. L., & Christensen, C. M. (1995). Disruptive technologies: Catching the wave. *Harvard Business Review*, January–February, 19–45.

Bowers–Brown, T. (2006). Widening participation in higher education amongst students from disadvantaged socio–economic groups. *Tertiary Education and Management, 12*(1), 59–74.

Brown, J. S. (2000). Growing up digital: How the web changes work, education, and the ways people learn. *Change: The Magazine of Higher Learning, 32*(2), 10–20.

Burgess, P. W. (2000). Real-world multitasking from a cognitive neuroscience perspective. *Attention and Performance, 18*, 465–472.

Camargo, M., Bary, R., Boly, V., Rees, M., & Smith, R. (2011). *Exploring the implications and impact of smartphones on learning dynamics: The role of self-directed learning.* Paper presented at the Concurrent Enterprising (ICE), 2011 17th International Conference, 20–22 June 2011 (pp. 1–11).

Chen, G. D., Chang, C. K., & Wang, C. Y. (2008). Ubiquitous learning website: Scaffold learners by mobile devices with information-aware techniques. *Computers and Education, 50*, 77–79.

Chen, J., Park, Y., & Putzer, G. J. (2010). An examination of the components that increase acceptance of smartphones among healthcare professionals. *Electronic Journal of Health Informatics, 5*(2), e16.

Christensen, C. M. (1997). *The innovator's dilemma: When new technologies cause great firms to fail.* Boston, MA: Harvard Business School Press.

Clough, G., Jones, A. C., McAndrew, P., & Scanlon, E. (2008). Informal learning with PDAs and smartphones. *Journal of Computer Assisted Learning, 24*(5), 359–371.

Clough, G., Jones, A., McAndrew, P., & Scanlon, E. (2009). Informal learning in online communities of mobile devices enthusiasts. In M. Ally (Ed.), *Mobile learning: Transforming the delivery of education and training* (pp. 100–112). Athabasca: Athabasca University Press.

Cochrane, T. (2006). *Learning with wireless mobile devices and social software.* Paper presented at the 23rd ASCILITE Conference, 3–6 December 2006. Sydney.

Cochrane, T., & Bateman, R. (2010). Smartphones give user wings: Pedagogical affordances of mobile Web 2.0. *Australasian Journal of Educational Technology, 26*(1), 1–14.

Cohen, L., Manion, L., & Morrison, K. (2000). *Research methods in education* (5th ed.). New York, NY: Routledge.

Corbeil, J., & Valdez-Corbeil, M. J. (2007). Are users ready for mobile learning? *Educause Quarterly, 11*, 51–58.

Costello, S. (2012) How many apps are in the iPhone app store? *About.com Guide.* Retrieved from http://ipod.about.com/od/iphonesoftwareterms/qt/apps-in-app-store.htm

Davis, H., & White, S. (2012). *Institutional personal learning environments: Paradise or paradox?* Keynote paper presented on 17 April 2012 at 4th International Conference on Computer Supported Education, 16–18 April 2012. Porto, Portugal.

Dearman, D., & Pierce, J. S. (2008). It's on my other computer! Computing with multiple devices. In *Proceedings of the twenty-sixth annual SIGCHI conference on human factors in computing systems (CHI '08)*. ACM, New York, NY.

Disobedient Media. (2010, October 18). 3D Crystal Viewer app released [Web log post]. Retrieved from http://disobedientmedia.co.uk/blog/2010/10/18/news18oct10/

Edwards, M. B., & Gronlund, S. D. (1998). Task interruption and its effects on memory. *Memory, 6*(6), 665–687.

Fischer, S. C., Morris, K. A., & Joslyn, S. (2003, July). *Measuring multi-tasking ability.* Report prepared for the Office of Naval Research by Anacapa Sciences, Inc. (157 pp.) Retrieved from http://handle.dtic.mil/100.2/ADA417039

Franklin, T. (2011). Mobile learning: At the tipping point. *Turkish Online Journal of Educational Technology, 10*(4), 261–275.

Han, J., Chung, S., & Sohn, Y. (2009). Technology convergence: When do consumers prefer converged products to dedicated products? *Journal of Marketing, 73*(4), 97–108.

Hembrooke, H., & Gay, G. (2003). The laptop and the lecture: The effects of multitasking in learning environments. *Journal of Computing in Higher Education, 15*(1), 46–64.

Hendery, S. (2009, July 9). Great gadget, stratospheric price. *New Zealand Herald,* B4. Retrieved from http://www.nzherald.co.nz/technology/news/article.cfm?c_id=5&objectid=10583290

Huang, Y.-M., Chiu, P.-S., Liu, T.-C., & Chen, T.-S. (2011). The design and implementation of a meaningful learning-based evaluation method for ubiquitous learning. *Computers & Education, 57*(4), 2291–2302.

Huang, Y. M., Jeng, Y. L., & Huang, T. C. (2009). An educational mobile blogging system for supporting collaborative learning. *Journal of Educational Technology and Society, 12*(2), 163–175.

Hwang, G., Chen, B., Chu, H., & Cheng, Z. S. (2012). *Development of a Web 2.0-based ubiquitous learning platform for schoolyard plant identification.* Paper presented at the 2012 Seventh IEEE International Conference on Wireless, Mobile and Ubiquitous Technology in Education. Retrieved from http://ieeexplore.ieee.org.lcproxy.shu.ac.uk/stamp/stamp.jsp?arnumber=06185043

Janis, I. L. (1972). *Victims of groupthink: A psychological study of foreign-policy decisions and fiascoes.* Boston, MA: Houghton Mifflin.

Jeng, Y. L., Wu, T. T., Huang, Y. M., Tan, Q., & Yang, S. J. H. (2010). The add-on impact of mobile applications in learning strategies: A review study. *Educational Technology & Society, 13*(3), 3–11.

Jewell, S. (2011). Productivity via mobile phones: Using smartphones in smart ways. *Journal of Electronic Resources in Medical Libraries, 8*(1).

JISC. (2006). Designing *space for effective learning: A guide to 21st century learning space design.* Retrieved from http://www.jisc.ac.uk/uploaded_documents/JISClearningspaces.pdf

JISC. (2009). *Effective practice in a digital age: A guide to technology-enhanced learning and teaching.* Retrieved from http://www.jisc.ac.uk

JISC. (2011a). *Mobile learning info kit* (pp. 55–57). University of Leeds Medical School. Retrieved from https://files.pbworks.com/download/ukYXA3QiTL/mobilelearninginfo-kit/50760424/mobile-learning-infokit.pdf

JISC. (2011b). *Mobile learning info kit* (pp. 50–54). University of Bradford. Retrieved from https://files.pbworks.com/download/ukYXA3QiTL/mobilelearninginfokit/50760424/mobile-learning-infokit.pdf

Jones, C., Ramanau, R., Cross, S., & Healing, G. (2010). Net generation or Digital Natives: Is there a distinct new generation entering university? *Computers & Education, 54*(3), 722–732.

Kennedy, G., Krause, K., Judd, T., Churchward, A., & Gray, K. (2006). *First year students' experiences with technology: Are they really digital natives?* Melbourne: University of Melbourne. Retrieved from https://www.griffith.edu.au/data/assets/pdf_file/0008/39266/NativesReport.pdf

Kukulska-Hulme, A., & Traxler, J. (Eds.). (2005). *Mobile learning: A handbook for educators and trainers. Open and flexible learning series.* London: Routledge.

Lee, I. (2006). Ubiquitous computing for mobile learning. *Asia-Pacific Cybereducation Journal, 2*(1), 17–28.

Lohnes, S., & Kinzer, C. (2007). Questioning assumptions about students' expectations for technology in college classrooms. *Innovate, 3*(5). Retrieved from http://www.innovate online.info/index.php?view = article&id = 431

Mayes, T., Morrison, D., Mellar, H., Bullen, P., & Oliver, M. (2009). *Transforming higher education through technology enhanced learning.* New York, NY: Higher Education Academy.

Middleton, A. J., & Nortcliffe, A. (2009a). *Audio, autonomy and authenticity: Constructive comments and conversations captured by the learner.* Poster presented at the ALT-C 2009 "In Dreams Begins Responsibility" – Choice, Evidence, and Change, 8–10 September 2009, Manchester, UK.

Middleton, A., & Nortcliffe, A. (2011). *Smartphone feedback: Pervasive and meaningful exchanges and interventions.* Paper presented at the ALT-C 2011 – Thriving in a Colder and More Challenging Climate, 6–8 September 2011, Leeds, UK.

Middleton, A., Nortcliffe, A., & Owen, R. (2009). *iGather: Learners as responsible audio collectors of tutor, peer and self reflection.* Paper presented at the A Word in User Ear – Audio Feedback Conference, 18 December 2009, Sheffield, UK. Retrieved from http:// research.shu.ac.uk/lti/awordinuserrear2009/

Mitchell, K., Race, N. J. P. & Clarke, M. (2005). *uLearn: Facilitating ubiquitous learning through camera equipped mobile phones.* In *Proceedings of the IEEE International Workshop on Wireless and Mobile Technologies in Education* (pp. 274–281), Washington, DC: USA.

Murphy, D. (2012, March 3). Apple's App Store hits 25 billion downloads: How many per iPhone? *PCMag.Com.* Retrieved from http://www.pcmag.com/article2/0,2817,2401122,00.asp

Nicol, D. J., & Macfarlane-Dick, D. (2006). Formative assessment and self-regulated learning: A model and seven principles of good feedback practice. *Studies in Higher Education, 31*(2), 199–218.

Nortcliffe, A. (2010). iPhone supervision and feedback: A case study. In A. Middleton (Ed.), *Media-enhanced feedback: Case studies and methods.* Paper produced to support the Media–Enhanced Feedback event, 27 October 2010, Sheffield, UK. Retrieved from http://ppp.chester.ac.uk/images/4/43/Middleton-Media-enhanced_feedback_proceedings-final.pdf

Nortcliffe, A. L. & Middleton, A. (2006). Audio lecture notes: Supplementary lecture materials with added value. *NADO News* (The Official newsletter of the National Association of Disability Officers Ltd.), Summer.

Nortcliffe, A. & Middleton, A. (2007). Audio feedback for the iPod generation. In *Proceedings of international conference on engineering education*, September 2007, Coimbra, Portugal.

Nortcliffe, A., & Middleton, A. (2008). A three year case study of using audio to blend the engineer's learning environment. *Engineering Education: Journal of the Higher Education Academy Engineering Subject Centre, 3*(2), 45–57.

Nortcliffe, A. L., & Middleton, A. (2009a). Understanding effective models of audio feedback. In R. Roy (Ed.), *Engineering education perspectives, issues and concerns.* Delhi: Shipra Publications.

Nortcliffe, A., & Middleton, A. (2009b). Effective assignment feedback through timely and personal digital audio engagement. In J. O'Donoghue (Ed.), *Technology-supported environments for personalized learning: Methods and case studies* (pp. 409–428). Hershey: IGI Global.

Nortcliffe, A., & Middleton, A. (2010). Student audio notes project: Lessons from the autonomous use of MP3 recorders by students to enhance their learning. In I. Moore, J. ElfvingHwang, K. Garnett & C. Corker (Eds.), *CPLA centre for promoting learner autonomy a centre for excellence in teaching and learning case studies*, (Vol. 1, pp. 151–164). Retrieved from http://extra.shu.ac.uk/cetl/cpla/resources/CPLA_Case_Studies_Volume_1.pdf

Nortcliffe, A., & Middleton, A. (2011). Smartphone feedback: Using an iPhone to improve the distribution of audio feedback. *International Journal of Electrical Engineering Education Special Edition, 48*(3), 280–293.

Nortcliffe, A., Middleton, A., & Woodcock, B. (2011). *Evaluating the use of audio smartphone apps for higher education learning*. Paper presented at the Audio Engineering Society 130th Conference, May 2011, London, UK.

Nortcliffe, A., Rossiter, J. A., & Middleton, A. (2009). *Students using digital audio interventions to enhance their learning experience*. Paper presented at The Higher Education Academy Annual Conference 2009 "The Future of the Student Learning Experience", 30 June–2 July 2009, Manchester, UK.

Oblinger, D. (Ed.), (2006). *Learning spaces*. Boulder, CO: EDUCAUSE, Retrieved from http://net.educause.edu/ir/library/pdf/PUB7102a.pdf

Oliver, B., & Goerke, V. (2007). Australian undergraduates' use and ownership of emerging technologies: Implications and opportunities for creating engaging learning experiences for the net generation. *Australasian Journal of Educational Technology, 23*(2), 171–186. Retrieved from http://www.ascilite.org.au/ajet/ajet23/oliver.html

Ophir, E., Nass, C., & Wagner, A. D. (2009). Cognitive control in media multitaskers. *Proceedings of the National Academy of Sciences of the United States of America, 106*(37), 15583–15587.

Paul, I. (2012, February 27). Android market hits 450K apps, challengers abound. *PC World*. Retrieved from http://www.pcworld.com/article/250765/android_market_hits_450k_apps_challengers_abound.html

Röpke, J., & Schneider, G. (2012). *MORE – Mobile referencing system for printed media*. Paper presented at the 4th International Conference on Computer Supported Education, 16–18 April 2012, Porto, Portugal.

Rossiter, J. A., Nortcliffe, A., Griffin, A., & Middleton, A. (2009). Using student generated audio to enhance learning. *Engineering Education: Journal of the Higher Education Academy Engineering Subject Centre, 4*(2), 52–61.

Ruth, A. (2012). Chalkface; interface; screen face: Moving the metaphor of teaching toward the nexus of teaching and learning. *Research in Learning Technology, 20*(2).

Sakamura, K., & Koshizuka, N. (2005). Ubiquitous computing technologies for ubiquitous learning. *Proceeding of the International Workshop on Wireless & Mobile Technologies in Education*, 11–18.

Santos, N. S. R. S., Valdeni de Lima, J., & Krug Wives, L. (2012). *Integration of technologies in the development of interactive educational content*. Paper presented at the 4th International Conference on Computer Supported Education, 16–18 April 2012. Porto, Portugal.

Sharples, M., Arnedillo-Sánchez, I., Milrad, M., & Vavoula, G. (2009). Mobile learning: Small devices, big issues. In N. Balacheff, S. Ludvigsen, T. Jong, A. Lazonder & S. Barnes (Eds.), *Technology-Enhanced learning*, Part IV (pp. 233–249). Dordrecht: Springer.

Sharples, M., Taylor, J., & Vavoula, G. (2007). A theory of learning for the mobile age. In R. Andrews, & C. Haythornthwaite (Eds.), *Sage handbook of elearning research* (pp. 221–247). London: Sage.

Shin, D., Shin, Y, Choo, H., & Beom, K. (2011). Smartphones as smart pedagogical tools: Implications for smartphones as u-learning devices. *Computers in Human Behavior*, *27*(6), 2207–2214.

Song, L., & Hill, J. (2007). A conceptual model for understanding self-directed learning in online environments. *Journal of Interactive Online Learning*, *6*(1), 27–42.

Traxler, J. (2009). Learning in a mobile age. *International Journal of Mobile and Blended Learning*, *1*(1), 1–12.

Traxler, J. (2010). Students and mobile devices. *ALT-J, Research in Learning Technology*, *18*(2), 149–160.

Tucker, T. G., & Winchester, III., W. W. (2009). Mobile learning for just-in-time applications. In *Proceedings of the 47th annual southeast regional conference (ACM-SE 47)*. ACM, New York, NY, USA. Retrieved from http://doi.acm.org/10.1145/1566445.1566469

Vavoula, G., & Sharples, M. (2008). *Challenges in evaluating mobile learning*. Paper presented at the mLearn 2008 conference. October 7–8 2008, Wolverhampton, UK.

Vozenilek, J., Huff, J. S., Reznek, M., & Gordon, J. A. (2004). See one, do one, teach one: Advanced technology in medical education. *Academic Emergency Medicine*, *11*(11), 1149–1154.

Whitney, L. (2012). *iOS, Android apps surpass 1 billion downloads in final week of 2011, CNET*. Retrieved from http://news.cnet.com/8301-1023_3-57351300-93/ios-android-apps-surpass-1-billion-downloads-in-final-week-of-2011/

Woodock, B., Middleton, A., & Nortcliffe, A. (2012a). Considering the smartphone learner: Developing innovation to investigate the opportunities for students and their interest. *Student Engagement and Experience Journal*, *1*(1). Retrieved from http://research.shu.ac.uk/SEEJ/index.php/seej/article/view/38/Woodcock

Woodock, B., Middleton, A., & Nortcliffe, A. (2012b). *Smart device potential for student learning*. Paper presented at the 4th International Conference on Computer Supported Education, 16–18 April 2012, Porto, Portugal.

Wu, T. T., Yang, T., Hwang, G., & Chu, H. (2008). *Conducting situated learning in a context-aware ubiquitous learning environment*. Paper presented at Wireless, Mobile, and Ubiquitous Technology in Education, 2008. WMUTE 2008. Fifth IEEE International Conference, 23–26 March 2008 (pp. 82–86). Retrieved from http://ieeexplore.ieee.org/stamp/stamp.jsp?tp=&arnumber=4489792&isnumber=4489772

Yan, C. (2009). *How to implement collaborative learning in Web2.0: Take three applications for example*. Paper presented at the Symposium on IT in Medicine and Education, 14–16 August 2009 (pp. 627–631).

ENGAGING TEACHERS (AND STUDENTS) WITH MEDIA STREAMING TECHNOLOGY: THE CASE OF BOX OF BROADCASTS

Vicki Holmes, Wilma Clark, Paul Burt and Bart Rienties

ABSTRACT

Information and Communication Technology offers powerful Web 2.0 tools that can benefit learners with different learning preferences. The rise of video streaming, the increased proliferation of 'on demand' televisual media and new smartphone streaming opportunities have generated a range of web-based media that may usefully support teachers and learners in accommodating these varied learning styles. At the same time, media streaming technologies such as YouTube have distinct drawbacks for students, teachers and their institutions, particularly in relation to appropriate content and the ethical issues around the uploading of student materials to a public repository.

Two studies are reported. In Study 1, two case studies of how teachers engaged students with a media-streaming system called Box of Broadcasts

Increasing Student Engagement and Retention using Mobile Applications: Smartphones, Skype and Texting Technologies
Cutting-edge Technologies in Higher Education, Volume 6D, 209–238
ISSN: 2044-9968/doi:10.1108/S2044-9968(2013)000006D010

(BoB) are discussed using principles of design-based research. The result from the first case study indicated that BoB provided an improved efficiency for teachers who filmed students' presentations in a second language. The second case study illustrated how the integration of BoB into their classroom teaching led a psychology teacher to think differently about students and the design and delivery of teaching and learning resources. In Study 2, the use of a qualitative semi-structured interview approach with eight teachers indicated that staff felt that BoB was beneficial in supporting pedagogic practice. Furthermore, staff highlighted the opportunities for dialogue about theory, reality and practice that video materials offered to students as added value. Key limitations for some staff in their use of BoB as a support for video-enriched pedagogic practice were the restricted level of available content on BoB, some difficulties relating to the skills required for creating and using clips and technical stability when using clips.

YouTube is a treasure trove of resources from around the globe and nostalgic video from the past. ... However, YouTube is also a vast wasteland of garbage and social parody that adds nothing to the learning process (Jones & Cuthrell, 2011, p. 81).

INTRODUCTION

Information and Communication Technology (ICT) offers powerful Web 2.0 tools that can benefit learners with different learning needs (Clark, Logan, Luckin, Mee, & Oliver, 2009; Homer, Plass, & Blake, 2008; Tempelaar, Niculescu, Rienties, Giesbers, & Gijselaers, 2012). Among these, video and media streaming and sharing technologies in particular represent a rapidly evolving area in higher education (Anastasiades et al., 2010; Duffy, 2008; Homer, et al., 2008; Kaufman & Mohan, 2009), with a strong focus on the use of streaming media content as a support for synchronous and asynchronous learning. Those in higher education expect their use of video streaming and sharing in education to grow significantly (Bloom & Johnston, 2010; Kaufman & Mohan, 2009; Williams & Fardon, 2007). Throughout this chapter, when we refer to media streaming (such as YouTube), we also include the notion of media sharing (e.g. sharing comments, video replies).

The rise of video streaming and the increased proliferation of 'on demand' television such as BBC iPlayer or 4 on Demand in the United Kingdom, Uitzendinggemist.nl or RTL XL in the Netherlands, or FOX and ABC in the United States, and the rise of digital radio such as Spotify or Pandora Radio, have generated a new stream of web-based media that may be useful for teachers and learners in accommodating different learning preferences. At the same time, an increasing number of institutes are recording lectures to allow students to re-watch the lectures at a time and place of their convenience (Williams & Fardon, 2007). Some learners prefer audio-visual materials to learn, others prefer to learn through audio or through the reading of texts (Jones & Cuthrell, 2011; Mayer, 2003; Thornhill, Asensio, & Young, 2002). On demand television and radio services provide a variety of digital materials that not only have the capacity to enhance the formal learning experience of students but also offer opportunities to engage students with the wider contexts of current events and real-world scenarios, either accessing these services from 'traditional' PCs or laptops or from handheld devices or smartphones. At the same time, media streaming technologies such as YouTube are often considered to have distinct drawbacks for students, teachers and their institutions. These include the appropriateness of content (both of clips and related social interactions in the form of comments made by students and 'externals') (Jones & Cuthrell, 2011), sharing of TV series and films and related copyright issues; inclusion of advertising, issues around privacy (Bloom & Johnston, 2010) and the ethics of uploading student materials to a public repository. Legal and technical issues often thwart attempts to create institutional video and synchronous learning experiences and repositories (Olaniran, 2006).

In response to these issues, the University of Surrey implemented a customised university-wide media capture, storage and streaming system known as Box of Broadcasts (BoB). BoB allows staff to schedule and capture broadcast TV and radio services that can then be delivered for web-based or mobile viewing. Recordings stored in BoB can be integrated with other systems to further exploit the functionality offered by other technologies. One example is the integration of BoB with a virtual learning environment (VLE), enabling staff and students to engage in discussion forums within the VLE about videos stored in BoB via a safe and closed learning environment. Staff and students are also able to create personalised playlists.

Two years after BoB was first implemented, we felt it timely to explore and understand better how staff (and students) were using and engaging with BoB, which would in turn inform future developments in terms of professional development, training and support from the e-learning centre. As highlighted by Kinchin (2012b), 'pedagogy cannot be added to e-learning … as an after-thought as the implicit values and beliefs required to construct a pedagogy will already inhabit the digital media, and will underpin the pedagogic discourse that inevitably pre-empts the linear discourse of teaching methods'. In order to provide a powerful learning experience to students in 'traditional' higher education, a key starting point is to understand how teachers engage and integrate technology into their classroom teaching (Kinchin, 2012a, 2012b; Luppicini, 2007; Mishra & Koehler, 2005; Rienties & Townsend, 2012). While most students feel comfortable with streaming technology (Jones & Cuthrell, 2011; Williams & Fardon, 2007), limited research has been conducted to identify which barriers hamper or stimulate teachers to engage with streaming technology. Although we acknowledge that students' adoption of and satisfaction with the technology-enhanced learning environment is crucial for sustainable success of technology adoption, in this chapter we primarily focus on how teachers use streaming technology in general and BoB in particular in their teaching practice.

This book-chapter first discusses two case studies of how teachers engaged students with BoB. It then discusses the perceived constraints on effective use of the BoB system, using data derived from semi-structured interviews with eight members of the university teaching staff. A key aim of the study was to understand better the conditions (technical, pedagogical, organisation or social) that contribute to the development of effective practice in the use of media streaming technology as a support for teaching and learning at the university. Both studies were conducted at the University of Surrey, a UK research-intensive university belonging to the top 15% in the United Kingdom.

HOW TO CREATE A POWERFUL LEARNING ENVIRONMENT THAT WORKS FOR STUDENTS AND TEACHERS?

While in primary and secondary education teachers provide more room for engagement and interaction with students, in higher education a persistent and common practice of teachers is to use (one-way) lectures with limited interaction with students (Struyven, Dochy, & Janssens, 2011). But research evidence has shown that traditional teacher-centred forms of education such as lectures do not provide an optimal learning experience for all types of learners (Biggs & Tang, 2007; Nicholls, 2001). In a recent study of student perceptions of effective teaching in higher education, Onwuegbuzie et al. (2007) asked 225 students at two US universities to list the three key characteristics that they believed effective university instructors possess or demonstrate. Based upon 2991 statements, 9 themes of effective teachers surfaced: student-centred (59%), expert (44%), professional (41%), enthusiastic (30%), transmitter (23%), connector (23%), director (22%), ethical (22%) and responsive (5%). This demonstrates that while most academic scholars will be experts in their own field and enthusiastic to transmit their expertise to students, students are first and foremost expecting teachers to be student-centred, able to connect to students and to effectively communicate and respond to students' needs. The implication is that universities need to facilitate and support a greater range of strategies for teachers, particularly as demands for flexible learning strategies grow from an increasingly diverse group of learners.

Technology is seen as one of the strategies to provide a good learning experience. Yet despite an increased understanding of how students learn and recognition of the effectiveness of student-centred learning facilitated through ICT, pedagogical challenges remain: 'Simply implementing communication technologies for the sake of incorporating technology does not work and the nature or structure of the communication technology is often given less consideration' (Olaniran, 2006, p. 211). Many ICT innovations have not delivered the fundamental changes in higher education that many teachers and researchers hoped for (Mishra & Koehler, 2005; Resta & Laferrière, 2007; Rienties, Kaper et al., 2012). This has been attributed to a lack of organisational embedding of innovation (ICT in particular) and a lack of understanding of the essential parameters for effective teaching with ICT (Kinchin, 2012a; Mishra & Koehler, 2005; Rienties, Kaper et al., 2012).

One aspect of successfully implementing ICT in education is to the importance of adjusting the content of a module in line with the technology selected and pedagogical approach used. Mishra and Koehler (2006) designed the technological pedagogical content knowledge (TPACK) model for successful learning using ICT on this premise. The authors show that learning is most effective when teachers have appropriate awareness of the complex interplay between pedagogy, technology and discipline knowledge. In order to effectively address students' needs, teachers need to have sufficient content and pedagogical and technological knowledge.

In practice there is often an imbalance between the technological, pedagogical and content knowledge of a teacher and how academic development addresses these three key areas (Kinchin, 2012a; Lawless & Pellegrino, 2007). Technological knowledge is often seen as independent from content and pedagogical knowledge (Kinchin, 2012a; Mishra & Koehler, 2006; Rienties & Townsend, 2012; Ziegenfuss & Lawler, 2008). As an example, a science teacher thinking about using a new ICT tool in education may consult a direct colleague or a teacher educator or a learning technologist for advice on how to effectively implement the technology into science education (Ziegenfuss & Lawler, 2008). If the science teacher decides to use video cases about optimising the performance of an internal combustion engine, it would be important to incorporate the videos into the module design (e.g. by having a task where students search for and share alternative videos of engine building in an online repository and then critically reflect on peers' contributions), into the content (e.g. by discussing the various internal combustion mappings in class based upon the discourse in the online repository) and into the pedagogy (e.g. by using a collaborative learning approach rather than using a traditional lecture-based approach) (Rienties, Brouwer, Lygo-Baker, & Townsend, 2011; Ziegenfuss & Lawler, 2008). Otherwise, it is likely that many of the students will not actively share videos and/or use the online repository and opportunities for deep and/or collaborative reflection among peers may be lost or overlooked. As a result, the teacher's motivation to use an ICT system like BoB may fade and there may be a negative impact on the perceived affordance and usability of BoB.

Research has also suggested that content knowledge often determines the pedagogical approach taken and the adoption of particular technologies (Koehler & Mishra, 2005; Mishra & Koehler, 2006). For example, in a review of 118 course designs for transitional, remedial education, Rienties, Kaper et al. (2012) found that teachers from 22 countries consistently aligned content with their pedagogical approach. However, the use of technology in these 118 courses was not found to be related to the teachers' content or pedagogical approach. As a specific example, math teachers who taught a basic algebra course to undergraduate business students adopted a similar pedagogical approach, but the affordances and ranges of ICT tools were extremely diverse.

MEDIA-STREAMING

Media streaming technology is a rapidly evolving area in higher education (Bloom & Johnston, 2010; Kaufman & Mohan, 2009) with much research already conducted in effective usage of videos in the classroom. For example, research by JISC (Joint Information Systems Committee) (Thornhill et al., 2002) focused on best practice in the use and development of video-enriched learning environments, with a particular emphasis on the use of streaming media content as a support for synchronous and asynchronous communication. The focus of this early research was largely on the transition from earlier historical modes of video use (e.g. educational television, VHS tapes, CD-ROMs and related multimedia to DVDs) and on instructional video materials, such as lecture content or subject-specific content (Williams & Fardon, 2007), particularly targeting distance learning (Luppicini, 2007; Mayer, 2003). The JISC 'Click and Go' (2002–2004) project sought to provide a guide for educators that clarified the 'tangled interplay between the various technical, pedagogical and infrastructure questions' linked to the use of audio-visual technologies and the 'learning materials and learning activities associated with them' (Thornhill et al., 2002). The JISC project identified five characteristics (Table 1) as being valuable in the use of media-streaming video technologies as a support for teaching and learning.

More recently, the rise of social media such as YouTube (Bloom & Johnston, 2010; Duffy, 2008) and the growth of 'on demand' television and radio has generated a new stream of mainstream and niche web-based audio and televisual media that is potentially useful for teachers and learners, particularly in terms of students' engagement with current events and real-world scenarios (Kaufman & Mohan, 2009; Smart, 2010). However, the ability to negotiate this wider media stream is an issue for educators as is the integration of such media into more formal learning environments, both face-to-face and at a distance. Jones and Cuthrell (2011) refer to this as the dichotomous nature of YouTube, whereby teachers can find excellent videos appropriate for their subject but at the same time find various social parodies and inappropriate, unreliable or non-scientific videos that may be off-putting and/or disrespectful for (some) students from different cultures. Although an essential graduate skill of students is to be able to select, interpret, use and re-create content from large databases like YouTube, in

Table 1.   Value-Added Characteristics of Video in Education.

Characteristic	Value
Visualisation	Video as a moving image helps the student to visualise a process, an event that might be difficult to represent through a text form
Illustration	Video reinforces the power of a still image or graphic; it can show an example of how something works, moves or performs
Validation	Video reinforces what is being said in the classroom; it validates knowledge through a moving image or representation
Explanation	Video helps to describe visually an explanation of a procedure or process through a 'show and tell' style
Motivation	Video can make content alive and bring it into the classroom

particular in the first 2 years of undergraduate programmes some students may be overwhelmed by the sheer amount of YouTube clips available on a given topic. Some students may lack an in-depth understanding of the discipline to select the most appropriate or relevant content and create their own mental maps.

The collation of educator perspectives on the pedagogical aspects of video streaming activity from mainstream and niche audio and televisual resources in teaching and learning environments therefore appears timely and desirable (Jones & Cuthrell, 2011; Kaufman & Mohan, 2009). Some commentators (Smart, 2010) are referring to this new stream of web-based broadcast technologies as the Web 3.0 Metaverse (i.e. the convergence of virtual and physical worlds). Trends and developments in the future shape of the Internet point to TV-quality open video, increased use of augmented reality interfaces and of pervasive broadband, wireless and sensory technologies. We are, as suggested by Duffy (2008) and Smart (2010, p. 9), in a time when 'the internet swallows the television'.

WHAT DOES BOX OF BROADCASTS DO?

BoB is a university-wide media capture, store and streaming system launched in March 2009 as an enhancement for teaching and learning across the university. BoB allows staff to schedule and capture broadcast TV and radio from both the United Kingdom and overseas, as illustrated in Fig. 1. Captured broadcasts are transcoded for multiple delivery formats, e.g. web-based or mobile viewing. Staff are also able to create a personalised repository through the use of a personal account area in *myBob* and, within that, to create and use individualised *playlists* as illustrated in Fig. 2. These playlists can be further enhanced for searching by adding relevant metadata and/or through user-generated naming of labels. Playback is streamed, allowing for quicker, non-linear playback and greater control over copyright materials. User control is also managed by the university through allocated rights at different levels, which currently at this university was set such that only staff and not students were allowed to record a broadcast.

Staff use is capped at 25 recordings scheduled at any one time. A particular merit for language, political science and sociology teachers is that 30 channels in French, German, Arabic, Russian, Spanish and Italian, which are commonly not part of TV subscriptions in the UK, are also available. A system buffer of 8 days is in place for 11 main TV channels and 6 main radio channels, so that if a teacher forgets to schedule in advance the

Fig. 1. Screenshot of Scheduling and Capturing Broadcast TV and Radio.

recording of a broadcast, they are still able to capture the desired video clip after the broadcast has taken place.

Copyright Issues

Complex rights exist around broadcasts, sound recordings and films, and copyright is an important but complex issue for any user of YouTube or

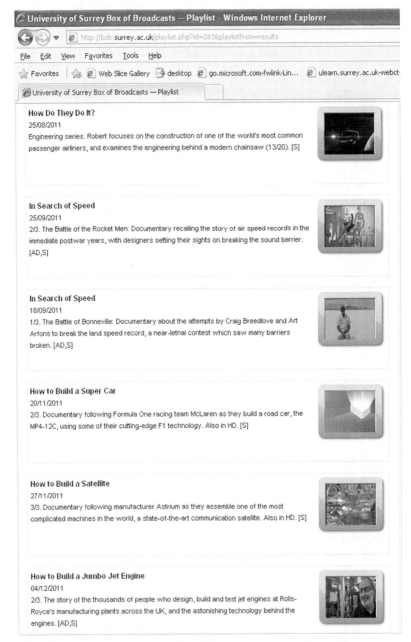

Fig. 2.   Screenshot of Playlist on Engineering.

BoB. A particular merit of BoB is that teachers are able to record, store and share off-air broadcast materials through the Educational Recording Agency + (ERA +) licence arrangements that govern use of BoB at the university. Access to BoB materials is restricted to University of Surrey staff and students and the UK geographical region. While BoB allows for content to be uploaded, the ERA + licence does not permit recordings of any non-broadcast material to be used such as commercial DVDs or YouTube content. This creates a dichotomous situation for staff and students who accessing both a 'walled garden' (BoB) and a 'wild meadow' (e.g. YouTube). While teachers are in full control of the videos and materials of BoB, the wild and vast meadows of YouTube are constantly changing. In YouTube, new videos appear at an unprecedented rate, but at the same time many 'flowers' are removed or repositioned, potentially leading to anxiety among teachers whether the materials in the shape and 'appropriate' format will actually be available during their module.

RESEARCH QUESTIONS

In Study 1, we explore two case studies about how a language teacher and psychology teacher redesigned their course model by implementing and integrating BoB in a pedagogically innovative manner. Following on from this, we explore the overarching research question of Study 2 which sought to ascertain the perceived benefits and limitations of the adoption and use of BoB as a support for teaching and learning within the University of Surrey. A related and subsidiary question focused on effective practice in the use of BoB. Three research aims, framed by Mishra and Koehler's TPACK model, were identified:
- To explore staff use of/perceptions of BoB (technological content knowledge, technological pedagogical knowledge)
- To contrast the benefits and constraints of YouTube versus BoB (technological focus)
- To understand potential benefits and constraints on the use of BoB and media streaming technology for staff members (TPACK)

METHOD

Study 1: Two Case Studies of Box of Broadcasts

To enhance the reader's understanding of how teachers at University of Surrey use BoB, we selected two case studies of teachers from psychology and languages who were using BoB. In Study 1, we use principles of design-based research (DBR) in order to critically reflect on how the two teachers have redesigned their courses by integrating BoB (Collins, Joseph, & Bielaczyc, 2004; Reeves, Herrington, & Oliver, 2005; Rienties & Townsend, 2012). According to Collins et al. (2004, p. 21), '[d]esign experiments bring together two critical pieces in order to guide us to better educational refinement: a design focus and assessment of critical design elements'. Although design research is set in real educational settings where teachers want to improve learning of their students, theoretical foundations (i.e. TPACK) and claims for design research are essential for identification of educational problems and possible solutions (Reeves et al., 2005; Rienties & Townsend, 2012). According to Reeves et al. (2005, p. 107), '[t]heory informing practice is at the heart of the [design research] approach, and the creation of design principles and guidelines enables research outcomes to be transformed into educational practice'.

Study 2: In-Depth Interviews of Teachers Using BoB

In a 2 month period across June and July 2011, we aimed to identify technical, organisational and/or social issues (real or perceived) that enhance or constrain the adoption and use of this media streaming technology using semi-structured interviews with selected staff. Study 2 aimed to identify examples of good (and 'bad') practice that can be used to support and encourage take up of BoB by the wider community of staff and students, or to extend and inform the ongoing practices of existing users.

Participation and Sampling

Participants in the study were selected from staff members across all four faculties of the university (Business Economics and Law, Engineering and Physical Sciences, Health and Medical Sciences, Arts and Humanities), who were identified as being users of BoB. Participant sampling was based on a range of criteria including usage levels, faculty/departmental affiliation and/or as being someone who has (based on user statistics drawn directly from BoB) an active interest in the use of BoB as a support for teaching and learning. Of the latter, an indicator used was the number of broadcasts recorded, with numbers scheduled ranging from a low of 54 to a high of 182 and total number of uploads. In addition, types of use were used to identify teaching staff with particular experiences of BoB, e.g. making playlists, using clips or uploading user-generated video materials. A selection of 18 potential interviewees was identified, whereby eight staff members were eventually interviewed, representing each of the four faculties. Of those who were approached and were unable to participate, a majority cited incompatible interview dates (e.g. they were on leave, had insufficient time due to other commitments, or had left the university in the interim period).

Procedure

The study adopted a largely qualitative approach alongside a small sampling of statistical data on user activity from the BoB system. Data were collected using individual semi-structured interviews of 45 minutes followed by a 15 minute talk-through of users' *myBoB* accounts with each participant. An interview schedule was used to guide participants using three basic themes: (1) use of BoB and media streaming technology more generally, (2) pedagogic implications of using BoB as a support for teaching and learning and (3) staff perceptions of what constitutes good practice in the use of BoB and media streaming technology. In line with TPACK, these three key themes were used to draw out, organise and analyse staff perceptions of the use of BoB and media streaming technology more generally as a support for teaching and learning. Consideration was also given to staff motivation, skills and experience in the use of technology generally and of technologies available. Participant interviews were transcribed and coded using a mixed inductive/deductive thematic approach which combined a priori themes from the interview schedule and *inductive* themes grounded in the data.

RESULTS

Study 1: Two Case Examples of Box of Broadcasts

Case 1: Language Learning, Student Portfolios and Video
A language teacher had designed a learning module whereby second language students were expected to present a topic of interest in a respective language; this was video recorded to facilitate review and reflection on presentation skills and language use, as recommended by Dlaska and Krekeler (2008). Prior to BoB, the procedure for capturing and disseminating student presentations with digital video was very onerous, both for the

departmental technician and for the teacher in charge of this area of students' learning, with each presentation being captured to camera, edited and stored on DVD for each individual student. The teacher also experimented with maintaining digital video recordings of individual student presentations on her hard disk and for students to call and collect these using a USB stick. Both designs were very time-consuming and deemed an inefficient process for students and the teacher.

> If you have 30 students coming with a USB – they have to plug it in, you do some small talk, shop talk with students while you're transferring the data. That – 30 times over – is not efficient use of tutor time.

Nevertheless, both formats worked well to establish procedures for capturing and assessing student performance with digital video. When BoB was introduced in the redesigned module, it was an easy matter to transfer this process across in BoB. In the current year, 130 (i.e. four times more students than in the original design) students made use of BoB as an interface for their professional presentations.

Using BoB meant that access to the videos could be streamlined, as illustrated in Fig. 3. While there was some work for the teacher in communicating individual access codes to students and some work for the technician in managing video data and uploading it, time was saved overall as the teacher no longer had to meet with students individually and the technician no longer had to create individual DVDs for each student. Furthermore, students could access their video data anywhere, anytime. The video data captured formed a part of students' Personal Development Plans and could be used to provide a supportive illustration of their skills to potential employers. For the teacher involved, BoB made a substantial difference to her practice and enabled the practice (which students view as highly valuable) to continue where, given the problematic logistics of the previous method and quadrupling of student numbers, it might well have been laid aside.

> BoB has made a real difference to something that was very cumbersome for everyone involved. It has cut the time and logistics. I actually think we would have left it aside and not continued with student presentations if we hadn't had this facility with BoB. Also, the fact that the technician is able to do this so efficiently means that it can be extended to other tutors – German, English, French – especially for colleagues who are perhaps not so confident with technology as I am.

In terms of the value to students, the teacher indicated that – in pedagogic terms – the advantage of videoing the presentations was to enable students to see their own performance. Using video data allowed students to detach

From: [redacted]
Sent: 07 February 2011 13:11
To: xxxxxxxxxxxxxxxx
Subject: FW: Enlace al video de la presentación
Importance: High

Dear xxxxxxx,

Below you have your personal code to watch your presentation in BoB:

XXXXXXXXXXX

To access your clip, open BoB in http://bob.surrey.ac.uk/. In the main page copy the code above in the box "Search the archive", which I have highlighted in a red circle in the image below:

Once you have viewed your clip, write your reflective report on it in Pebblepad, https://www.pebblepad.co.uk/surrey/, following the instructions below – the ones we went through in class. The deadline to write your reflection in Pebblepad and share it with me is Monday 14 de February at 5pm:

1. Write your University username and password to enter Pebblepad.
2. Create New
3. Ability
4. Give it a title: SPA1026 Presentación oral
5. Click 2: evidence. You don't have to do anything, but if you want, you can link here your clip from BoB
6. Click 3: reflection: Copy here your reflection of the presentation – no longer than 400 words.
7. Click 4: click Send to: click Gateway (for LTS students) y click person Law or BM with Spanish students.
8. If click Gateway > select languages 2010 PDP portfolio
9. If click person > write my name (Maria) and surname (Menendez-Lopez) and select the first email in the list.

If you have any questions please write me an email.

Fig. 3. Sample Instructions for Use of BoB in Language Case.

themselves from the process, and reflect upon their process in terms of writing a report. In this sense, it is important for effective use of video data that there is a coherent plan for student review and reflection on the content of the video, whether those elements are formally assessed or not (Bloom & Johnston, 2010; Olaniran, 2006). It is an activity that, by all accounts, students appreciated and valued highly.

Case 2: Using Playlists in BoB to Highlight Complexities in Psychology
A psychology teacher had developed effective practice by integrating broadcasts recorded off air via BoB with a VLE. This teacher's method of facilitating and guiding students in their use of video material through use of playlists and Q&A was also exemplary as a model of good practice. For

example, she organised her playlists by category (cognitive psychology, individual differences, personality, intelligence etc.) and created separate playlists for modules covering subject areas such as attitudes and behaviour, and psychology and education.

The teacher actively encouraged students to view her playlists, either as a source of additional contextual material or as a specific activity. In the case of the latter, she would tend to link the video to related Q&A activities or discussion tasks in the VLE, as recommended by Mishra and Koehler (2005). She also indicated that it was necessary to proactively engage and guide students in their use of video materials, helping them to understand that watching videos was not just about 'fun' or something different from reading but that it formed an active part of their learning. In terms of ways of using video for teaching and learning, she divided these into two types: classroom delivery and additional context. For the former, short clips were more suitable, and for the latter this might involve students watching a longer episode at home or outside of class or lecture time.

> I would never show more than a short clip in a lecture, unless it was really, really important to show something more substantial. At the same time, I do like to make resources available to students for their own study time. I have been surprised by how many of them actually go away and use these additional materials. In this way, my approach has evolved over the last few years. I give students a few little bricks to build upon, resources for self-study, and BoB is a large part of that, in terms of giving students the opportunity to look at things they might otherwise not look at or consider.

This had, over time, led the teacher to think differently about students and the teaching and learning resources she made available to them.

> BoB has been a big part in a shift of thinking for me. It has made me realise that there are opportunities to develop student's thinking – to engage them in independent and critical thinking outside of the lecture. It has also made me realise that what the student can do outside of the lecture is not just read papers, make notes and pull things together but is part of a bigger practice of thinking about things and assimilating ideas.

The increased range and variety of learning materials available to students was also identified as an important shift in her pedagogical values and in motivating students. Furthermore, BoB materials were identified as being particularly supportive for students in their final year, where modules tend to be more research-led and students follow specialised topics in smaller groups. It was felt that the range and variety of materials available via BoB was particularly well-suited to those circumstances.

> I think students engage with video in a better way. It provides variety as well. They do a lot of reading and I think it's nice, in study time, to do something a bit different and

I actually think it encourages more discussion amongst students. I've heard them in the lecture saying, oh, did you watch the documentary on so and so and what did you think about this bit – you know, actually discussing things and I suppose it's a bit more interesting for them and they want to talk about it more than say, they do with a paper.

Study 2: In-Depth Interviews of Teachers Using BoB

Use of BoB in Teaching and Learning

Analysis of user statistics for BoB for the period of April 2009–February 2012 show that the system at the University of Surrey had 334 unique users (teachers) who requested 3082 unique services. In total 29,729 services were watched, while teachers uploaded 618 unique videos, 412 playlists and 333 clips. According to the eight teachers interviewed, staff perceptions of BoB as a tool to enhance teaching and learning were generally positive. A range of technical and training issues were identified by a majority of staff, but it was not felt that these were insurmountable. Most staff recognised these as 'teething issues' of the kind generally associated with the adoption of new systems as identified by Olaniran (2006) and Rienties and Townsend (2012). In many cases, technical issues raised had been successfully resolved via the university's e-learning team.

Awareness of BoB and Decision to Use

Staff members became aware of BoB in a variety of ways with a majority citing interactions with staff from the e-learning team as being a dominant factor in their take up of BoB. Staff mainly identified their rationale or decision to use as being closely interlinked to their individual interests (in innovating pedagogy and technology) or to a specific need arising in their plans for teaching and learning.

- *I teach a particular module called 'Television Entertainment' and I needed materials and used some clips for that.*
- *I'm new to the university and to teaching and, having come out of clinical practice into teaching, I'm trying to use BoB to enhance my teaching ... so it's blended, varied, to promote discussion and to illustrate certain points/ themes.*
- *I'm a module convener and I chose to record some programmes about organisational behaviour in my role as module manager, it's useful to illustrate what happens in real life and how that relates to the theory we're teaching.*

Others suggested that it was only after their use of BoB that they generated ideas about its utility as a support for teaching and learning.

- *I first came across BoB about the time of the Haiti earthquake and I used BoB to record that and I used it in an Earthquake Engineering module.*
- *I realised it would allow me to make recordings. Previously, I got our technicians to tape things from TV and they put it on DVD so that I could show it in a lecture but this didn't allow students to watch it in their own time and I couldn't cut out a specific clip. Those kinds of things make BoB more flexible and probably more attractive to students as well.*

Overall, staff perceptions were that BoB was a useful technology in that it allowed them greater control and flexibility in their use of audio and televisual materials as a support for teaching and learning, as illustrated by the psychology teacher case study 2. Furthermore, it allowed them to target relevant, real-world scenarios that served to illustrate links between theory and practice to promote discussion among students and between staff and students and, as described in the language teacher case study 1, to provide a secure environment for easy dissemination of student-generated content (videos of student presentations). Staff mostly focused on the use of material from broadcast television. A smaller number, however, mainly from sociology and psychology, pointed to the utility of radio services, citing Radio 4 (a British discussion/news radio) in particular, as a useful support for dialogue, discussion and context-building for students.

Types of Use, Training, Confidence, Motivation and Skills
Staff were mainly using BoB to record and view services. The majority of staff were confident in their use of BoB at a basic level (i.e. recording, making playlists, etc.) but felt less confident about more complex activities such as making clips or uploading video. However, all expressed an interest in learning more about BoB's functionality. Similarly, staff tended not to use the search facility within BoB, indicating that either they did not know how to do so effectively or that when they used BoB, they did so with a specific purpose in mind and so went directly to the service they had decided to schedule/record. A majority of respondents made use of playlists, with only one staff member not having made any. Some staff were using this facility in effective and innovative ways such as matching playlists with course content or providing students with a set of relevant resources in a course-framed repository within VLE.

About half of the respondents had tried making and using clips, with varying degrees of success and failure. The general perception of staff was that clips were not only useful but potentially essential in terms of making effective and appropriate use of video with students in and beyond the classroom, with time being a key factor of import. At the same time, the generation and use of clips was one of the most cited issues raised in terms of the limitations of BoB in its current state. The general view of staff members who had used the clips feature was that it needed to be more reliable, that it would benefit from a tutorial video for updating skills that had not been used for some time and that a showcase video of effective and/or innovative clip use would be beneficial for staff wishing to use this feature. Only one member of staff was currently using BoB to upload and share user-generated content.

The Benefits and Limitations of YouTube
Staff perceived a benefit of YouTube over BoB as being the provision of a wider range of content as found by Jones and Cuthrell (2011). Other benefits identified by staff were that YouTube includes some commercial content unavailable via BoB; clips can be easily embedded in presentations and the brevity of YouTube clips is often more useful in a teaching and learning setting (Duffy, 2008). YouTube was also deemed particularly useful for language learning in terms of providing native source materials (Bloom & Johnston, 2010). YouTube is easily accessible to staff and students without need for additional logins (Olaniran, 2006).

- *The thing about YouTube is that people upload all kinds of things and I use it a lot to research things to do with mental health and psychiatry. There are lots of really interesting clips around psychology and things like that and I use those a lot and save them as bookmakers, then when I come to do a teaching session, I embed them as a URL in my session.*
- *Compared to YouTube, BoB is limited – you can only look at TV programmes, whereas YouTube has a mix of everything.*
- *I found some interesting clips on YouTube from an NHS (National Health Service) Trust which were really good for my teaching session.*
- *The beauty of YouTube is that the clips are very short. They are readymade clips of 2, 3 or 5 minutes which is really good just for capturing students' attention or relaxing their minds for reflection.*

Staff nevertheless recognised that there were definite limitations with YouTube as a support for teaching and learning, as recently also highlighted by Jones and Cuthrell (2011). These included appropriateness of content (both of clips and related comments); inclusion of advertising; instability of URLs; lack of control over continued availability of content (fear of useful clips disappearing); issues of potential copyright infringement; management of useful clip libraries/playlists; privacy and ethics of uploading student materials to a public repository and related issues of ownership and control of uploaded content.

- *The problem with YouTube is that they are not stable URLs and, of course, the copyright question on YouTube is such that content frequently appears and disappears.*
- *Some YouTube content is prefaced by advertising and you can't just say to students, now we're going to watch a 90 second commercial and then we'll get to the interesting part.*
- *With YouTube, there is the question of quality – some YouTube content goes down to the very minimum of what works on a projector screen.*
- *With YouTube, you either embed lots of clips somewhere or you're left wondering ... now where did I find that YouTube clip exactly? You know, which pathway did I go down to get there. So, BoB is better there because you can save your clips onto your own bit (myBoB).*
- *Where can we store student work? On YouTube? I don't want YouTube – that was an alternative we looked into, maybe having a closed group on there, but we wanted something more private in the end. You don't know what's going to happen with YouTube. Bob is private and we've got ownership as well.*

An interesting point was made by one member of staff regarding the appropriateness of related content on YouTube (i.e. user comments) insofar as her experience contrasted with most staff members' view of 'related content' on YouTube being a limitation. By contrast and in line with findings from Bloom and Johnston (2010), she argued that user comments could be a positive stimulus for student discussion, debate and reflection.

- *Some YouTube content is quite good as an illustration. Sometimes the comments around a YouTube clip are really useful, if you're looking at attitudes. Like 'Extreme Breastfeeding' – some comments are really quite controversial – that makes for a good discussion point, it's good for illustrating attitudes at large to certain areas of healthcare.*

Benefits, Limitations and Constraints in the Use of BoB (Technological Knowledge)
Staff perceptions on the benefits, limitations and constraints of using BoB were almost equally spread across all three of these indicators. Staff felt that the availability of BoB was useful, that it did offer enhanced functionality

for technology-supported, video-enriched learning, and that it had the potential to add value to students' learning through the easy availability of real-world scenarios, personalised content and integration with related formal learning environments such as VLE. The most valuable advantage was deemed to be the ability to store such media indefinitely and securely, without fear that it would disappear or be withdrawn overnight, thus enabling staff to reuse materials in parallel with related teaching and learning resources, year on year. In addition to these 'BoB-specific' advantages, staff highlighted the opportunities for dialogue between theory, real-world scenarios and practice that these video materials offered to students by way of added value. Key limitations of BoB as a technology tool focused on instability of the system, and issues relating to user authentication, which are highlighted by Olaniran (2006) as key concerns for successful campus-wide implementation. Constraints of BoB as a useful support for teaching and learning focused on lack of time for staff developing, maintaining and planning around resources, lack of access to certain useful content, low buffer period and copyright restrictions.

- *BoB is useful to illustrate what happens in reality ... how that reality relates to the theory we teach. Documentaries can support the key message of a lecture very well.*
- *BoB gives students' access to documentaries, e.g. about mental health care in the community.*
- *There may be some things that only become significant with hindsight, e.g. an emerging news story that might inform your teaching and students' learning.*
- *Visual images, especially moving images, are a great bonus in my subject area (geology) ... something like a volcano erupting or a landslip sliding ... video is so much better than a still image.*

Furthermore, even though bandwidth issues are less prevalent in 2012 than when Olaniran (2006) published his work, the comments of the respondents below do reflect his argument that universities need to take a holistic view when implementing new technology that is synchronous in nature and requires appropriate hardware in the classroom.

- *The University has failed to put in a reliable infrastructure across lecture rooms, sometimes there's no LAN or even a desktop, so you have to rely on your laptop and a wireless connection which isn't reliable and doesn't offer a reliable audio system so that makes playing video clips not worthwhile.*

- *One of the biggest limitations is that you go to use BoB in and it doesn't work in some of the teaching rooms.*
- *I was in a teaching room with computer access, had my PowerPoint up, went in to open BoB and it took a while because it seemed to think I was trying to log in remotely for some reason.*

User authentication in BoB was viewed by staff as both an advantage and a limitation, depending on how this was used. The privacy and security of authentication were valued as a means of controlling viewing of user-generated and/or sensitive content (e.g. medical or health-related video clips). At the same time the requirement for a dual login process for embedded or linked BoB services in VLE was viewed as a limitation that could easily be improved through the use of a single sign-on for both systems.

Constraints
Staff time.   Lack of time to fully engage with new technologies in terms of training, planning to use and identifying ways of embedding them in their everyday practice was the key constraint identified by staff members. The importance of time to learn to implement ICT effectively into education has already been extensively documented in the literature (Lawless & Pellegrino, 2007; Luppicini, 2007; Resta & Laferrière, 2007; Rienties, Brouwer et al., 2011; Stes, De Maeyer, Gijbels, & Van Petegem, 2011; Ziegenfuss & Lawler, 2008). Staff generally only found time when notice of a training course coincided with free time or when an urgent need to make use of video materials in their courses precipitated their participation in a course or their investigation of BoB as a possible technology to support video-enriched teaching and learning. Other than these approaches, the most often cited stimulus for getting involved in use of BoB was recommendation by a colleague who had used the tool already. Such recommendation might simply be a passing conversation or it might involve a more engaged introduction, incorporating either a demonstration, or an illustration and/or provision of informative or instructive materials (e.g. a user guide).

Scope and nature of available content.   Staff had mixed views about content, with some staff happy that it sufficed (e.g. humanities) and others feeling that it lacked coverage of certain key services/channels that were beneficial to their more industry-specific areas, e.g. engineering, film studies, languages. There was an awareness and understanding of copyright and

Table 2. Comparison of BoB (as Used in Surrey) and YouTube.

	YouTube	BoB	Notes
Web-based, ease of access with smartphone	★★★★	★★★★	Students and staff need to log into BoB using their university credentials
Richness of number of videos available	★★★★★	★★★★	Infinite amount of videos in YouTube; in BoB only what teachers have recorded or uploaded
Quality of videos available relative to number of videos	★★★	N.A.	YouTube has enormous wasteland of materials (Jones & Cuthrell, 2011)
Secure storage of student (sensitive) materials (e.g. presentations, clinical records, portfolio)	N.A.	★★★	Although YouTube allows 'private' video sharing of the URL with a maximum of 50 views, anyone who has the URL could watch this video
Secure storage of videos	★★	★★★★	
Lack of advertisements and comments non-relevant to educational setting	★	★★★★	
Ability of teachers to record TV and radio programmes	N.A.	★★★★	Teachers can record any programme within UK license restriction and share this with students. If a teacher has recorded a programme on separate medium (not YouTube), YouTube can still remove content
Ability of teachers to upload and edit videos and provide comments	★★★★	★★★	While both system uploads work similar, the editing functionality of BoB is more complex and cumbersome
Ability of students to upload videos and provide comments	★★★★	N.A.	This is a particular design decision by University of Surrey

Note: Rating is based upon (perceptions of) the authors of the functionalities and affordances of the system and use by academic staff at this institute at the time of writing. New functionalities of BoB and YouTube will influence the ratings.

budgetary constraints but nevertheless staff still wished to express their desire for more relevant content.

Staff were generally *au fait* with and accepting of copyright restrictions imposed by UK law and framed by the university's adherence to the ERA + licence. Although they understood the need for these, some expressed a desire that they could be a little more flexible, particularly in terms of extending use to overseas enrolled students of the university who they felt were being denied parallel distance learning opportunities to their UK counterparts. Some staff also expressed regret that services from YouTube could not be embedded in BoB as this would address a key issue of materials disappearing without notice. At the same time, they recognised that this was a difficult issue to address, given the open nature of YouTube content.

- *I used BoB to record a programme about the Haiti earthquake and I used it in the Earthquake Engineering module but I couldn't use it fully as I was up against restrictions in that this module was offered by distance learning (beyond the UK) and students couldn't access it. Three of our major MSc modules involve distance learning with overseas students and this is an issue as it means we wouldn't be treating all students in the same way in terms of available resources.*

In addition, one of the key limitations of BoB for many staff users related to the inability to bring in relevant YouTube clips to that environment. Staff recognised that this was an issue of UK copyright law and the potential for infringement of third-party materials and/or the way in which YouTube links through to recommend other videos that might be less appropriate in an educational setting. However, a majority expressed a strong desire to be able to bring in their YouTube finds to the BoB environment in cases where copyright was clear and materials were being offered by commercial broadcasters for educational or other public use. Based upon the discussions with staff and our own reflections, in Table 2 we highlight the main advantages and disadvantages of BoB and YouTube.

DISCUSSION

This book chapter addressed a new innovative media-streaming technology called BoB, which is used by 300 + staff at the University of Surrey to engage students with relevant and current video materials. Media streaming technology such as YouTube is a rapidly evolving area in higher education (Bloom & Johnston, 2010; Kaufman & Mohan, 2009). A unique feature of

BoB in comparison to YouTube is that it allows staff to schedule and capture broadcast TV and radio services, which are then transcoded for web-based or mobile viewing. A particular merit for language, political science and sociology teachers is that 30 channels in French, German, Arabic, Russian, Spanish and Italian are available, which are commonly not part of TV subscriptions in the United Kingdom. Staff and students are also able to create a personalised repository and can engage in discussions about the videos stored in BoB via a safe and closed learning environment. A key aim of the study was to better understand what TPACK conditions (technical, pedagogical, discipline-specific knowledge) contribute to the development of effective practice in the use of media streaming technology as a support for teaching and learning at the University.

Using principles of design-based research (Reeves et al., 2005; Rienties & Townsend, 2012) of two case studies of BoB usage in Study 1, we found that BoB provided an efficiency improvement for the language teacher who filmed her students' presentations in their second language. Furthermore, the videos could be used for students' Personal Development Plans as an illustration of their employability skills. In the second case study, a psychology teacher used topical playlists to broaden and extend the discussions in and outside her classroom. The integration of BoB into her classroom led the teacher to think differently about students and the teaching and learning resources she made available to them. Both case studies highlighted that teachers can successfully design and implement BoB in a range of pedagogical scenarios, which provided them with additional ways to provide feedback and engagement. At the same time, both teachers still experienced some technical and organisational difficulties, as was found in other studies (Olaniran, 2006; Ziegenfuss & Lawler, 2008). Both teachers were able to overcome these, but it stresses the need for teachers to become knowledgeable in pedagogy, discipline *and* technology (Mishra & Koehler, 2005; Rienties & Townsend, 2012).

Using a semi-structured interview qualitative method with eight teachers from four faculties, Study 2 indicated that overall staff felt that BoB was beneficial in supporting pedagogic practice. In particular, they felt that BoB provided a motivating and engaging alternative to text-based curricula that also had a capacity to enable students to make relevant connections between their learning and the wider everyday contexts in which that learning would ultimately be implemented. The most valuable advantage was deemed to be the ability to store such media indefinitely and securely, without fear that it would disappear or be withdrawn overnight, thus enabling staff to reuse materials in parallel with related teaching and learning resources, year on year. Furthermore, staff highlighted the opportunities for dialogue between theory, real-world scenarios and practice that these video materials offered to students by way of added value.

A key limitation for some (but not all) staff in their use of BoB as a support for video-enriched pedagogic practice was the restricted level of available content on BoB as well as some difficulties relating to service length and skills required for, and stability in use, of clips. Key constraints on effective long-term use of BoB for staff were competing priorities in terms of general workload and time (Stes et al., 2011; Ziegenfuss & Lawler, 2008) required to view, review and plan for the inclusion of video materials into teaching and learning. Furthermore, even if staff were able to overcome these initial barriers, some of the facilities in the classroom itself hampered effective usage, as highlighted by one teacher who noted that university infrastructures in the classrooms were not appropriate for showing media streaming activities. Finally, most staff used BoB on a relatively basic (pedagogical and technological) level, primarily as a repository of online materials, rather than actively promoting more collaborative and Web 2.0 functionalities for students to actively discuss, comment and share alternative materials and opinions.

Several reasons may be put forward to explain the lack of engagement among some teachers to embrace all the Web 2.0 affordances of BoB. Some argue that the institutional culture may be a limiting factor (Kinchin, 2012a; Kinchin, Lygo-Baker, & Hay, 2008; Rienties, Kaper et al., 2011). For example, a conscious decision was made to restrict recording and uploading content to 'teachers-only' in order to prevent similar meadows of vast but (mostly) irrelevant videos in YouTube. Others argue that teachers are insufficiently trained and equipped with appropriate technological and pedagogical skills (Jimoyiannis & Komis, 2007; Lawless & Pellegrino, 2007; Mishra & Koehler, 2006; Rienties & Townsend, 2012). Although specific workshops and training manuals are provided, and most staff interviewed indicated that BoB was easy to use, creating an awareness and understanding of the complexities of integrating pedagogy and technology within a discipline probably requires a more substantial investment by both teachers and university (Kinchin, 2012a, 2012b; Mishra & Koehler, 2005; Rienties, Kaper et al., 2012). Finally, the almost infinite possibilities and affordances of modern VLE systems and BoB and YouTube in particular may be overwhelming and deter teachers in effectively engaging with technology. For many, this is caused through anxiety or negative attitudes towards technology that occur through uncertainty (Jimoyiannis & Komis, 2007).

Future Research and Implications for Practice

This research focused on staff; it would be valuable to conduct additional research on how students perceived and used BoB, whether the design choices and implementations made by the teachers were actually leading to improved learning of students, and whether students actually found it easy to watch streaming videos on BoB using smartphones. As found by our own research (Clark et al., 2009; Giesbers, Rienties, Tempelaar, & Gijselaers, in press; Rienties et al., 2012; Tempelaar et al., 2012) and others (Kinchin, 2012a; Kinchin, et al., 2008; Mishra & Koehler, 2005), the pedagogical design decisions by teachers are not always understood and interpreted in exactly the same manner by students. For example, in an online economics course using discussion forum tools, Rienties et al. (2012) found that a small increase in the scaffolding learning process in order to stimulate more balanced discussions had a substantial negative impact on how students shared knowledge and expertise in an online team setting. In follow-up research, Giesbers et al. (in press) redesigned the online economics course by allowing students to interact synchronously with each other and the teacher using online video conferencing. Giesbers et al. (in press) found that students using a rich online video conferencing tool in comparison to using 'simple' discussion forums were more satisfied about the instructional support, but to our surprise were less satisfied about the self-determination of their actions and the assessment strategy. In a study among 700+ students using a mathematics programme, Tempelaar et al. (2012) found that emotional factors (i.e. anxiety, boredom) strongly influenced whether students were active users of the online system or not. Therefore, future research should address whether the design decisions made by the institute and teachers in particular actually led to increased learning among students.

Most of the literature (Bloom & Johnston, 2010; Duffy, 2008; Kaufman & Mohan, 2009; Smart, 2010) available on the use of media-streaming and YouTube in particular is (extremely) positive about the affordances and potentials of media-streaming for learning and teaching. However, most of this literature appears to be primarily descriptive in nature. More studies are required which apply greater scientific rigor. Although we acknowledge that media-streaming services such as YouTube provide an enormous wealth of information, we agree with the notion of 'dichotomous nature of YouTube' introduced by Jones and Cuthrell (2011) in that teachers can find excellent videos on psychology or engineering experiments alongside inappropriate videos. Therefore, we encourage further (evidence-based) research on how teachers and students alike are using media-streaming technology. In particular given recent findings by Luppicini (2007) and Tempelaar et al. (2012), it is important to understand how personal characteristics of learners influence how learners with different learning strategies engage with media-streaming technology. Therefore, in a follow-up study we intend to conduct a study on how learning styles influence usages of BoB by students in order to further fine-tune the configuration of BoB. Furthermore, in line with recommendations by Mishra and Koehler (2005), it is important to focus research on how teachers can develop both technological as well as pedagogical knowledge in order to effectively implement media-streaming into their module design. Preliminary findings from research conducted in a Dutch online teacher professionalisation programme (Rienties, Brouwer et al., 2011) as well as a Belgium blended teacher programme (Stes et al., 2011) seem to indicate that designing effective ICT training services is complex.

REFERENCES

Anastasiades, P. S., Filippousis, G., Karvunis, L., Siakas, S., Tomazinakis, A., Giza, P., & Mastoraki, H. (2010). Interactive videoconferencing for collaborative learning at a distance in the school of 21st century: A case study in elementary schools in Greece. *Computers & Education, 54*(2), 321–339.

Biggs, J., & Tang, C. (2007). *Teaching for quality learning at University* (3rd ed.). Maidenhead, UK: Open University Press.

Bloom, K., & Johnston, K. M. (2010). Digging into YouTube videos: Using media literacy and participatory culture to promote cross-cultural understanding. *Journal of Media Literacy Education, 2*(2), 113–123.

Clark, W., Logan, K., Luckin, R., Mee, A., & Oliver, M. (2009). Beyond Web 2.0: Mapping the technology landscapes of young learners. *Journal of Computer Assisted Learning, 25*(1), 56–69.

Collins, A., Joseph, D., & Bielaczyc, K. (2004). Design research: Theoretical and methodological issues. *The Journal of the Learning Sciences, 13*(1), 15–42.

Dlaska, A., & Krekeler, C. (2008). Self-assessment of pronunciation. *System, 36*(4), 506–516.

Duffy, P. (2008). Engaging the YouTube Google-eyed generation: Strategies for using Web 2.0 in teaching and learning. *Electronic Journal of e-Learning, 6*(2), 119–130.

Giesbers, B., Rienties, B., Tempelaar, D. T., & Gijselaers, W. H. (in press). Why increased social presence does not automatically lead to improved learning. *E-Learning and Digital Media.*

Homer, B. D., Plass, J. L., & Blake, L. (2008). The effects of video on cognitive load and social presence in multimedia-learning. *Computers in Human Behavior, 24*(3), 786–797.

Jimoyiannis, A., & Komis, V. (2007). Examining teachers' beliefs about ICT in education: implications of a teacher preparation programme. *Teacher Development, 11*(2), 149–173.

Jones, T., & Cuthrell, K. (2011). YouTube: Educational potentials and pitfalls. *Computers in the Schools, 28*(1), 75–85.

Kaufman, P. B., & Mohan, J. (2009). *Video use and higher education: Options for the Future*. New York, NY: Intelligent Television.

Kinchin, I. M. (2012a). Avoiding technology-enhanced non-learning. *British Journal of Educational Technology, 43*(2), E43–E48.

Kinchin, I. M. (2012b). Visualising knowledge structures of university teaching to relate pedagogic theory and academic practice. In J. Groccia, M. Al-Sudairi & W. Buskist (Eds.), *Handbook of college and university teaching: A global perspective* (pp. 314–332). Thousand Oaks, CA: Sage.

Kinchin, I. M., Lygo-Baker, S., & Hay, D. (2008). Universities as centres of non-learning. *Studies in Higher Education, 33*(1), 89–103.

Koehler, M. J., & Mishra, P. (2005). What happens when teachers design educational technology? The development of technological pedogogical content knowledge. *Educational Computing Research, 32*(2), 131–152.

Lawless, K. A., & Pellegrino, J. W. (2007). Professional development in integrating technology into teaching and learning: Knowns, unknowns, and ways to pursue better questions and answers. *Review of Educational Research, 77*(4), 575–614.

Luppicini, R. (2007). Review of computer mediated communication research for education. *Instructional Science, 35*(2), 141–185.

Mayer, R. E. (2003). The promise of multimedia learning: Using the same instructional design methods across different media. *Learning and Instruction, 13*(2), 125–139.

Mishra, P., & Koehler, M. J. (2005). What happens when teachers design educational technology? The development of technological pedagogical content knowledge. *Journal of Educational Computing Research, 32*(2), 131–152.

Mishra, P., & Koehler, M. J. (2006). Technological pedagogical content knowledge: A framework for teacher knowledge. *Teachers College Record, 108*(6), 1017–1054.

Nicholls, G. (2001). *Developing teaching and learning in higher education*. London: Routledge.

Olaniran, B. A. (2006). Applying synchronous computer-mediated communication into course design: Some considerations and practical guides. *Campus-Wide Information Systems, 23*(3), 210–220.

Onwuegbuzie, A. J., Witcher, A. E., Collins, K. M. T., Filer, J. D., Wiedmaier, C. D., & Moore, C. W. (2007). Students' perceptions of characteristics of effective college teachers: A validity study of a teaching evaluation form using a mixed-methods analysis. *American Educational Research Journal, 44*(1), 113–160.

Reeves, T. C., Herrington, J., & Oliver, R. (2005). Design research: A socially responsible approach to instructional technology research in higher education. *Journal of Computing in Higher Education, 16*(2), 96–115.

Resta, P., & Laferrière, T. (2007). Technology in support of collaborative learning. *Educational Psychology Review, 19*(1), 65–83.

Rienties, B., Brouwer, N., Lygo-Baker, S., & Townsend, D. (2011). Changing teacher beliefs of ICT: Comparing a blended and online teacher training program. In S. Greener & A. Rospigliosi (Eds.), *Proceedings of the 10th European conference on elearning* (pp. 670–677). Brighton, UK: Academic Publishing Limited.

Rienties, B., Giesbers, B., Tempelaar, D. T., Lygo-Baker, S., Segers, M., & Gijselaers, W. H. (2012). The role of scaffolding and motivation in CSCL. *Computers & Education, 59*(3), 893–906.

Rienties, B., Kaper, W., Struyven, K., Tempelaar, D. T., Van Gastel, L., Vrancken, S., ... Virgailaitė-Mečkauskaitė, E. (2012). A review of the role of Information Communication

Technology and course design in transitional education practices. *Interactive Learning Environments, 20*(6), 563–581.

Rienties, B., & Townsend, D. (2012). Integrating ICT in business education: Using TPACK to reflect on two course redesigns. In P. Van den Bossche, W. H. Gijselaers, & R. G. Milter (Eds.), *Learning at the crossroads of theory and practice* (Vol. 4, pp. 141–156). Dordrecht: Springer.

Smart, J. M. (2010). *How the television will be revolutionized: The future of the iPad, Internet TV and Web 3.0 (The Metaverse): Plus: Other uses, political challenges, and how tablet PCs could have started in 1993.* Retrieved from http://accelerating.org/downloads/SmartJ-2010-HowTVwillbeRevolutionized.pdf. Accessed on 12 December 2011.

Stes, A., De Maeyer, S., Gijbels, D., & Van Petegem, P. (2011). Instructional development for teachers in higher education: Effects on students' learning outcomes. *Teaching in Higher Education, 17*(3), 295–308.

Struyven, K., Dochy, F., & Janssens, S. (2011). Explaining students' appraisal of lectures and student-activating teaching: Perceived context and student characteristics. *Interactive Learning Environments, 20*(5), 391–422.

Tempelaar, D. T., Niculescu, A., Rienties, B., Giesbers, B., & Gijselaers, W. H. (2012). How achievement emotions impact students' decisions for online learning, and what precedes those emotions. *Internet and Higher Education, 15*(3), 161–169.

Thornhill, S., Asensio, M., & Young, C. (2002). *Video streaming: A guide for educational development.* Manchester, UK: JISC.

Williams, J., & Fardon, M. (2007). *'Perpetual connectivity': Lecture recordings and portable media players. ICT: Providing choices for learners and learning.* Paper presented at the Ascilite, Singapore. 2–5 December.

Ziegenfuss, D. H., & Lawler, P. (2008). Collaborative course design: Changing the process, acknowledging the context, and implications for academic development. *International Journal for Academic Development, 13*(3), 151–160.

BUSINESS STUDENTS' LEARNING ENGAGEMENT AS A FUNCTION OF READING ASSIGNED E-TEXTBOOKS

Susan Stites-Doe, Patricia E. Maxwell and Jennifer Little Kegler

ABSTRACT

In this chapter we report findings from a quantitative and qualitative pilot study of students from a single university setting in the northeastern United States. The majority of participants were enrolled in either face-to-face or online sections of a business course in organizational behavior, and the textbook modality included both open (PDF) and proprietary (CourseSmart) digital formats. The key research questions focus on the degree to which students feel satisfied with electronic textbooks (e-textbooks). We also explore correlates of students' satisfaction and their positive attitudes regarding the functionality of the use of e-textbooks by examining the impact of prior coursework and students' concurrent use of other Internet sites, e.g., social media networks, while reading e-textbooks. Specifically, we explore the extent to which students' positive attitudes toward the functionality of e-textbook use is sufficient

Increasing Student Engagement and Retention using Mobile Applications:
Smartphones, Skype and Texting Technologies
Cutting-edge Technologies in Higher Education, Volume 6D, 239–270
ISSN: 2044-9968/doi:10.1108/S2044-9968(2013)000006D011

to result in students' engagement. Engagement is measured via their intentions to buy additional e-textbooks in the future, their course grades, and their perceptions of comprehension of the material over time. Students' overall satisfaction with the e-textbook is likewise explored to determine impact on the same measures of engagement.

INTRODUCTION

It would appear that electronic and open textbooks are now fully on the radar of colleges and universities in the United States. To understand why this is so, one must cast a wide net around driving factors. They span from campus strategic priorities and resource constraints to national level concerns over access to education, and from student behaviors to economic realities. In the decision to adopt an electronic textbook (e-textbook), faculty preferences matter. Student preferences also matter, and publishers' electronic offerings matter. That operating resources on college campuses are uncertain, and that administrators are worried about being able to invest in capital improvements and human resources in future decades is a vast understatement. Campus leaders across the nation are spending increasing amounts of their time strategizing ways in which they can protect the academic core of their institutions, and at the same time keep the educational engines revving in the midst of dramatic cutbacks in support from state and federal sources.

In this chapter, we first briefly explore the factors that are causing renewed interest in e-textbooks on college campuses. Some forces center on student behavior and the learning strategies they employ, and others are driven by harsh economic realities. By knowing more about these forces we can better understand the e-textbook usage trends, students' reactions to e-textbooks, and the ways in which e-textbooks stand to alter engagement in the future. These forces prompt change, and it is important to put them in the proper context as we explore students' satisfaction with e-textbooks, and the possible promulgation of e-textbook use across the higher education landscape. In this discussion we share findings from previously published research on students' reactions to e-textbook use, and on the associated student learning outcomes when e-textbooks are used. We also explore possible precursors and correlates of students' satisfaction with e-textbooks as suggested by the literature. Lastly, we present research questions that informed a pilot study of student outcomes associated with e-textbook use at a single public university in the northeast United States over the course of three semesters (Fall 2010, Spring 2011, and Fall 2011). Both quantitative and qualitative findings from this study are reported. Results indicate that while students appreciate the benefits e-textbooks offer both in terms of access to learning materials and in terms of engagement, student grades decreased as satisfaction increased. We explore the implications of these findings, offer suggestions for future research, and provide practical advice on the use of electronic resources in college classrooms.

THE TEXTBOOK QUESTION

Public Outcry Over the Cost of Textbooks

The fact that textbook prices have begun to represent a serious problem for both colleges and students is no secret. The average cost of textbooks required of a student in a given semester has risen substantially over the last two decades, at a rate estimated to be well over twice that of inflation, according to a report produced by the U.S. Government Accountability Office (GAO, 2005). And, as a percentage of total tuition costs per year, the GAO report indicates that the estimated cost of textbooks and supplies as a percentage of tuition and fees per year ranges from 8% at a private non-profit 4-year school to 26% at a public 4-year school to 72% at a public 2-year school. On average, a single college textbook costs $125, but in some disciplines this price climb is much higher (Miller & Baker-Eveleth, 2010, p. 39). Textbooks are one of the few one-time large-scale purchases made during a semester, and may possibly be the only one for which there are multiple competing sources for the same product, available in multiple formats, and at vastly differing price structures (Beliveau, Hicks, & Stone, 2011). Textbooks are often bought last, after all other college expenses have been settled, and are often paid for out of pocket. When low- and middle-income students do receive grant money to support their college expenses, many fail to receive sufficient funds to cover the cost of their assigned books, and when they do, financial aid checks are often received late, after classes have started (Advisory Committee on Student Financial Assistance, 2007, p. 2).

These factors result in textbook costs falling squarely under a large and very bright spotlight, and there is a nationally growing degree of protest and push back about costs from consumers (Nicholas, Rowlands, & Jamali, 2010). A network called the Textbook Rebellion, supported by the Student Public Interest Groups, is reaching out to broad audiences spanning campus

administrators, faculty, parents, and students (Allen, 2011). The Higher
Education Opportunity Act of 2008 was passed in an attempt to lessen
student debt by, in part, controlling the manner with which faculty and
college bookstores report books selected for courses and the associated costs
of each book at the time that students are able to register for courses. The
Act is intended to give students ample time to search for the least expensive
outlet from which to purchase their books (Smith, 2010). The upshot of
these factors is that students have plenty of motivation to reduce their
financial burden by buying books via online wholesalers, purchasing illegal
copies of reproduced books, or sharing copies with other students (Young,
2010a). Reacting to the increasing cost of textbooks, one student newspaper
put it this way, 'Give us cheap books, and we will give you expensive minds'
(The Journal, 2011, para. 11).

Access to Higher Education and Assessment of Student Learning Outcomes

What is the real cost of students' inability to pay for textbooks? It boils
down to access to education; access is the most compelling driver of e-
textbook consideration for campuses. As an element of the overall cost of
higher education, climbing physical textbook costs have resulted in students
deciding to go without textbooks for classes in which they are enrolled
and, in some cases, have kept students from enrolling in college at all. For
those who do enroll, one can assume that students who are not reading
assigned books are not learning at an optimal level. Thus, the assessment of
learning outcomes has become an important goal of researchers who study
the impact of alternative textbook models, e.g., electronic and open texts
(e.g., Baker-Eveleth, Miller, & Tucker, 2011; Ovadia, 2011; Petrides, Jimes,
Middleton-Detzner, Walling, & Weiss, 2011).

The State Council of Higher Education for Virginia reports that about
40% of their students did without some of the required books for one
semester (Dawkins, 2006, p. 30). According to the National Association of
College Stores [NACS] (2011), approximately 60% of college students
choose not to buy all of their course materials. The U.S. Public Interest
Research Group, a consumer-advocacy organization, found a full 70% of
1905 undergraduate survey respondents reported not buying a textbook at
least once because they could not afford to do so. Among this sub-group,
78% "expected to perform worse" (Redden, 2011, para. 4) in classes for
which they did not purchase the book. These statistics are staggering when
one considers that without textbooks the student relies only on his or her

ability to learn from classroom experiences or summaries of materials posted, for example, on course learning management systems. How can we expect students to learn effectively without required books (Bell, 2010)? And, how can we prevent grade inflation and regression to the mean in terms of the quality of instruction on the faculty side of the equation when students come to class so inadequately prepared to learn?

Officials at Daytona State College in Florida were so concerned about the increasing percentage of textbook costs in their students' budgets that they developed a relationship with several textbook publishers to secure cheaper digital editions of textbooks by buying them in bulk. Books were then made available to students for a vastly reduced course materials fee that substantially lowered their overall textbook expense (Young, 2010a). Though this program is now in question following a change in leadership and mixed student satisfaction reports (Graydon, Urbach-Buholz, & Kohen, 2011; Kolowich, 2011), the model stands as an important benchmark from which other schools might learn. Centralizing the purchase of textbooks at the college level to permit economies of scale is what one administrator at Indiana University at Bloomington refers to as "moving the tollbooth" (Young, 2010a, para. 14). At Indiana an experimental arrangement with a company called Courseload was initiated to determine the value of a books-for-fees system for both their students and academic departments. In this arrangement Courseload provided digital content by striking agreements with multiple publishers, including McGraw-Hill, Pearson, and John Wiley. Projections of fees to be charged to students were anticipated to be $35 per course per semester (Young, 2010a).

Bookstores report extremely low profit margins on books, and their sales are declining. One bookstore manager stated that the profit margins on textbooks are surprisingly low and in fact, potato chip sales have a higher profit margin. That same bookstore manager describes herself as a "buggy whip salesman" (Young, 2010b, para. 4), referring to the obsolete nature of the traditional college textbook and the need to explore new ways to add value to the campus operation. In what may be an illustration of the changing preferences of students and the obsolescence of hard-copy textbooks, the NACS is now building its own software to deliver e-textbooks (Young, 2010b). On average, the cost of digital textbooks is reported to be 52% lower than the cost of physical, printed textbooks (Allen, 2010, p. 5). Despite this fact, many research reports claim that students still prefer to read books the traditional way, via the printed page. A 2011 study conducted by OnCampus Research reports that 75% of students prefer printed textbooks over digital books (NACS, 2011).

LITERATURE REVIEW

Student Reactions to E-textbook Features

One of the reasons commonly given for students' failure to embrace e-textbooks is dissatisfaction with their initial experiences using an e-textbook (Baker-Eveleth et al., 2011). Digital reading requires an additional set of skills for learning, comprehending, and interacting with technology (Coiro, 2003). These skills rely on a foundation of traditional literacy, research skills, technical skills, and critical analysis (Jenkins, Clinton, Purushotma, Robison, & Weigel, 2006, p. 4), leading to a new participatory culture "that make[s] it possible for average consumers to archive, annotate, appropriate, and recirculate media content in powerful new ways" (p. 8). It could be that reported dissatisfaction with e-books is a reflection of the students' need to develop some of these new literacies skills. This is indicated by the Daytona State report that students are particularly sensitive to the complications of downloading and using reader software necessary to utilize e-textbooks. These students also struggled with basic e-textbook functionality, e.g., locating readings, creating bookmarks, using highlighting tools, and writing notes (Kolowich, 2011). Conversely, students' confidence with their computer skills were suggested to be one possible predictor of self-selection into class sections for which e-textbooks were used (Miller & Baker-Eveleth, 2010). It may be that additional preparedness in other courses using digital technologies, such as English composition (which includes research using online databases), could have an impact on e-textbook reading comprehension and retention, but heretofore there is no evidence of such a link in the literature. New literacies research, specifically in cognitive conceptions of reading comprehension, is in its infancy, "… further complicated by the fact that the technologies of online reading continue to evolve at a rapid pace" (Hartman, Morsink, & Zheng, 2010, p. 154).

Research indicates a positive, significant relationship between a person's attitude toward and intent to use technology based on what they perceive to be its usefulness and ease of use (see Chung, 2010; Davis' Technology Acceptance Model (TAM), 1989; Sun, Tsai, Finger, Chen, & Dowming, 2008). Weisberg (2011) observed this during his 2-year longitudinal study of college business student attitudes and behaviors toward the use of digital textbooks in the classroom. Early in the study, students considered e-textbooks as "two generations away from readiness" (p. 191). At the study's close, 87% of participants reported a preference for e-textbooks and 91% were very interested in using an e-reader as a primary or secondary textbook

(p. 194). Portability, note taking, and the ability to find information easily are common features explored in research on students' use of e-textbooks.

Some students report their belief that technology helps them do their work faster (Dahlstrom, Grunwald, de Boor, & Vockley, 2011; Weisberg, 2011). Sixty-one percent to 78% of surveyed students have confidence in their ability to use e-textbooks (Dahlstrom et al., 2011; Roscorla, 2011), while a growing minority (31%) prefer their instructors use more e-books or e-textbooks (Dahlstrom et al., 2011). In fact, 50% of students in a 2010 survey identified e-books and e-textbooks as technologies having a significant impact on their overall learning (Cengage Learning and Eduventures, 2010, p. 23). At least one research report suggests that up to 42% of students say they would use additional e-textbooks if only given a chance to do so (Garneau, n.d.; Dahlstrom et al., 2011).

One way faculty and students can increase e-textbook use is by selecting open textbooks. Faculty members will consider adopting an open textbook in order to save students money as long as the text is of high quality and easy for the student to access and use (Petrides et al., 2011, p. 43). Likewise, Petrides et al. found that 67% of the students in their study preferred using the open textbook because of its ease of use in terms of being able to access specific locations in the book via the instructor's use of a URL, and due to their ability to access the book from a lab, in the classroom, on public transport, during class breaks, etc. This easy access to content provided students the ability to better manage their time in light of other family and work obligations (p. 44).

Predictors of E-textbook Use: Subject Engagement

Reading an e-textbook presents opportunities that a printed text does not: The reading device, often a laptop, can be an effective study and research tool as well as a gateway to deeper subject engagement via the Internet. There is a positive correlation between student use of technology and measures of engagement in certain online learning activities such as discussion boards and accessing library databases (Chen, Lambert, & Guidry, 2010). Today's students view the Internet as an indispensable part of their lives (Chou, Wu, & Chen, 2011), where they can participate in both formal and informal learning cultures. They recognize the "importance of online information to broadening their knowledge base, to enabling them to do creative and interesting things, to facilitating their school work and life routines, and to societal progress" (p. 944). When asked to name the one website a student could not live without, Google and Wikipedia were the top two identified (Dahlstrom et al., 2011). Eighty-two percent of students surveyed use Wikipedia as a starting point for background information, and the strongest predictor of Wikipedia use was also using Google for course-related work (Head & Eisenberg, 2011). Wikipedia exemplifies an "online collective intelligence community" (Jenkins et al., 2006, p. 43) where students must draw on critical analysis and judgmental literacy skills. The motivated student will expand their search beyond Wikipedia (Chung, 2010).

Instructional technology can increase the amount of time a student spends on a given subject, and there is a positive and relatively strong relationship between effective education practices, student self-reported educational gains, and the use of learning technology (Chen et al., 2010; Coiro, 2003; Laird & Kuh, 2005). Eighty-six percent of students report their academic engagement has improved as they have increasingly used digital tools in their coursework; 31% identify e-textbooks as having the potential to improve engagement and learning outcomes (Cengage Learning & Eduventures, 2010).

Business students, in particular, seem to have an affinity for e-books. In the United Kingdom, study business and management titles were found to have been viewed more frequently for longer periods of time, and the use of business titles over time increased at a rate that was higher than that for other subjects (Nicholas et al., 2010). The management title, *Organisational Behaviour and Analysis: An Integrated Approach*, was the most popular e-book, attracting "82,787 page views in the 14-month survey period" (p. 269), and "used by 955 students in the entry survey and by 1068 in the exit survey" (p. 270). It was also the most recommended e-book (by 21.1% of business and management staff). Across survey administrations of the same students, positive recommendations increased by 10.4% for the business e-textbook.

Correlates of Student Success Using E-textbooks: Multitasking and Preparedness

There is evidence suggesting the number of hours spent studying with digital or print textbooks is not as important as the techniques students employ while reading the textbook. Students completing annotations while reading e-texts performed better in their tests and exams (Dominick, 2005; Ertuk & Keen, 2010). Students who multitask while studying have been found to take longer to complete their task and have a lower academic performance

(Bowman, Levine, Waite, & Gendron, 2010; Gurung, 2004; Kraushaar & Novak, 2010). Gurung (2005) correlated reported study techniques with exam scores of 229 introductory psychology students and found that reading notes, reading the text, and using mnemonics were significantly related to exam scores. Multitasking activities such as listening to music or the TV and responding to emails while studying were negatively correlated with exam grades. Experiments by Poldrack (2006) indicate high-frequency multitaskers use a different part of their brain (the stratium) to gain knowledge and are unable to generalize that knowledge when tested. Interestingly, a study comparing student reading task performance under three conditions (active multitasking, passive multitasking, or reading in silence) indicated students who were comfortable with the subject material performed best when there was a video playing in the background while studying (Lin, Robertson, & Lee, 2009).

In today's participatory culture, students must learn "how to distinguish ... between being off task and handling multiple tasks simultaneously" (Jenkins et al., 2006, p. 36), as these are the challenges they will face in their future work environment. Research shows that students are judiciously managing how and when they access the other programs on their laptop or mobile devices (Head & Eisenberg, 2011). Hundreds of students from all types of U.S. campuses were interviewed to learn how they balance productivity while surrounded by technology. Many of the students considered technology management to be a "practical necessity" (p. 28) when studying, especially in the final weeks before exams. After a self-defined period of reading time or completion of a specific task, students describe rewarding themselves by checking for messages or taking a Facebook break (Head & Eisenberg, 2011).

Continued research in student attitudes toward and experience with e-textbooks is required due to the constantly evolving format and delivery platforms. "We live in a society that is experiencing an explosion of alternative texts" (as cited in Coiro, 2003, p. 14). Jenkins et al. (2006) remind us:

> The range of opportunities and the transformative possibilities for learning at all levels as a result of readily available and emergent digital technologies are broad. The transformation in knowledge conception and production as a result of these new technological practices must be considered (p. 194).

In that spirit this study was conducted to (1) explore student satisfaction with e-textbooks; (2) analyze whether prior coursework predicts students' satisfaction with e-textbooks; (3) investigate the impact of students' concurrent use of other Internet sites while reading; (4) consider how student satisfaction and positive attitudes with e-textbooks correlate with student engagement. Research propositions follow:

Proposition One
Students' prior preparation in key disciplines such as English composition, math, and computer literacy will positively impact their level of satisfaction with the use of e-textbooks.

Proposition Two
Students' multitasking use of social networking sites, online shopping sites, and Wikipedia while reading e-textbooks will positively impact their level of satisfaction with the use of e-textbooks.

Proposition Three
Students' level of satisfaction with the use of e-textbooks will positively impact their level of engagement with the coursework.

METHODOLOGY

Sampling Frame and Research Design

Field survey methodology was employed to gather both quantitative and qualitative data. A single public university setting in the northeastern United State served as the field site. Human subject review approval was sought and received for the use of the surveys. Sample size varied across the three survey administrations. Twenty variables were utilized to address the main hypotheses. Qualitative data was gathered through open-ended questions in the survey and group interviews.

Over the course of three semesters, undergraduate students ($N = 138$) used a digital format of their required course text. One hundred twenty-four of the students were enrolled in an upper-level organizational behavior course with both online and face-to-face (F2F) sections, all taught by the same instructor. There were also 14 students enrolled in non-business courses (English, health science, education, and geology) who responded to a flyer seeking participants for a study of student use of e-textbooks. The flyer-stated participants would receive one free e-textbook for a class within which they were currently enrolled (value to $65). All participants received their e-textbook at no cost. The majority of participants (112, 81%) attended F2F classes. Seventy-seven (56%) of the students were male;

61 female (44%). Participants were predominantly between 18 and 24 years of age (112, 81%) and business majors (120, 87%). Non-business majors included the 14 self-selected participants. While there was a risk that self-selection would introduce a bias, the volunteers made it possible for us to deplete remaining funds and survey a small sample of students in other subject areas for comparative purposes.

This study utilized pre- and post-survey administrations and focus groups. Survey items were adapted from previously validated research work of Davis, Bagozzi, and Warshaw (1989), Schcolnik (2001), Dominick (2005), and the National Survey of Student Engagement (2010). Focus group qualitative findings are reported herein only to the extent they may help us to understand the empirical results and provide guidance for future research. The pre-survey was designed to gather data about possible pre-cursors to student success using an e-textbook while also establishing a baseline measurement of student attitudes toward printed and e-textbooks. Students were asked to select statements which best described their use of any course textbook and previous experience with e-textbooks specifically. Participants were also asked how many hours they spent per week engaged in eight Internet activities such as visiting social networking sites, shopping online, or researching by way of Wikipedia or the Library's website. Attitudes toward print/e-textbooks were measured through a duplicate set of statements wherein the first set referenced printed textbooks and the second referenced e-textbooks. Statements about print/digital books used a five-point Likert scale from 1 (strongly disagree) to 5 (strongly agree). The statements measured perceived usefulness ("I can easily find the information I need"), perceived ease of use ("… is portable"), study behavior ("I always highlight"), and intent ("I prefer reading an e-textbook").

The post-survey repeated the pre-survey's print/e-textbook statements in order to measure any changes in attitudes or behavior, followed by a series of structured and open-ended questions intended to measure: (1) subjective satisfaction with the e-textbook experience; (2) how the e-textbook was used; (3) multitasking while reading the e-textbook; (4) intent to continue using e-textbooks; (5) student learning engagement and e-textbook use. Sample items include, "Which of the following statements best describes how you used the e-textbook for this course?" and "Did you visit any of the following sites while reading your e-textbook?" Finally, survey measures of engagement included indicating agreement (five-point Likert scale) with statements such as "When reading the textbook for this class online, I find that I am often motivated to do on-the-spot Internet research or other Internet browsing related to the topics I read about in the book."

Focus group questions investigated student experience with the e-textbook in the context of the course, as well as the electronic device being used to access the digital book. Participants were invited to discuss how they used the e-textbook, any difficulties they were having with it, and whether they were printing any content.

Procedures

There were three semesters of data collection with some variance in the e-textbook title students used. In the first and second semesters (Fall 2010; Spring 2011), 68 students enrolled in an organizational behavior course were provided access codes for their course textbook through the CourseSmart website. During the second semester, an additional 14 student volunteers read different titles in non-business subjects. Most of these other e-textbooks were published by CourseSmart; there were also a few NookStudy and Kindle titles. The third semester participants were exclusively those enrolled in the organizational behavior class. This time, students read an open version of their course textbook available online at FlatWorld Knowledge. At any point in the study, participants could elect to purchase at their own expense a print version of their text from the campus bookstore.

Pre- and post-surveys were collected directly from the students during class visits by the researchers without the instructor present. Students were informed the instructor would not see any of their survey responses until after final grades were posted. Since all participants were enrolled in for-credit courses, the instructor wanted to ensure there were no immediate barriers to learning that might prevent the students from reading their book. The pre-survey visits provided an opportunity for the researchers to demonstrate e-textbook features and answer any questions the students might have regarding e-textbook access or the research in general. Midway through each semester, the researchers conducted focus groups. In all semesters, online students unable to be on campus were asked to complete an online survey containing the focus questions.

Measurement

As shown in Fig. 1, student preparedness for the use of e-textbooks is modeled as being predictive of student satisfaction. Students' preparedness

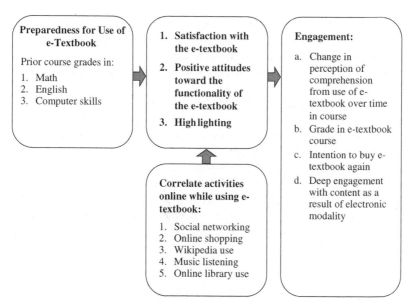

Fig. 1. A Research Model of Student Engagement with Electronic Textbooks. *Note*: This figure illustrates student preparedness and correlate online activities are predictive of student satisfaction and level of engagement with e-textbooks.

is captured via archival methods, by determining their grades in the highest math course taken and required in their degree programs. As the vast majority of students in our sample came from business programs, this course was almost always calculus. The computer literacy course was likewise most often Computer Information Systems, a required course for all business majors. The English literacy course was English composition, a required course for all students at the college.

Students' satisfaction with their e-textbooks was operationalized via the use of single items and of factor analytic methods across multiple items; factor analytic results are reported in the next section. In total, three aggregated measures for satisfaction and one single item measure are employed: overall satisfaction, satisfaction with e-textbook functionality early in the semester, satisfaction with e-textbook functionality late in the semester and, because of its prominence in the literature we explored, a single item to measure students' satisfaction with the ability to highlight text in the e-textbook.

Students' correlated activities while they were using the e-textbook included measures for social networking, online shopping, listening to music, online library use, and Wikipedia use. These were captured in single-item measures designed to determine whether or not students accessed these sites while reading their e-textbooks.

Lastly, students' engagement with the course material was analyzed using a multi-measure approach. First, to gauge students' change in their perceptions regarding their own comprehension of the material over time, repeated items were utilized in pre- and post-survey administrations and an index of change was calculated. Second, archival methods were used by capturing students' actual grades in the courses for which e-textbooks were used. Third, students' intentions to buy e-textbooks again were captured via single-item measures. Lastly, students' "deep engagement" with the material was captured using the survey's engagement measures.

RESULTS

Hypothesis Testing

A total of 20 variables were utilized in the primary analyses. Descriptive statistics for these 20 variables are reported in Table 1, and correlations in Table 2. Exploratory factor analytic methods were utilized in order to explore the relationships between the variables in the research and thereby create clusters of key variables. All retained factors have eigenvalues of greater than or equal to one. Cronbach's alpha measures of reliability were used to measure internal consistency (reliability) of the clusters of key variables. The general guideline is to use survey item variables that have a Cronbach's alpha measure of .70 or greater. Our key variables are positive attitudes toward e-textbooks early in the semester (1 factor with an eigenvalue of 3.065 and Cronbach's alpha reliability of .80), positive attitudes toward e-textbooks late in the semester (1 factor with an eigenvalue of 2.757 and a Cronbach's alpha reliability of .788), overall satisfaction with e-textbooks (1 factor with an eigenvalue of 2.398 and a Cronbach's alpha reliability of .763), and students' engagement (1 factor with an eigenvalue of 4.332 and a Cronbach's alpha reliability of .891) with the e-textbooks. Factor analyses are reported in Table 3. Propositions were tested using ordinary least squares regression. Results are reported in Tables 4–13. A summary of findings appear below.

Table 1. Descriptive Statistics for Undergraduate Students Reading E-Textbooks at a Public University.

	N	Minimum	Maximum	Mean	Standard Deviation
Age[a]	152	1	4	1.25	.567
Gender[b]	153	0	1	.55	.499
Class type (Online or F2F)[c]	155	0	1	.83	.381
Math grade[d]	117	1	4	2.98	.881
English grade[d]	129	0	4	3.24	.758
End-user computing grade[d]	100	2	4	3.59	.621
Overall satisfaction[e]	117	1.00	5.00	3.41	.823
Positive attitude at study start[e]	82	1.67	4.67	3.14	.620
Positive attitude at study end[e]	105	1.67	5.00	3.30	.688
Visits social networking sites[f]	86	0	1	.76	.432
Visits Wikipedia[f]	86	0	1	.28	.451
Visits online shopping sites[f]	86	0	1	.22	.417
Visits library website or databases[f]	86	0	1	.35	.479
Visits music sites[f]	86	0	1	.26	.439
Visits other online sites[f]	86	0	1	.14	.349
Engagement[e]	37	1.13	5.00	3.15	.781
Grade in e-textbook course[d]	137	0	4	3.15	.898
Comprehension change index[e,g]	54	−.75	1.00	.08	.371
Would recommend e-textbooks[f]	107	0	1	.82	.384
Highlights in e-textbook[e]	103	1	5	2.22	1.163

[a]Age was presented in four categories: 1 = 18–24 years; 2 = 25–34 years; 3 = 35–44 years; 4 = 45 and older.
[b]Nominal scale: 1 = male, 0 = female.
[c]Nominal scale: 1 = F2F, 0 = online.
[d]Grades computed on four-point scale, with 4 = A.
[e]Likert scale with 5 = strongly agree, 1 = strongly disagree.
[f]Nominal scale: 1 = Yes, 0 = No.
[g]Measure of the average change over time in the respondents' perceived ability to comprehend the content in the e-textbook.

Control Variables

Three control variables are utilized in each of the equations: age, gender, and whether the student took a F2F course (coded as 1) or an online course (coded as 0).

Proposition one findings

Proposition one states students' prior preparation in key disciplines such as English composition, math, and computer literacy will impact their level

Table 2. Correlations.

		(1)	(2)	(3)	(4)	(5)	(6)	(7)	(8)	(9)	(10)	(11)	(12)	(13)	(14)	(15)	(16)	(17)	(18)	(19)	(20)
(1) Age	R	1.0	0	-.221**	0	0	0	0	.217	.108	-.105	-.052	.202	.199	-.176	-.082	.331*	.114	.094	.016	.048
	Significance (2-tailed)		.151	.006	.212	.368	.450	.115	.053	.279	.340	.636	.064	.067	.108	.455	.046	.188	.502	.873	.634
	N		152	152	117	129	100	115	80	103	85	85	85	85	85	85	37	136	53	105	101
(2) Gender	R		1.0	.304**	.003	-.047	-.119	.143	.048	.111	-.184	.284**	-.035	.016	.047	-.072	.010	-.227**	-.126	.056	-.083
	Significance (2-tailed)			.000	.978	.595	.237	.128	.674	.264	.091	.008	.754	.882	.671	.511	.953	.008	.368	.569	.412
	N			153	117	129	100	115	80	103	85	85	85	85	85	85	37	136	53	105	101
(3) Class type (online or F2F)	R			1.0	-.010	-.019	-.143	-.107	.060	.011	.126	.048	-.017	.057	.224**	.031	-.034	-.114	-.408**	-.013	-.110
	Significance (2-tailed)				.916	.829	.155	.252	.590	.908	.249	.658	.875	.602	.038	.774	.841	.184	.002	.896	.268
	N				117	129	100	117	81	103	85	85	85	85	85	85	37	137	53	105	101
(4) Math grade	R				1.0	.126	.218*	-.040	-.032	.015	-.011	.163	-.013	-.069	.029	-.121	.076	.014	.137	-.059	.025
	Significance (2-tailed)					.182	.035	.705	.798	.894	.928	.192	.920	.582	.818	.333	.683	.887	.362	.592	.827
	N					114	100	117	82	105	86	86	86	86	86	86	37	137	54	107	103
(5) English grade	R					1.0	.226*	-.139	-.090	.030	-.080	-.005	.252*	-.005	.060	-.047	-.128	.254**	.062	-.161	.039
	Significance (2-tailed)						.024	.165	.460	.779	.501	.969	.030	.969	.613	.689	.458	.005	.678	.128	.719
	N						94	93	68	82	66	66	66	66	66	66	31	111	46	84	81
(6) End-user computing grade	R						1.0	-.206	-.030	-.116	-.189	-.130	-.025	.034	-.302*	.009	-.267	.426**	.237	-.051	-.103
	Significance (2-tailed)							.070	.824	.342	.156	.333	.850	.803	.021	.949	.170	.000	.140	.675	.404
	N							99	70	90	74	74	74	74	74	74	36	122	47	91	89
(7) Overall satisfaction	R							1.0	.399**	.700**	.011	.240*	.073	-.031	-.084	.037	.688**	-.152	.062	.664**	.314**
	Significance (2-tailed)								.001	.000	.920	.026	.505	.775	.443	.738	.000	.112	.655	.000	.001
	N								58	69	58	58	58	58	58	58	28	94	40	70	68
(8) Positive attitude at study start	R								1.0	.610**	-.068	.011	-.044	.068	.065	-.048	.260	-.022	-.270*	.320*	.432**
	Significance (2-tailed)									.000	.637	.939	.757	.637	.650	.737	.297	.850	.048	.011	.001
	N									105	86	86	86	86	86	86	35	110	54	107	103
(9) Positive attitude at study end	R									1.0	-.044	.186	.041	-.038	.032	-.030	.441**	-.161	.143	.471**	.539**
	Significance (2-tailed)										.693	.090	.711	.734	.773	.787	.008	.113	.302	.000	.000
	N										58	51	51	51	51	51	18	75	54	63	58
(10) Visits social networking sites	R										1.0	-.250*	.172	-.038	.147	-.162	-.178	-.100	-.138	.073	-.194
	Significance (2-tailed)											.020	.113	.726	.176	.137	.364	.376	.356	.510	.078
	N											86	84	84	84	84	35	98	54	100	103
	N											86	86	86	86	86	28	80	47	85	84

		(11)	(12)	(13)	(14)	(15)	(16)	(17)	(18)	(19)	(20)
(11) Visits Wikipedia	R	1.0	−.081	.089	−.008	−.026	.318	−.221*	.076	.259*	.155
	Significance (2-tailed)		.456	.418	.940	.811	.100	.049	.612	.017	.159
	N		86	86	86	86	28	80	47	85	84
(12) Visits online shopping sites	R		1.0	.081	.202	.028	−.121	.049	−.063	.150	−.173
	Significance (2-tailed)			.460	.063	.796	.538	.667	.676	.172	.116
	N			86	86	86	28	80	47	85	84
(13) Visits library website or databases	R			1.0	−.150	−.224*	.211	.157	−.269	.109	−.052
	Significance (2-tailed)				.169	.038	.280	.165	.067	.322	.640
	N				86	86	28	80	47	85	84
(14) Uses music sites	R				1.0	.072	.149	.061	−.139	.027	−.153
	Significance (2-tailed)					.513	.449	.593	.352	.805	.164
	N					86	28	80	47	85	84
(15) Visits other online sites	R					1.0	−.032	−.269*	.233	−.031	−.011
	Significance (2-tailed)						.871	.016	.115	.779	.922
	N						28	80	47	85	84
(16) Engagement	R						1.0	−.157	.034	.436*	.403*
	Significance (2-tailed)							.361	.894	.013	.016
	N							80	47	85	84
(17) Grade in e-textbook class	R							1.0	.005	−.149	−.189
	Significance (2-tailed)								.974	.140	.066
	N							36	18	32	35
(18) Comprehension change index	R								1.0	−.023	.191
	Significance (2-tailed)									.871	.166
	N								52	100	96
(19) Would recommend e-textbooks	R									1.0	−.029
	Significance (2-tailed)										.774
	N									53	54
(20) Highlights in e-textbook	R										1.0
	Significance (2-tailed)										
	N										99

R = Pearson's correlation.
*Correlation is significant at the 0.05 level (2-tailed).
**Correlation is significant at the 0.01 level (2-tailed).

Table 3. Factor Analysis.

Variables	N	Cronbach's alpha	Factor	Eigenvalue
Positive attitude toward the functionality of the electronic textbook at beginning of semester: 1. E-textbooks are easy to use. 2. E-textbooks are portable. 3. I can easily find the information I need when using e-textbooks. 4. The text in my e-textbook is easy to read (no eye strain). 5. I always highlight text in my e-textbook. 6. I prefer reading an e-textbook.	66	0.801	1	3.065
Positive attitude toward the functionality of the electronic textbook at end of semester: 1. E-textbooks are easy to use. 2. E-textbooks are portable. 3. I can easily find the information I need when using e-textbooks. 4. I prefer reading an e-textbook.	91	0.788	1	2.757
Undergraduates' overall satisfaction with the electronic textbook: 1. The e-textbook was a useful addition to the class. 2. I would recommend using e-textbooks for other classes in the future. 3. I would prefer to have all of my textbooks in electronic format. 4. Participation in this study influenced my enthusiasm for e-textbooks.	101	0.763	1	2.398
Undergraduates' engagement: 1. Time spent reading/reviewing e-textbook compared to all other classes. 2. Time spent reading/reviewing e-textbook compared to all other business classes. 3. Motivation to perform assignment-related research on the Internet when reading the e-textbook. 4. Motivation to ask more questions in class than in other classes. 5. Feeling connected to the assigned subject. 6. Confidence about subject matter. 7. Using e-textbook to learn more after viewing podcasts/videos. 8. Using ANGEL (LMS) to read supplemental course materials posted there. 9. E-textbook increases interest in the course. 10. Videos/audios posted by instructor makes student want to learn more.	34	0.891	1	4.332

of satisfaction with the use of e-textbooks. Results shown in Tables 4–6 indicate that proposition one is not supported. There were no findings in support of students' altered satisfaction as a direct result of students' prior coursework and, therefore, preparedness for the use of e-textbooks. Thus, using the three course grades in English, Math, and computer literacy as representative of preparedness, students seem to require no preparation to be satisfied with the use of the e-textbooks that they employed.

Table 4. Impact of Students' Preparedness for Use of E-Textbooks on Overall Satisfaction.

Variable	β	Significance	N
Constant	4.768	0.000	72
Math grade	−0.007	0.952	
English composition grade	−0.061	0.662	
Computer literacy grade	−0.281	0.113	
Age	0.103	0.684	
Gender[a]	0.367	0.074	
Online/F2F[b]	−0.529	0.046	
R^2	0.140		
F	1.761		

[a]Male was coded as "1."
[b]Face-to-face (F2F) courses were coded "1."

Table 5. Impact of Students' Preparedness for Use of E-Textbooks on Early and Late Positive Attitudes Toward E-Textbook Functionality.

Variable	Dependent Variable					
	Early positive attitude			Late positive attitude		
	β	Significance	N	β	Significance	N
Constant	3.122	0.000	55	3.701	0.000	63
Math grade	−0.083	0.447		−0.012	0.921	
English composition grade	−0.029	0.827		0.049	0.735	
Computer literacy grade	−0.004	0.978		−0.156	0.369	
Age	0.156	0.473		0.057	0.821	
Gender[a]	0.075	0.728		0.390	0.055	
Online/F2F[b]	0.148	0.618		−0.341	0.175	
R^2	0.031			0.094		
F	0.255			0.175		

[a]Male was coded as "1."
[b]Face-to-face (F2F) courses were coded "1."

Proposition Two Findings

Proposition two states that students' use of social networking sites, online shopping sites, and Wikipedia while reading e-textbooks will have a positive impact on their level of satisfaction with the use of e-textbooks. Results shown in Tables 7–9 indicate that proposition two is only partially

Table 6.   Impact of Students' Preparedness for Use of E-Textbooks on
Importance of Highlighting.

Variable	β	Significance	N
Constant	3.701	0.000	63
Math grade	−0.012	0.921	
English composition grade	0.049	0.735	
Computer literacy grade	0.156	0.369	
Age	0.057	0.821	
Gender[a]	0.390	0.055	
Online/F2F[b]	−0.341	0.175	
R^2	0.094		
F	0.971		

[a]Male was coded as "1."
[b]Face-to-face (F2F) courses were coded "1."

Table 7.   Impact of Multitasking Correlates on Overall Satisfaction.

Variable	β	Significance	N
Constant	2.938	0.000	77
Social networking	0.300	0.211	
Wikipedia use	0.485	0.034	
Online shopping	0.051	0.839	
Online library use	−0.088	0.684	
Listening to music	−0.152	0.533	
Other online activities	0.166	0.556	
Age	0.264	0.298	
Gender[a]	0.167	0.427	
Online/F2F[b]	−0.201	0.419	
R^2	0.110		
F	0.920		

[a]Male was coded as "1."
[b]Face-to-face (F2F) courses were coded "1."

supported. Among the correlate activities explored, i.e., social networking, Wikipedia use, online shopping, library use, and listening to music, only Wikipedia use was found to be related to one of the measures of student satisfaction: their overall satisfaction. The Wikipedia use variable was found to be significant in predicting students' overall satisfaction at the .05 level of significance.

Table 8. Impact of Multitasking Correlates on Satisfaction with Highlighting in E-Textbooks.

Variable	β	Significance	N
Constant	2.402	0.000	83
Social networking	−0.281	0.426	
Wikipedia use	0.390	0.221	
Online shopping	−0.415	0.216	
Online library use	−0.210	0.470	
Listening to music	−0.202	0.537	
Other online activities	−0.067	0.868	
Age	0.348	0.313	
Gender[a]	−0.115	0.685	
Online/F2F[b]	−0.248	0.476	
R^2	0.109		
F	0.993		

[a]Male was coded as "1".
[b]Face to Face (F2F) courses were coded "1".

Table 9. Impact of Multitasking Correlates on Early and Late Positive Attitudes Toward E-Textbook Functionality.

	Dependent Variable					
	Early positive attitude			Late positive attitude		
Variable	β	Significance	N	β	Significance	N
Constant	2.957	0.000	50	2.852	0.000	83
Social networking use	−0.131	0.541		0.050	0.818	
Wikipedia use	−0.015	0.940		0.299	0.133	
Online shopping	−0.119	0.592		0.037	0.860	
Online library use	0.123	0.585		−0.123	0.497	
Listening to music	0.174	0.420		0.085	0.677	
Other online activities	−0.089	0.715		−0.066	0.792	
Age	0.179	0.536		0.281	0.193	
Gender[a]	−0.063	0.736		0.108	0.539	
Online/F2F[b]	0.015	0.955		−0.089	0.679	
R^2	0.038			0.071		
F	0.175			0.617		

[a]Male was coded as "1."
[b]Face to Face (F2F) courses were coded "1."

Table 10.   Impact of Satisfaction on Engagement with Content.

Variable	β	Significance	N
Constant	0.783	0.625	18
Overall satisfaction	0.809	0.024	
Early functionality positive attitude	0.080	0.770	
Late functionality positive attitude	−0.345	0.578	
Highlighting importance	0.168	0.590	
Age	0.234	0.670	
Gender[a]	−0.306	0.478	
Online/F2F	N/A	N/A	
R^2	0.608		
F	2.847		

Note: Type of course (online or F2F) was omitted as a variable in this model because all students were enrolled in F2F classes.
[a]Male was coded as "1."

Table 11.   Impact of Satisfaction on Grades in E-Textbook Course.

Variable	β	Significance	N
Constant	3.204	0.000	51
Overall satisfaction	−0.359	0.062	
Early functionality positive attitude	−0.172	0.412	
Late functionality positive attitude	0.404	0.155	
Highlighting importance	−0.075	0.549	
Age	0.539	0.195	
Gender[a]	0.262	0.225	
Online/F2F[b]	−0.140	0.637	
R^2	0.167		
F	1.229		

[a]Male was coded as "1."
[b]Face-to-face (F2F) courses were coded "1."

Proposition Three Findings
Proposition three maintains students' level of satisfaction with the use of e-textbooks will positively impact their level of engagement with the coursework. Results shown in Tables 10–13 indicate that there is mixed support for proposition three. Table 10 results indicate that, among the variables explored, overall satisfaction has a direct and positive impact on students' deep engagement with the content of the course. Table 11 findings

Table 12. Impact of Satisfaction on Change in Perception of Reading Comprehension.

Variable	β	Significance	N
Constant	0.638	0.058	48
Overall satisfaction	−0.080	0.340	
Early functionality positive attitude	−0.331	0.001	
Late functionality positive attitude	0.245	0.052	
Highlighting importance	0.061	0.301	
Age	0.119	0.457	
Gender[a]	0.045	0.638	
Online/F2F[b]	−0.347	0.013	
R^2	0.388		
F	3.627		

[a]Male was coded as "1."
[b]Face-to-face (F2F) courses were coded "1."

Table 13. Impact of Satisfaction on Positive Recommendation to Buy More E-Textbooks.

Variable	β	Significance	N
Constant	−0.389	0.167	51
Overall satisfaction	0.172	0.015	
Early functionality positive attitude	−0.006	0.946	
Late functionality positive attitude	0.240	0.025	
Highlighting importance	−0.094	0.053	
Age	−0.077	0.585	
Gender[a]	0.017	0.839	
Online/F2F[b]	0.152	0.184	
R^2	0.562		
F	7.892		

[a]Male was coded as "1."
[b]Face-to-face (F2F) courses were coded "1."

indicate that among the variables explored, students' overall satisfaction has the most significant impact on students' grades in the course in which the e-textbook was used, but the direction is not as predicted; as found here, the satisfaction level predicted lowered course grades. Table 12 shows more promise in supporting the proposition: Both early and late satisfaction with the e-textbook functionality predict the change in reading comprehension index, at .01 and .052 levels of satisfaction, respectively. Similarly, results from Table 13 show some support for the proposition. Among the variables explored, students' overall satisfaction, and their late semester perceptions of the functionality of e-textbooks are both predictive of their willingness to recommend e-textbooks, at .015 and .025 levels of significance, respectively. Counter to expectations, students' perceptions regarding the importance of highlighting is shown to have a negative impact on their willingness to recommend the use of e-textbooks again.

Experimental Variables

The majority of survey respondents (70%) indicate they are willing to use more e-textbooks in the future; an even larger majority (83%) would recommend e-textbooks to other students. There appears to be a slightly stronger preference for e-textbooks among males (74% compared to 65% of females willing to read more e-textbooks); however, 33% of these male students report they will only use more e-textbooks if they are free. Women are more willing to pay for an e-textbook (48% compared to 41% of men willing to pay for an e-textbook).

Focus groups and open-ended questions provide further insight into the digital reader's experience with an e-textbook. Table 14 lists e-textbook features most liked/disliked by participants, as well as some of the difficulties students reported.

In the study's first semester, students expressed frustration with CourseSmart server issues that resulted in slow page loadings and delayed highlighting. One student stated, "I only tried highlighting at first but I never used it [again] because you had to click on too many things and couldn't tell if it was on." Twenty-six percent of post-survey participants reported waiting for pages to load or highlighting to apply. Midway through the first semester (Fall, 2010), CourseSmart upgraded its reader platform. In following semesters, student comments such as, "Highlighting was great because it really helped during tests and quizzes" became more common. Students found the keyword search function very easy to use and a time saver: "It [the search function] was, in my opinion, the best part of having an e-textbook. It made everything so easy and it helped with cutting down re-reading EVERYTHING [participant's emphasis]." Many students reported using the search function to find answers for quizzes and homework.

Very few students reported using other tools included with the e-reader software such as annotation, bookmarking, or even copy/paste. During each

Table 14. Free Text Responses About Using E-Textbooks.

Likes (*N* = 46)	Dislikes (*N* = 55)	Challenges Noted
• Cost: free! (19 of 46)	• "Tied to Internet" (16 of 55)	• Not an object (to remind me to read) (5 of 15)
• Accessibility (from any computer) (19 of 46)	• Network/Server lag (15 of 55)	• Prefer eReader/ Tablet format (6 of 15)
• Searchability (including TOC navigation) (11 of 46)	• Eye fatigue (13 of 55)	• Learning how to use (5 of 15)
• Can print (8 of 46)	• View/Zoom options (9 of 55)	• Distractions (4 of 54)
• Easy to use (7 of 46)	• Referencing page numbers (7 of 55)	• Printing multiple pages (2 of 15)
• Notetaking features (highlighting, tagging, sharing) (5 of 46)	• Navigating through e-textbook (7 of 55)	• Initial setup (1 of 15)
	• Making handwritten notes while reading from computer (5 of 55)	
	• Can't access while in class (3 of 55)	

initial class visit by the researchers, several students would complain the text size was too small. These students expressed surprise to learn the software included a zoom feature that would enlarge the size of their text font.

Students describe pursuing deeper engagement with the subject by switching between the e-textbook, their Learning Management System (LMS), and Internet sites such as the Library, Google, and Wikipedia: "I used other sites like Google if I was making a discussion post and had to relate the chapters to Internet articles." Another participant wrote, "I access[ed an] ... internet site that is about same textbook. I obtained practice questions there and studied before each chapter quiz." Many of these same students reported it was "hard to stay on one site when using it [e-textbook]," finding themselves "drifting" into a Facebook break or "checking email." Other focus group participants responded this was often a challenge even if reading a printed textbook.

The low cost (free) of the e-textbook was very appealing to students. This was noted 19 times in quotations such as "I really enjoyed not paying for a book that would have cost me over a hundred dollars. It made me less stressed. I also did not need to carry a book around which made my life easier." Another student wrote, "If the price is cheap it is worth it because it's not hard to use at all. Just need to know if the teacher would be okay with it."

Hearing other students share their experience reading an e-textbook on their dedicated e-reader or smartphone inspired other participants to want to try the same. "I liked it but I think I would have enjoyed it more if I had a Kindle or an iPad, something easier to access and carry around," was a frequent comment. At a Fall 2011 focus group of 28 students, 5 (18%) indicated they intended to ask for an e-reader as a Christmas gift. As one student stated, "To me it just seems more convenient. If I could just bring a Kindle to all my classes it would mean I wouldn't have four textbooks – in addition to other supplies to carry around all day." In another focus group, a student (who was reading the book on her smartphone) observed, "You know what the problem is with reading the e-textbook? Sometimes I read too much!" She explained that the phone's small screen size limited any clues to book location, and so she tended to read beyond the assigned number of pages.

Post-survey comments about the open text format suggest that readers who prefer printed textbooks will use the e-textbook as a secondary reference source. Eight of 24 (33%) students who chose to purchase a printed version of this study's open textbook reported alternating between both the digital and print versions throughout the semester. One student explained:

> I never used an e-textbook before. This semester I alternated between both the digital and print. I now feel more comfortable with an e-textbook from now on. I will buy e-textbooks if they are available on my iPad ... It [is] ... so much easier and faster.

DISCUSSION

The most interesting findings of this research center on students' positive perceptions of the functionality of e-textbooks. These positive attitudes prove to be quite resilient, irrespective of their prior coursework in English, math, and computer literacy courses, and regardless of the multitasking students engaged in while reading e-textbooks. Only one multitasking activity was found to increase students' favorable attitudes toward the use of e-textbooks: the use of Wikipedia. It is reasonable to assume that students are using Wikipedia in support of their reading and homework assignments as described by Chung (2010) and Head and Eisenberg (2011). Importantly, students' positive perceptions of e-textbooks were found to predict their engagement with the course materials, much like that reported in the

Cengage Learning and Eduventures (2010) survey and Dahlstrom et al.'s (2011) *ECAR National Study of Students and Information Technology in Higher Education*. These findings give pause, and cause us to think broadly about the future of e-textbooks in the college classroom.

That students report they can adapt readily to e-textbook formats and functionality, and that they can multitask successfully without regard to satisfaction with the experience of reading electronically, speaks to the powerful potential of the medium. When one considers all of the drivers of the use of e-textbooks reviewed at the outset of this paper, spanning from financial incentives to the reduction of operating budgets on college campuses, these findings, in combination with the proliferation of e-reading devices in the college student population, would seem to suggest that students are ready and willing to use e-textbooks. In fact, only 30% of this study's participants continue to prefer print, compared to earlier studies reporting up to 75% (NACS, 2011).

As noted by Nicholas et al. (2010), business students may be particularly receptive to the use of e-textbooks. One possible reason for this receptivity may be the values that underlie a business education. Students may be encouraged to be open to ambiguity and to practice adaptive behaviors in order that they may find success in the labor market as practitioners after they graduate. In order to judge the generalization of these findings beyond one discipline, one may also need to explore the extent to which faculty themselves are open to the e-textbook technology, and the values that are inculcated in students within those unique disciplinary areas. Further, faculty must consider the new literacies skill set advocated by leaders such as Coiro (2003), Jenkins et al. (2006), and Davidson and Goldberg (2010) for success in digital and participatory learning.

These findings are indeed important to better understand student learning and engagement. They are also important to college administrators who are in search of ways to engage students more fully in the college experience, with their coursework, and with their programs. Students may very well continue to clamber for cheaper books. If, as this study suggests, they need not be uniquely prepared to succeed in terms of mastery of preparatory coursework, and if we need not worry about the impact of multitasking on students' positive perceptions of the experience of reading e-textbooks, it may be possible to meet both students' low-cost motives and the campus's goals of increased engagement at the same time. Both campus-level personnel and students have something to gain by paying attention to the new offerings in e-textbooks. As providers improve the delivery mechanisms and formats through which students may read the books, and as more and more publishers come aboard with the medium, we will all face wider choices. While there may continue to be holdouts among the faculty who continue to prefer traditional print books, the use of these paper media can be joined side-by-side with e-textbooks in order that students may engage in the learning process fully.

Research Limitations, Unexpected Findings, and a Research Agenda

Study Limitations

Because the majority of participants were enrolled in the F2F version of an upper level business course primarily composed of business majors, findings might have limited applicability to students enrolled in other subject areas. Non-business participants' intent to purchase more e-textbooks was slightly lower than the business students: 75% were likely to use more e-textbooks (compared to 85% of the business students). Some participants completed the final survey even though they had switched to a printed version or only briefly used the e-textbook. Only a small percentage of the participants were adult learners, thus presenting another challenge in terms of extrapolation. Throughout the various waves of data collection employed in the survey there are relatively small sample sizes, which make interpretation of the data more precarious. At the same time, we note that many of the previous studies reporting on the use of e-textbooks have a similar limitation. Because of this shortcoming in the data, we prefer to view this as a pilot study and look forward to using the data in the future to further validate the measures and secure greater generalization across disciplines.

Unexpected Findings

In this study student grades decreased as satisfaction increased. Though this finding was probably a function of small sample size, it does present tantalizing research questions regarding the possible deleterious impact of being "too satisfied" or too comfortable in the course of learning. It may be that first, students are lacking new literacies skills in support of a digital environment, and second, students' motivation was lowered as a result of their perceived ease of use of e-textbooks. Earlier, we stated students are willing to use an e-textbook. But, their neutrality toward using digital study tools accompanying the e-reader software (copy/paste, annotate, bookmark) and the apparent lack of initiative of some participants to discover how to make the text font larger suggests students are lacking technical skills at best, new literacies skills at worst.

In consideration of student comments regarding not having to re-read passages, their satisfaction with keyword searching to find quiz and homework answers, and their "drifting" off to Facebook, it could be that some students are not effectively employing the multitasking discipline observed by Head and Eisenberg (2011), nor committing the acquired subject knowledge to long-term memory as suggested by Poldrack, Gurung, and others. Additional insight into this dynamic may be found in terms of students' use of highlighting, for which the mean on a response scale of 1 to 5 was 2.22. This suggests most students did not highlight passages when using their e-textbooks. Early focus group conversations confirmed that many students had difficulty with highlighting, finding the process to be cumbersome and unreliable. It may be that because they did not highlight, students did not enjoy the same level of motivation or engagement as when using a printed textbook, thus causing their performance to suffer.

It should be noted that there are additional facilities-related complications surrounding the use of e-textbooks in the classroom. For example, in terms of laptop use, 77% of students surveyed by Petrides et al. reported not ever taking their laptops into the classroom (2011, p. 45). One probable cause we have observed on our own campus relates to the issue of classroom furniture and the instability of the students' desks; students openly voice their discontent over the safety of their laptops when using wobbly tablet-style desks that they deem to be unwise for laptop use. We echo the call of Davidson and Goldberg (2010) that over time universities will need to align student learning behaviors with their own master plans for classroom instruction. Students also complain that the physical weight of the laptop, when added to their books in their backpack, is too burdensome. For now, it may well be that students are avoiding using e-textbooks because they do not want to risk dropping their laptops, carrying them around all day, or loss due to theft.

A Research Agenda
Further exploration of the impact of the use of e-textbooks on students' learning and academic performance is warranted in order to understand how instructors can help students "master the skills and knowledge they need to function in a hypermediated environment" (Jenkins et al., 2006, p. 57). Since the time of this data collection, new purveyors of e-textbooks have announced their foray into the distribution process, and features continue to improve as comparative prices continue to go down. These conditions will need to be explored for their relative impact on students' receptivity to the medium. In addition, we would like to explore the factors

that motivate and propel faculty to adopt e-textbooks. Lastly, we would like to better understand the sources of resistance to the electronic medium for other campus personnel, including librarians. In our conversations with broad audiences, and in our review of the literature, we find that there continue to be barriers to entry to the fuller use of e-textbooks. Only by studying these factors may we fully understand what might be holding back what we view as a natural progression in the use of resources that are critical to teaching and learning processes.

REFERENCES

Advisory Committee on Student Financial Assistance. (2007, May). *Turn the page: Making college textbooks more affordable*. Retrieved from http://www2.ed.gov/about/bdscomm/list/acsfa/turnthepage.pdf

Allen, N. (2010, September). *A cover to cover solution: How open textbooks are the path to textbook affordability* [press release]. Retrieved from http://www.copirgstudents.org/sites/student/files/reports/A-Cover-To-Cover-Solution_1.pdf

Allen N. (2011, April 6). *Exorbitant costs spur launch of national 'Textbook Rebellion'* [press release]. Chicago, IL: Student PIRGs. Retrieved from http://studentpirgs.org/news/exorbitant-costs-spur-launch-national-%E2%80%98textbook-rebellion%E2%80%99

Baker-Eveleth, L. J., Miller, J. R., & Tucker, L. (2011). Lowering business education cost with a custom professor-written online text. *Journal of Education for Business, 86*(4), 248–252. doi: 10.1080/08832323.2010.502911.

Beliveau, B., Hicks, L., & Stone, R. (2011). Why college students sell back their textbooks. *College Student Journal, 45*(2), 288–295.

Bell, S. (2010). Textbook turmoil: The library's role in the textbook revolution. *Library Issues, 31*(1), Retrieved from http://www.libraryissues.com/sub/PDF3101Sep2010.pdf

Bowman, L. L., Levine, L. E., Waite, B. M., & Gendron, M. (2010). Can students really multitask? An experimental study of instant messaging while reading. *Computers & Education, 54*, 927–931. doi: 10.1016/j.compedu.2009.09.024.

Cengage Learning and Eduventures. (2010). Instructors and students: Technology use, engagement and learning outcomes. Retrieved from http://www.cengage.com/trends/pdf/CL-EduventuresSurvey2010.pdf

Chen, P. D., Lambert, A. D., & Guidry, K. R. (2010). Engaging online learners: The impact of Web-based learning technology on college student engagement. *Computers & Education, 54*, 1222–1232. doi: 10.1016/j.compedu.2009.11.008.

Chou, C., Wu, H., & Chen, C. (2011). Re-visiting college students' attitudes toward the Internet-based on a 6-T model: Gender and grade level difference. *Computers & Education, 56*, 939–947. doi: 10.1016/j.compedu.2010.11.004.

Chung, S. (2010). Factors influencing the use of social media in learning: A case of Wikipedia. *Proceedings of Interactive Computer-aided Learning, Belgium, 2010*, 490–500.

Coiro, J. (2003). Reading comprehension on the Internet: Expanding our understanding of reading comprehension to encompass new literacies. *Reading Teacher, 56*(5), 458–464.

Dahlstrom, E., Grunwald, P., de Boor, T., & Vockley, M. (2011). ECAR national study of students and information technology in higher education: Key findings. Boulder, CO: EDUCAUSE Center for Applied Research. Retrieved from http://net.educause.edu/ir/library/pdf/ERS1103/ERS1103pdf.pdf

Davidson, C. N., & Goldberg, D. T. (2010). *Future of thinking: Learning institutions in a digital age*. Cambridge: MIT Press.

Davis, F., Bagozzi, P., & Warshaw, P. (1989). User acceptance of computer technology: A comparison of two theoretical models. *Management Science, 35*(8), 982–1003.

Davis, F. D. (1989). Perceived usefulness, perceived ease of use, and user acceptance of information technology. *MIS Quarterly, 13*(3), 319–340.

Dawkins, W. (2006). Textbooks: The big squeeze. *Black issues book review, 8*(5), 30–32.

Dominick, J. L. (2005). *The in-situ study of an electronic textbook in an educational setting*. UMI No. 3170422. Retrieved from Dissertations and Theses database.

Ertuk, N., & Keen, R. (2010). An investigation of using textbook annotations as a study aid for college students. In J. Chen (Ed.), *EDULEARN Proceedings* (pp. 6594–6601). Barcelona, Spain: International Conference on Education and New Learning Technologies.

Garneau, E. (n.d.). *The digital generation doesn't want digital textbooks* [Web log post]. Retrieved from http://education-portal.com/articles/The_Digital_Generation_Doesnt_Want_Digital_Textbooks.html

Graydon, B., Urbach-Buholz, B., & Kohen, C. (2011). A study of four textbook distribution models. *Educause Quarterly, 34*(4), 1–11.

Gurung, R. (2004). Pedagogical aids: Learning enhancers or dangerous detours? *Teaching of Psychology, 31*(3), 164–166. doi: 10.1207/s15328023top3103_1.

Gurung, R. (2005). How do students really study (and does it matter)? *Teaching of Psychology, 32*(4), 238–240.

Hartman, D. K., Morsink, P. M., & Zheng, J. (2010). From print to pixels: The evolution of cognitive conceptions of reading comprehension. In E. A. Baker (Ed.), *The new literacies: Multiple perspectives on research and practice*. New York, NY: The Guilford Press.

Head, A., & Eisenberg, M. (2011). *Balancing act: How college students manage technology while in the library during crunch time*. Retrieved from http://projectinfolit.org/pdfs/PIL_Fall2011_TechStudy_FullReport1.2.pdf

Jenkins, H., Clinton, K., Purushotma, R., Robison, A. J., & Weigel, M. (2006, October 19). *Confronting the challenges of participatory culture: Media education for the 21st century*. Retrieved from http://www.macfound.org/press/publications/white-paper-confronting-the-challenges-of-participatory-culture-media-education-for-the-21st-century-by-henry-jenkins/

Kolowich, S. (2011, December 23). Daytona State reins in its push toward e-textbooks. *Inside Higher Ed*. Retrieved from http://www.insidehighered.com/news/2011/12/23/daytona-state-reins-its-push-toward-e-textbooks.

Kraushaar, J. M., & Novak, D. C. (2010). Examining the affects of student multitasking with laptops during the lecture. *Journal of Information Systems Education, 21*(2), 241–251.

Laird, T. F., & Kuh, G. D. (2005). Student experiences with information technology and their relationship to other aspects of student engagement. *Research in Higher Education, 46*(2), 211–233.

Lin, L., Robertson, T., & Lee, J. (2009). Reading performances between novices and experts in different media multitasking environments. *Computers in the Schools, 26*, 169–186.

Miller, J. R., & Baker-Eveleth, L. (2010). Methods of use of an online economics textbook. *American Journal of Business Education*, *3*(11), 39–44.

National Association of College Stores. (2011). *Electronic book and ereader device report*. Retrieved from http://www.nacs.org/research/industrystatistics/oncampusresearchbriefs.aspx.

National Survey of Student Engagement (NSSE). (2010) *The college student report*. Retrieved from http://nsse.iub.edu/pdf/US_paper_10.pdf

Nicholas, D., Rowlands, I., & Jamali, H. R. (2010). E-textbook use, information seeking behaviour and its impact: Case study business and management. *Journal of Information Science*, *36*(2), 263–280. doi: 10.1177/0165551510363660.

Ovadia, S. (2011). Open-access electronic textbooks: An overview. *Behavioral & Social Sciences Librarian*, *30*(1), 52–56. doi: 10.1080/01639269.2011.546767.

Petrides, L., Jimes, C., Middleton-Detzner, C., Walling, J., & Weiss, S. (2011). Open textbook adoption and use: Implications for teachers and learners. *Open Learning*, *26*(1), 39–49. doi: 10.1080/02680513.2011.538563.

Poldrack, R. (2006). Modulation of competing memory systems by distraction. *Proceedings of the National Academy of Sciences of the United States of America*, *103*(31), 11778–11783. doi: 10.1073/pnas.0602659103.

Redden, M. (2011, August 23). 7 in 10 students have skipped buying a textbook because of its cost. *Chronicle of Higher Education*. Retrieved from http://chronicle.com/article/7-in-10-Students-Have-Skipped/128785/

Roscorla, T. (2011, March 14). CSU system shares e-book pilot results. *Converge*. Retrieved from http://www.convergemag.com/classtech/California-State-University-Shares-E-book-Pilot-Results.html

Schcolnik, M. (2001). A study of reading with dedicated e-readers. Unpublished doctoral dissertation. Nova Southeastern University, Fort Lauderdale. Retrieved from http://www.planetebook.com/downloads/schcolnik.pdf

Smith, D. (2010, July 22). New federal rules aim to help college students with textbook costs. *Fort Worth Star-Telegram*. Retrieved from http://www.star-telegram.com/2010/07/21/2352490/new-federal-rules-aim-to-help.html

Sun, P., Tsai, R., Finger, G., Chen, Y., & Dowming, Y. (2008). What drives a successful e-learning? An empirical investigation of the critical factors influencing learner satisfaction. *Computers & Education*, *50*, 1183–1202. doi: 10.1016/j.compedu.2006.11.007.

The Journal. (2011, September 1). Survey says: Students can't afford books. *The Journal*. Retrieved from http://websterjournal.com/2011/09/01/editorial-survey-says-students-cant-afford-books/

U.S. Government Accountability Office (GAO). (2005). *College textbooks: Enhanced offerings appear to drive recent price increases*. GAO Report 05-806. Retrieved from http://www.gao.gov/cgi-bin/getrpt?GAO-05-806

Weisberg, M. (2011). Student attitudes and behaviors towards digital textbooks. *Publishing Research Quarterly*, *27*(2), 188–196. doi: 10.1007/si2109-0JI-9217-4.

Young, J. R. (2010a, October 24). To save students money, colleges may force a switch to e-textbooks. *Chronicle of Higher Education*. Retrieved from http://chronicle.com/article/The-End-of-the-Textbook-as-We/125044/

Young, J. R. (2010b, November 14). As textbooks go digital, campus bookstores may go bookless. *Chronicle of Higher Education*. Retrieved from http://chronicle.com/article/As-Textbooks-Go-Digital/125363

FACILITATED WORK BASED LEARNING: A NEW METHOD FOR CONTINUING EDUCATION?

Anja Overgaard Thomassen

ABSTRACT

In this chapter the notion of 'the third context' is presented as a useful perspective in order to reduce the gap between work and continuing education, as continuing education is argued to be an activity different from work as well as education, namely as something 'third'. Consequently, 'the third context' is an alternative to the predominant understanding of work and education as two incompatible entities based on different paradigms. The understanding of incompatibility between work and education had extensive influence on learner engagement and learning outcome in two continuing education courses based on Facilitated Work Based Learning (FWBL). FWBL focuses extensively on integrating work and continuing education with the purpose of increasing employee involvement and engagement: Theoretically, FWBL is inspired by John Dewey and Problem Based Learning. Obstacles occurred during the FWBL courses, especially in relation to the question of 'how can work and continuing education be integrated?' More extensive use of information technology is argued to be a method supporting the alignment of processes between the FWBL course and the workplace.

Increasing Student Engagement and Retention using Mobile Applications: Smartphones, Skype and Texting Technologies
Cutting-edge Technologies in Higher Education, Volume 6D, 271–296
Copyright © 2013 by Emerald Group Publishing Limited
All rights of reproduction in any form reserved
ISSN: 2044-9968/doi:10.1108/S2044-9968(2013)000006D012

INTRODUCTION

Globalisation, technological revolutions, competition, knowledge and competence development are issues highly placed on the agenda of politicians as well as businesspeople, the reason being that we live in a world changing at an ever faster pace. Hence, in order to stay on the forefront of development, new innovative initiatives and solutions based on the latest knowledge must continually be developed. Global developments and tendencies have a major impact on the entire educational system, including the area of continuing education. Within recent years the area of continuing education has experienced a tremendous growth in the number of students as well as different types of continuing education. In a Danish context, the number of part-time master education has exploded during the last decade or so. However, part-time master education is 'slow' education from a company point of view, as the master programmes normally takes 2 years. Furthermore, the master programmes are founded on an academic approach and do not have practical problem solving as the main focus. For this reason companies are becoming more and more interested in continuing education that to a higher extent focuses on direct application of new knowledge in problem solving designed for the special need of each company and its employees. The transfer and application of new knowledge in problem solving become faster providing better opportunities for developing competitive advantage.

Universities have to respond to the request for new types of flexible continuing education structured according to the needs of individual or smaller groups of companies. Hence, the area of continuing education is changing from supply-driven to demand-driven, implying that 'the primary product of the university is no longer the content but rather services to transform changes resulting from the learning experiences facilitated through academic studies' (Choy & Delahaye, 2011, p. 170). The use of information technology plays a central role in the process of offering new and flexible continuing education as it supports fast and easy communication between university staff and companies. Furthermore, methods like e-learning and mobile learning provide new opportunities for offering flexible and special design continuing education. Traditionally, communication between teacher and student has taken place through face-to-face interactions, now it takes place via Skype, e-mail or other types of learning programmes. However, this does not remove the fact that student and teacher are interacting, but now the interaction is mediated through PCs, ipads, iphones, smartphones etc.

A recurrent discussion within continuing education is how work and education can be more closely connected as these are often perceived as incoherent activities: The common understanding is that it is difficult to combine the new knowledge gained during continuing education and the daily work in the organisation (Billett, 2001; Boud & Garrick, 1999; Choy & Delahaye, 2011; Eraut, 2004; Mulcahy, 2011; Stegeager & Thomassen & Laursen, 2012; Tennant, 1999). Normally, Facilitated Work Based Learning (FWBL) is presented as a method for continuing education in which work and education are perceived, not as separated and incoherent activities, but as activities that can be integrated. The latter is a fundamental aspect within FWBL, which theoretically is inspired by philosopher John Dewey's pragmatic thinking.

Two FWBL courses conducted in collaboration between two software engineering companies and Aalborg University (AAU), Denmark form the empirical foundation of the chapter. The FWBL content and time schedule were designed according to the special needs of the employees and the companies in general. The FWBL course took place in the companies and in each case 2–4 employees participated. Each case was assigned a facilitator (university teacher/researcher) possessing extensive knowledge within the theoretical field. The facilitator undertook the teaching and facilitated the employees' learning processes during the FWBL courses. The duration of each FWBL course was approximately 9 months and the engineers participating had university degrees. The empirical data consists of 15 qualitative interviews conducted with employees, facilitators, project managers, and administrative staff from the university several times during the courses along with four tape recordings of meetings and learning activities. The empirical material stems from the Ph.D. dissertation *Facilitated Work Based Learning – analysed from a Pragmatic Perspective* (Thomassen, 2009).

Based on the two FWBL cases it became apparent that the understanding of the difference between work and education has had an extensive impact on the engineers' as well as the facilitators' understanding of FWBL, especially in relation to their understanding of whether work and education can be integrated. Furthermore, it became clear that the understanding of incompatibility has had an extensive impact on the processes during the FWBL course and consequently on the learning outcome of the participating engineers (Thomassen, 2009, 2011). As an alternative to continue the discussion of work opposed to education, the perspective of 'the third context' is put forward. It is argued that within this perspective continuing education at workplaces can benefit from being understood on its own terms. This implies that continuing education is neither work nor education, but a 'third' something that arises and develops when engineers and facilitators interact around continuing education. 'The third context' is a perspective that provides the possibility of transcending the distinction between work and education. John Dewey's pragmatic pedagogical thinking and his notion of experience-based learning inspires the argument as to why it is expedient and possible to transcend this distinction and instead integrate work and education. A corner stone within Dewey's thinking is the necessity of having practical real-life problems as the starting point for education followed by the argument that neither practise nor education can stand alone, instead they presuppose each other (Dewey, 1988).

This chapter has three parts. In the first part the method of FWBL is outlined. Attention is paid to setting the historical theoretical frame of FWBL. The frame is set through descriptions of Problem Based Learning (PBL) and main elements within John Dewey's pragmatic thinking. The second part of this chapter focuses on the two FWBL courses and outlines the participants' difficulties in grasping FWBL. In particular it becomes evident that the perception of work and education belonging to two different contexts has extensive impact on the participants' difficulties in removing their feeling of not understanding FWBL. In the last part of the chapter, the Dewey-inspired notion of 'the third context' is presented as a way of thinking within which FWBL and context are integrated elements developing simultaneously. Furthermore, it is outlined that if FWBL is to become successful, actors must transcend the understanding of incompatibleness between work and education via reflective thinking.

The investigation of the FWBL courses did not have a special focus on the use of information technology. However, the issues presented and discussed throughout this chapter are perceived to be highly relevant for continuing education incorporating a high level of information technology, the reason being the overall theme of how to combine and connect work and education.

FROM PROBLEM BASED LEARNING TO FWBL

The development of PBL is inspired by a number of different philosophical and theoretical learning perspectives. PBL can be perceived as a patchwork centred on central elements like participant engagement and learning through problem solving. Originally PBL was developed due to an increasing discontent with the traditional method of education in which students were perceived as passive participants absorbing the information presented by the teacher. During the 1960s and 1970s, it became increasingly clear that this traditional method of education did not provide the students with the skills necessary in order to cope with the increasing complexity in society and in working life in particular. Thus, a growing interest in PBL occurred, as it was perceived as a method of education that could provide students the requisite skills and competencies (Savin-Baden & Major, 2004).

In the late 1960s, PBL was developed as a method of education within medicine at McMaster University, Canada with Howard Barrows being the main figure (Kolmos, 2008). Since then, PBL has spread to an increasing number of countries, and today PBL is used in a range of disciplines such as engineering, social science and humanities. Savin-Baden and Major (2004) argue that in general PBL is characterised by the following:

1. an acknowledgement of the base of experience of learners;
2. an emphasis on students taking responsibility for their own learning;
3. a crossing of boundaries between disciplines;
4. an intertwining of theory and practice;
5. a focus on the processes rather than the products of knowledge acquisition;
6. a change in the tutor's role from that of instructor to that of facilitator;
7. a change in focus from tutors' assessment of outcomes of learning to student self-assessment and peer assessment;
8. a focus on communication and interpersonal skills so that students understand that in order to relate their knowledge, they require skills to communicate with others, skills that go beyond their area of technical experience (Savin-Baden & Major, 2004, p. 4).

In a Danish context PBL was introduced when AAU and Roskilde University Centre (RUC) were established in the beginning of the 1970s. Hence, PBL has been the educational method used since the beginning and it is applied in all faculties. As mentioned above, PBL is inspired by a number of theoretical perspectives; however, in a Danish context the German philosopher Oskar Negt and the American philosopher John Dewey have been the main sources of inspiration (Berthelsen & Illeris & Poulsen, 1977; Graff & Kolmos, 2003; Kolmos, 2008; Krogh & Olsen & Rasmussen, 2008). An important aspect to be aware of in relation to the Danish context is the fact that the teaching is PBL oriented and organised in projects. This implies that approximately 50% of the time students are working in groups of 3–6 students focusing on how to solve a practical problem. Collaborating students are expected to 'argue for, select, apply, and assess specific theories and methods in regard to their appropriateness for dealing with the specific problem they have chosen for their area of

Table 1.   The Difference in Goal on the Basis of Problem Solving (Fink
& Holifield, 2004).

Learning by Problem Solving	Engineering Problem Solving
• The problem is a tool • Learning is the goal	• Professional skills are the tools • The goal is to solve the problem

inquiry' (Jørgensen & Strand & Thomassen, 2012, p. 444). It is the students
and not the teacher who define the problem with which to deal. The problem
must lie within the topic and frame of the semester. Each project group is
assigned a university teacher being a facilitator supporting the students'
learning processes. The remaining 50% of the time students participate in
lectures and workshops relevant to the theme of the semester. This 'Aalborg
model' of PBL is the main source of inspiration for developing the FWBL
method (Fink & Nørgaard, 2006).

Around 10 years ago a group of researchers at AAU got interested in
applying the principles of PBL in continuing education. They perceived PBL
as a useful method for continuing education providing the possibility of
handling the many challenges and problems that over time have been put
forward concerning continuing education, e.g., the difficulty of applying
new knowledge in the workplace. The idea was to transform the problem
based and project organised way of educating students at AAU into a
practice-oriented method for continuing education of highly educated
employees working in companies (Fink & Nørgaard, 2006; Thomassen,
2009). The notion of FWBL was applied in order to underline this particular
focus.

From the outset, it was recognised that the interest in and objective
related to problem solving differs between companies and university
(Nørgaard & Fink, 2004). The difference is illustrated in Table 1.

The vision and the objectives of FWBL are the following:

• To provide knowledge to busy employees within the industry without
  necessarily having to spend time on participation in traditional courses
• To integrate knowledge directly and make it immediately applicable in the
  job functions of the employee
• To plan tailor-made learning which matches the qualification needs of the
  company

- To apply the pedagogical model of AAU – the problem based and project organised way of learning
- To ensure that the course of learning as far as possible is related to a development project relevant to the company (Nørgaard & Fink, 2004, p. 2)

The FWBL course is centred on work-related problems experienced by the engineers that they find relevant and interesting. Furthermore, the theoretical level within the FWBL course is defined according to the present knowledge of each engineer. Both elements are included in order to support the engagement and motivation of the participants, making it visible how and why a FWBL course is relevant and useful. A 'learning agreement' is made stating the number of participants, the topic of the FWBL course as well as the duration. The learning agreement is signed by the participants, the project manager, the facilitator and the university's manager of FWBL (Fink & Holifield, 2004).

The FWBL course takes place in the company when the engineers find it relevant. This requires a high level of flexibility within the FWBL structure. The flexibility is incorporated in order to secure that, e.g., a presentation of new theoretical knowledge takes place in close connection to its actual use. The objective is to avoid a long timespan between presentation and application, as new knowledge is quickly forgotten, implying that the application aimed at becomes more difficult. Hence, the idea is to offer a FWBL course designed and executed according to the specific needs and requests of the participating engineers.

A facilitator, being a university teacher, possessing extensive knowledge about PBL, is affiliated with the FWBL course. The facilitator is involved right from the beginning when the overall topic of the FWBL course is defined to the end when the learning outcomes of the engineers are evaluated. In between, the facilitator is responsible for presenting relevant theoretical theories and models to the participants as well as supporting the participants' learning processes during the participants' problem-solving processes. The role of the facilitator is very important as he/she is interacting directly with the participants during teaching and facilitation. Hence, it is very important that the facilitator possesses the ability to analyse the knowledge level of the participants, the practical problems they are working on and combine these into a FWBL course. Therefore, a high level of responsibility is placed on the shoulders of the facilitator both in regard to teaching and facilitator competencies, but also in regard to flexibility, because a FWBL course cannot be planned in detail as it follows the learning processes of the participants (Fink & Nørgaard, 2006).

JOHN DEWEY'S PRAGMATIC THINKING

The following section contains a brief presentation of the most important elements and perspectives within John Dewey's pragmatic thinking, especially elements related to his pedagogic thinking. The presentation of Dewey has three purposes. First, the presentation is used in order to highlight how Dewey's pragmatic pedagogic thinking is visible in FWBL. Second, the presentation is used in the analysis of some of the obstacles that occurred in the two FWBL courses. Third, the theoretical elements are used in the presentation of the notion of 'the third context'.

Dewey developed his pragmatic pedagogy as a critique of the traditional way of educating students within which students are perceived as passive participants absorbing the presented content, and where the students are evaluated according to their ability to replicate the content. Dewey highly disliked the traditional perspective, as he perceived it to be based on a dualism separating mind and body. Furthermore, Dewey criticised the strict division between subjects, as students would 'only' gain knowledge about the subject as such prohibiting the students from integrating different subjects in problem-solving processes. Dewey's argument was that traditional education, which solely focuses on passing on theory, does not support the students in developing the necessary competencies for dealing with real-world problems outside the school system. Thus, the school system does not live up to what it is obliged to, namely prepare students for handling situations outside education (Dewey, 1988).

Instead of having education centred on theoretical phenomenon, Dewey argued in favour of having empirical problems as the starting point. The argument was that an empirical starting point enhances the possibility of creating a close connection between what is thought during education and the life lived outside. Opposite to the perspective that students must be silent and passive, Dewey argued that active involvement and actions are the starting point in learning processes. This implies that it is not enough that students read or get lectures about certain theories and models, it is the application of the theories and models that is crucial.

Dewey heavily underlined the importance of involving the students throughout the learning process, the reason being that experience is developed on the basis of a feeling of surprise, a feeling which cannot be enforced from the outside, but develops within the person. In relation to education, this implies that a teacher can in perfect terms explain a certain theory and the problems related to its application. However, at this stage the presented problems/theory are merely facts, as the student has not himself felt the problems related to the application of the theory in problem solving. It is not until the student himself actively has used the presented theory in a problem-solving process that real experience will be gained. Once again it is emphasised that action is the key to new experiences, as it is via the interaction (transaction) between subject and world that experience develop (Dewey, 1988).

Reflective thinking develops out of the transaction between actors and context. An action is made and a given response is expected. Incongruence in the transaction is experienced if the response differs from what was expected. Inquiry is the process leading actors from a situation within which they feel that they are facing a problem until they have the feeling that the problem is removed. Reflective thinking constitutes a main element within the inquiry process through which experience is gained. Reflective thinking makes us capable of solving present problems; however, more importantly reflective thinking enhances future problem solving as it supports the development of experiences. Therefore, a better and more comprehensive foundation on which to base problem solving is acquired. Our actions become more qualified enhancing the likeliness of reaching a situation of harmony between action and context, even though, from Dewey's point of view, harmony is a transient situation quickly replaced by new problems. Hence, transaction is the interaction (interplay) between actor and context, and reflective thinking is the content of the transaction (Dewey & Bentley, 1991[1949]). According to Dewey, reflective thinking is made up of five phases. The five phases are not necessarily run through in the presented order and the weighting can differ; however, all elements are to some degree included in reflective thinking.

> In between, as states of thinking, are (1) *suggestions*, in which the mind leaps forward to a possible solution; (2) an *intellectualization* of the difficulty or perplexity that has been felt (directly experienced) into a *problem* to be solved, a question for which the answer must be sought; (3) the use of one suggestion after another as a leading idea, or *hypothesis*, to initiate and guide observation and other operations in collection of factual material; (4) the mental elaboration of the idea or supposition as an idea or supposition (*reasoning*, in the sense in which reasoning is a part, not the while, of inference); and (5) testing the hypothesis by overt or imaginative action. (Dewey, 1933, p. 107)

A main concept within Dewey's thinking is continuity, implying that we gain new experience on the basis of the experiences we already have. In relation to education, this underlines the importance of placing the students and their level of knowledge in the centre, because if, e.g., the presented theories and methods are too far away from the students present experience he/she does not have any experience on which to base the enquiry of the problem. Instead it is important that the students feel they can relate to the problem combined with a feeling of surprise, a feeling that will be the motivation for engaging in inquiry. The overall objective of structuring education this way is to support the students' engagement in education, as when students are engaged and motivated they will truly engage themselves in education. This underlines the argument that experience is developed from within a person and cannot be enforced from the outside, a perspective having extensive influence on the role and position of the teacher (Dewey, 1988).

Traditionally, the teacher has been the one on the pedestal defining the subjects to be dealt with during education not taking the knowledge and interest of the students into consideration. Dewey disliked this traditional understanding of a teacher. He argued that the teacher should take on a position as facilitator. Hence, the task of the teacher is, due to his more extensive insight, to evaluate the actions and processes unfolding among the students in order to support the students' learning processes. Consequently, the teacher does not possess the 'right' knowledge that the students must replicate. Instead the teacher is a guide inspiring the students for engaging in inquiry processes (Dewey, 1988; Thomassen, 2009).

FWBL AND DEWEY'S PRAGMATIC PEDAGOGY

Based on the above presentation of main elements within Dewey's pedagogic thinking a strong correlation to FWBL is apparent. First and foremost the argument that the starting point of the FWBL course is the participants' everyday practice and especially the problems they face. Therefore, FWBL has adopted the Dewey perspective, that education must be based on problems that the participants themselves have discovered, and not due to the interests of a facilitator. Furthermore, it is clearly defined that the FWBL course must take into consideration the interest and knowledge level of the participants, elements identifiable in Dewey's thinking. Also, the facilitator has a strong and very important role within Dewey's thinking and in FWBL, being a main figure in relation to support the learning processes of the participants. All in all the theoretical inspiration within FWBL is very evident.

Discussing the theoretical inspiration of FWBL, the context within that it is executed is important to bear in mind. FWBL takes place in workplace surroundings and not in an educational environment like a university. This change of context is very important, as within Dewey's thinking context has extensive impact on experience, as experience develops due to ongoing transactions between the individual and the world (Biesta, 2009; Elkjaer, 2003). Hence, when the context is a company and not a university, the experience will differ because the learning process is influenced by different elements.

FWBL TURNS CONTINUING EDUCATION UPSIDE DOWN

As mentioned, an ongoing discussion is how education and work can be more closely connected. Very often the same problems and challenges as to why it is difficult to integrate work and education are mentioned again and again. One major reason is that the literature in general is based on the understanding that work and learning belong to two different paradigms having significant problems in reaching each other. Consequently, the literature focusing on continuing education often focus on giving answers to very specific and practical problems not questioning the fundamental issue regarding the suitable in perceiving work and education as two different worlds.

To a high extent FWBL challenges the traditional understanding of work and education, as the point of departure is not separation but integration of work and education through a PBL inspired perspective on learning. This change in perspective implies that FWBL has the potential of eliminating and overcoming some of the very traditional challenges mentioned in relation to continuing education. The following list summarises some of the common problems mentioned in connection to continuing education:

- Educational institutions predefine the content of the continuing education programme without taking the participants and workplace into consideration.
- General and standardised courses do not fit the needs of the participants and the company.
- New knowledge gained during continuing education is difficult to apply in the workplace.
- New knowledge is forgotten due to timespan between education and actual use in the workplace.

- Difficulty in detecting the potential outcome due to participation – thus motivation is reduced.
- Difficult to find time for continuing education.
- The theoretical level is too low or too high.
- The return on investment in continuing education is difficult to identify.

Traditionally, universities and other educational institutions have had the power to define the content within continuing education leading to a theoretical orientation (Bottrup & Clematide, 2005; Gustavsson, 2003; Svensson & Randle, 2006). For that reason the issues dealt with have very often been of a general character, and have not had the specific participants and their work settings as the point of departure. Consequently, a distance often occurs between the subjects dealt with during continuing education and the participants specific work assignments implying that the participants find it difficult to apply the new gained knowledge in problem solving. According to Billett (2001), this situation occurs due to the fact that knowledge in educational settings and in work settings are contextualised differently. The reason being that knowledge is generated, evaluated and applied on the basis of different perspectives and objectives (Illeris, 2011; Wahlgren, 2010). The starting point within FWBL is fundamentally different from this traditional perspective in regards to who is in power of defining right from wrong, which affects the content of the continuing education programme. Within FWBL the participants, their present knowledge, their present work assignments and present work-related challenges are the point of departure. Hence, it is not the educational institution, in this case AAU, which forces certain predefined theoretical subjects on the participants. Thus, FWBL turns the traditional under-standing of continuing education upside down arguing in favour of a bottom up process in which the participants are actively engaged in defining the subject of the continuing education programme and not a standardised programme applying a top-down approach to content. The intention is to decrease and hopefully eliminate the distance between work and continuing education.

Very often participants in continuing education are adults possessing extensive experience along with an understanding of who they are privately as well as professionally. Therefore, they are very selective in relation to the types of activity they want to be engaged in. In order to engage adults, it is commonly acknowledged that the activity must be meaningful, implying that the potential outcome and benefit of participating in continuing education must be immediately apparent (Illeris, 2011). As the gap between continuing education and the participants' work setting is often wide, it becomes increasingly difficult to see the relevance in participating, thereby removing the motivation for participating (Bottrup & Clematide, 2005). FWBL is diametrically opposite of this, as it tries to engage the participants by directly connecting the course to their present work-related problems, thereby making the benefits in participating very clear. In relation to this, another commonly known problem is taken into consideration, often the theoretical level is either too high or too low which creates a loss of interest by the participants. This problem is reduced within FWBL, as the theoretical level is defined according to the knowledge level and interest of the participants.

A major asset within FWBL is the high level of flexibility that reduces the timespan between educational activities and application. Valuable new knowledge is applied immediately, an aspect that supports the learning outcome as well as the participants' motivation because the outcome and benefit of the participation becomes evident. Consequently, FWBL can be perceived as a method that provides concrete answers to the managers and experts that find it difficult to determine the effect of continuing education.

Based on the above argumentation, FWBL stands forward as an alternative to more traditional approaches to continuing education, and it possesses the potential of overcoming some very crucial problems related to that area. Hence, it must be expected that when applied in continuing education FWBL delivers what it promises by strengthening its position as an alternative to traditional continuing education methods that focus solely on knowledge of a theoretical and general character. In the subsequent section, the two FWBL courses conducted in collaboration between two different software development companies and AAU are presented. Special attention is paid to some of the most profound challenges detected during the FWBL courses. When applied in practice, it becomes evident that challenges occur that the FWBL method does not have any ready-made 'answer' for at the moment.

CAN WORK AND CONTINUING EDUCATION BE INTEGRATED?

A recurring question asked by the participants throughout the FWBL course is 'how can work and continuing education be integrated?' This question illustrates the participants' difficulties in grasping FWBL, a difficulty that has an extensive impact on the FWBL courses and the engagement and learning outcome of its participants. The following will outline (1) why the question 'how can work and continuing education be integrated?' is present throughout the FWBL courses, and (2) why this question has major impact on the processes unfolding during the FWBL courses.

The Motivation for Participating

It is relevant to take a closer look at the interest in and motivation for participating in FWBL, as these elements indicate the participants' understanding of the FWBL course including the objectives they perceive as obtainable. The following quotation stems from an interview conducted with one of the project managers illustrating the general understanding present among the participating engineers and project managers.[1]

> Early in the process I mentioned to [the FWBL managers at the university] that they should not believe that we had the same values and norms for this Work Based Learning process. The norms and objectives are very different. My need is, that my software developers understand a specific problem and that they can solve the problem [...] the university is more focused on the learning process, which I am not in this course, absolutely not. The objective is to acquire some basic knowledge. (Thomassen, 2009, p. 112)

In the quotation the project manager clearly explains that he has one objective and the university has another, a situation which does not appear to be a problem from the project manager's point of view, to him this is just a fact. Based on the quotation it becomes evident that the project manager perceives participation in FWBL as a tool he can use in order to solve a problem in the company, namely the software developers' lack of competence in solving a specific software engineering problem. This illustrates the project manager's interest in problem solving and not in the learning process as such.

The project manager makes a clear distinction between problem solving and learning. When applied to the aspect of production paradigm vs. school paradigm (Jørgensen, 2004), it becomes evident that the project manager makes a clear distinction between the two. He is positioned within the production paradigm and the FWBL course belongs to the educational paradigm, and he is not interested in orienting himself in the direction of the educational paradigm. From the project manager's point of view there is no argument for doing so. The quotation highlights the fact that the understanding of work and education belongs to two different paradigms as applied by the project manager in the process of grasping the relation between problem solving in the company and the FWBL method's interest in supporting learning processes.

Having presented the general perspective of the companies through the lens of a project manager, it is relevant likewise to present the university's point of view. This is presented in the following quotations stemming from an interview with the two FWBL administrative staff at the university.

> The objective is that they [the participants] learn something. Perhaps they can learn something from a consultant if they are sitting next to him doing the same; however, this is not the purpose within FWBL. A consultant is supposed to solve a specific problem in the company. We are also solving a problem, but our task is to teach the participants how they on their own can solve the problem. This is what we aim for. (Administrative person no. 1 in Thomassen, 2009, p. 138)

> Well, the goal for "Company B" is not that they have solved a concrete problem, the goal is that 2–30 engineers have learned to use a new software development method [the subject dealt with during the FWBL course]. If their problem is solved at the same time, that is a different story. The objective is that they have learned something that they can use in future development projects as well. (Administrative person no. 2 in Thomassen, 2009, p. 138)

The above clearly illustrates the different perspectives and objectives brought into the FWBL course along with the fact that work and education are perceived as two different activities. The project manager is highly focused on solving a specific problem in the company, and from the project manager's perspective FWBL is the tool that can eliminate the problem. The project manager's goal does not comply with the goal of the university. From a university perspective, FWBL is a method that can *educate* the participants not only making them capable of solving the present problem but also future problems that may arise. Thus, a more fundamental and idealistic perspective on education is the foundation on which the facilitators and the administrative staff act during the FWBL course. Based on the above, it is evident that the companies and the university are not striving for the same objective. The companies as well as the university continue throughout the FWBL courses to pursue their own goals (Thomassen, 2009). This has a major impact on the FWBL courses, as no mutual platform for the collaboration is developed. Instead the 'collaboration' proceeds as two separate trajectories incapable of finding common ground.

The above presentation illustrates a class between the production paradigm and the educational paradigm (Jørgensen, 2004). However, it also illustrates that the paradigm within which one is placed has extensive impact on the understandings gained of new issues, aspects, methods etc. presented to you. The project manager, e.g., creates meaning about FWBL on the basis of his position within the production paradigm and the facilitators and administrative staff create meaning on the basis of the educational paradigm. To follow Dewey's line of thinking, context and present experience influence the new meaning created (Dewey, 1933).

FWBL Does Not Fit In

Dewey's notions of continuity and reflective thinking are useful in order to outline why the participants' express difficulties in grasping FWBL. Continuity implies that present experience is the platform for gaining new experience. Hence, the perspectives and experiences that the involved actors (from the companies and university) bring into the FWBL course have impact on the new understandings and experiences they gain. Specifically, this implies that a participant through the application of reflective thinking tries to create a link between his present understanding and the new issue or problem he is confronting. However, it is not always possible to create an understanding of the new as it is too different; in other words, the actor does not possess the concepts and understanding necessary in order to develop an understanding of the new (Dewey, 1974[1936]).

Throughout the FWBL courses it was evident (Thomassen, 2009) that the participants from the companies had difficulties grasping that FWBL is based on the idea that problem solving and learning can be integrated, a difficulty which overshadowed the entire FWBL course. First of all, the participants applied the understanding that work and education belong to two separate paradigms as the platform for understanding FWBL. Continually, they tried to understand FWBL on the basis of this separation, every time increasing the level of frustration and not the level of understanding. The frustration occurred because the rationale applied by the participants was fundamentally different from the rationale on which FWBL is based. It is like comparing apples and bananas. Second, it was evident that the participants applied a traditional understanding of learning and education within which the teacher holds the knowledge to the right answer beforehand. Added to this was a strong belief that the facilitator should in a very direct manner guide the problem-solving process informing the participants about how to solve their problems. These perspectives are exemplified in the following quotations. An engineer said that:

> I would like if we together with the facilitator took a closer look at one issue or function and said 'well, let us take this one and let us work it through. Then we do this, and then

this' So we can see how things are connected, and how we do it – what is the process? (Thomassen, 2009, p. 103)

And the project manager says:

There is no doubt that I expected that it was an educational program, however, I also expected that the facilitator possessed the required competencies. I expected that it was more than supervision because we received new knowledge from the outside via a person who knew the problems and worked within the area, so we expected more or less to receive the answer [...] I had expected to receive some clear statements saying "do this and do that," because based on experience this is what works. (Thomassen, 2009, p. 114)

The main reason why participants and project managers express difficulties in grasping FWBL is the fact that they cannot 'see' the difference between their traditional understanding of learning and the understanding applied in FWBL. The fundamental problem is that the participants approach FWBL through a lens which is fundamentally different from the one on which FWBL is founded.

From an educational point of view, it is problematic that the main focus is directed towards the process of trying to understand FWBL and not in the direction of learning processes as intended. Thus, the learning outcome is negatively influenced due to the major problems in grasping what FWBL is all about.

FWBL IS UNDER PRESSURE IN THE WORKPLACE

In both cases it became apparent that the FWBL courses had difficulties in gaining a legitimate position in the organisations implying that the FWBL courses were relatively quickly placed on the sideline not perceived as an activity of high importance. The following outlines why FWBL got under pressure in the workplaces.

FWBL was placed on the sidetrack because the starting point was a practical problem that had to be solved within a short period of time. Thus, having an extensive influence as a paradox as within FWBL, it is explicitly stated that the starting point must present a practical problem the participant finds relevant (Fink & Holifield, 2004). However, a tension emerged between the request for solving the problem and the possibility of spending time on learning processes.

All things being equal, it takes more time to solve a problem if educational activities are connected – time that is seldom available in organisations. Combined with the fact that employees in general are obliged to solve problems and deliver products within strict deadlines, it becomes the production paradigm that sets the agenda. In education a number of different methods and theories are often tried out, as the main focus is the application and the learning processes connected to this (Savin-Baden & Major, 2004). Hence, sometimes the problem dealt with is solved and sometimes it is not. This is not good enough in company settings, in companies useful solutions must be found every time.

Within FWBL it is made clear that the course must follow the needs of the participants. Combining with a strict focus on real-life problems implies that the focus is directed towards concrete hands-on assignments. The FWBL course is so tightly connected to practice that it has influence on each participants' work assignments; therefore, it becomes very difficult to create convergence between the FWBL course and the participants' work-related problem solving, as the processes and activities change very quickly. Consequently, the processes in the workplace outrun the FWBL course, meaning that the problem-solving processes develop much faster than the FWBL course is able to support. As the participants are in a work setting facing concerns of problem solving within a certain deadline, they do not have the luxury to wait for the FWBL course. The participants must continue the problem-solving process leaving the FWBL course behind.

Another difficulty is that it continually creates a feeling of uncertainty for participants and managers, which in turn places a decisive influence on why it is put on a sideline. This turns focus away from the pivotal learning processes. Furthermore, the feeling of uncertainty implies that the possible outcome of the FWBL course is not clear. The participants and project managers start questioning whether it is worth the trouble to continue the engagement in the FWBL course. The companies do not, as indicated in the quotation earlier in the chapter, have the perception that their goals are fulfilled. The position on the sideline can be seen as the companies' way of signalling a difference between the time and money invested in the FWBL course and the level of problem solving obtained. The participants did not receive what they expected prompting the decrease in engagement and interest in participating. A self-reinforcing process has started pushing the FWBL course even further out on the sideline.

In general problems occurring during the FWBL courses are illustrations of an ongoing discussion between the production paradigm and the education paradigm, a discussion centred around which one should be in power and set the agenda. Consequently, two different agendas are present with both aiming for different objectives. This leaves the impression that the two paradigms are continually trying to eject the other. In the FWBL cases, the education paradigm appears to have sizeable problems in gaining a significant position in the workplace. An essential reason is that the educational paradigm is not only moved into the workplace, it is also very tightly connected to the core of the production paradigm, namely the solving of concrete work assignments. Therefore, the education paradigm is placed in a line of activities already well established and influenced by very influential currents that are very difficult to affect and change.

In the remaining part of this chapter, an alternative to the traditional perspective on the relationship between work and continuing education is presented.

THE THIRD CONTEXT

I have demonstrated that the understanding of work and learning as two incompatible entities based on different paradigms has had an extensive negative impact on learner engagement and learning outcome. In order to overcome these obstacles, the notion of 'the third context' is presented. First, it is outlined that Dewey's ontological understanding of us being *in* the world and in particular the notions of transaction, experience, and reflective thinking constitute the theoretical foundation of 'the third context' (Thomassen 2009, 2011). For that reason 'the third context' is first of all a mental construction, implying that it is a way of thinking in regards to continuing education and the relation between workplaces and universities. Second, it is argued that from a company perspective participation in FWBL is interesting for two reasons: The practical problem is solved, and more importantly, the employees acquire competencies in reflective thinking. Third, it is argued that if the potential of 'the third context' is to unfold the involved actors, from the companies as well as the university, have to overstep their existing understandings and perspectives of work and education and instead perceive work and continuing education as integrateable. The aspect of reflective thinking is perceived to have a major impact on the possibility for developing such new perspectives. Therefore, reflective thinking is argued to be of the utmost importance in the process of overcoming the gap between work and continuing education.

As the previous presentation of the two FWBL courses made evident, problems and challenges occurred during the application process despite the special focus on overcoming the gap between work and education. The following is an elaboration of how the notion of 'the third context' can be useful in the process of overcoming the previously mentioned problems.

The notion of 'the third context' is based on the argument that continuing education is neither work nor education in its pure form, but something that is a 'third'. Furthermore, the notion is in line with Dewey's ontological perspective concerning the way in which we interact in social contexts, and not least, the influence that social contexts have on experience via transaction. Consequently, 'the third context' illustrates the meeting between the actors from the workplace and the educational institution. Integrated in 'the third context' is the aspect that FWBL is continuing education based on a pragmatic learning theory, and that continuing education unfolds in 'its own context'.

'The third context' is illustrated in Figure 1. 'The third context' does not pre-exist, it emerges and unfolds as the actors from the company and the university interact. 'The third context' is not to be perceived as a still photograph. Instead it is to be perceived as a context that emerges *in* the meeting between the involved actors and which is under continual development and change (Dewey, 1988; Mulcahy, 2011; Thomassen, 2011). However, the context disappears when the interaction between the actors ends. Therefore, 'the third context' is at the same time a result as well as a dynamic frame, as the context is framed in a specific way at a specific point in time; however, at the same time it constantly changes due to the actions and experience development of the involved actors.

In the outset 'the third context' is by default a fragile construction, as actors from the different organisations are often interacting for the first time. Consequently, there are no solid rules or mutual understandings on which to base the collaboration. The limited acquaintance combined with the actors' existing experiences laid the foundation for the transaction. Hence, in order to create a positive and fruitful collaboration, it is of utmost importance to develop a strong 'third context'. Based on Dewey's pragmatic thinking, this becomes important as the context has a major impact on the learning processes due to the transaction unfolding between actor and context (Biesta, 2009; Dewey, 1933).

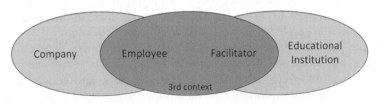

Fig. 1. The Third Context.

It is important to note that it is not enough just to present the FWBL method and the idea of 'the third context' to potential participants and project managers and assume that the perspective is understood. In the outset the FWBL method and 'the third context' are only presented entities to which no 'real' experience is connected. Hence, an understanding of the two does not exist beforehand; instead, the experience is continually developed on the basis of active involvement in the FWBL course.

As mentioned the investigated FWBL courses are placed at the companies' sideline, which can be argued to be a bit of a surprise when related to the argumentation above. First, one might assume that participation would provide an increasing level of insight and understanding of FWBL. As earlier described, it is the frustration of not understanding FWBL that increases and not the level of understanding as such. The frustration occurs as the company-actors apply an understanding of work and education belonging to two fundamentally different paradigms in the process of grasping FWBL. Continually the company-actors make a comparison between their present understanding and what they are confronted with during the FWBL course.

Piaget's notions of assimilation and accommodation are useful in describing how the participants' try to reach an understanding of FWBL. Assimilation is the individual's adaptation of the environment 'i.e. the taking in of impressions from the environment into previously developed psychological structures' (Illeris, 2004, p. 29) and accommodation being 'a changing of the structures already developed in relation to new conditions in the environment' (Illeris, 2004, p. 30). As mentioned earlier, the participants continually relate FWBL to their present understanding of education and work belonging to separate entities implying that they use assimilation. However, their present schemes cannot cope with the new type of continuing education they face. Thus, they experience a problematic situation. Based on Piaget's thinking the participants would most likely apply accommodation, thereby changing their mental structures and reaching a new and different understanding of FWBL. However, the case studies show that this does not occur at a significant level. This is underlined by the following quotation stemming from an interview with one of the participants at the end of the FWBL course.

> I still do not know what this is all about, and what would have been the right thing to do. Actually it would be interesting to know [...] what it [FWBL] was all about? I would like to know that, because it appears to me that our understanding is very different from yours [the university's]. (Thomassen, 2009, p. 101)

The above indicates that reflective thinking has not been applied in a profound manner in order to remove the feeling of not understanding

FWBL. This underlines the importance of inviting the company-actors into applying reflective thinking with the purpose of them grasping the alternative that FWBL and the notion of 'the third context' offers.

Consequently, it cannot be assumed that the company-actors from the outset have an understanding of FWBL and the notion of 'the third context', the understanding is developed as the FWBL course unfolds and 'the third context' becomes a more solid social construction. Hence, the interactions of the actors within 'the third context' become crucial, the reason being that 'the third context' develops and changes on the basis of their actions. The transactions unfolding between the actors within 'the third context' are able to support or reduce the participants' possibility of developing a new understanding of FWBL as well as 'the third context'. Consequently, the outcome of the FWBL course to a high extent depends on the development of 'the third context'.

In the FWBL courses it was evident that the company-actors and university-actors stayed within their own trajectory. As previously mentioned, the focus on own objectives had a negative impact on the interaction (Thomassen, 2009). Hence, the company-actors as well as university-actors have to change their understanding of the other and the relation between them. There is a need for each of the collaborative partners to work together in order to reach a common objective, namely development of the participants' knowledge and ability to solve practical work-related problems. Yet, it is assumed that the company-actors will not engage in collaboration and engage in a process of reflective thinking unless they feel they will gain from it.

THE NEW ARGUMENT FOR ENGAGING IN FWBL

As it concerns continuing education, companies traditionally focus on the employees gaining new knowledge about something specific, e.g., a new software development method or project management methods, a situation evident in the two cases included in this chapter. Much attention is paid to the new method or theory as such. Less, if any, attention is paid to the application process of the new method, wherein the application process is meant to increase the employees' thinking processes, as these are the ones where new knowledge the converted into actual use. Consequently, the employees' ability to think reflectively has enormous impact on how the new method is used and its return on investment that companies gain in competence development. Hence, it can be argued that the companies do not only acquire information about new methods or theories as such, but that simultaneously the employees' competence in reflective thinking is developed. Thus, they do not have to stick to the traditional way of solving problems – new innovative solutions can be made due to the problem-solving process unfolding via reflective thinking. Hence, the companies enhance the likeliness of developing new competitive advantages due to the employees' ability to engage in reflective thinking, an ability that can be used every time a new engineering problem is discovered.

FINAL REMARKS

What does the notion of 'the third context' offer? It provides a useful language for describing and handling the complicated process of conducting practically oriented continuing education. In particular it suggests consent that the understanding of work and continuing education are two fundamentally different practices and offers a concept based on integration. This offers a way of thinking about the relation between work and continuing education inspired by John Dewey. Furthermore, the notion points out that the FWBL course and 'the third context' become integrated, and development within the FWBL course and 'the third context' occurs simultaneously.

The suggestion that FWBL and 'the third context' develop simultaneously is crucial for further development of FWBL as a method for continuing education. This is verified through the courses conducted in this research where processes unfolded at a faster pace within the company than within the FWBL course. Consequently, the company-actors, due to impending deadlines, did not have the luxury to wait for the FWBL course. Therefore, daily work practices and the FWBL course became detached. Hence, it is vital that a stronger focus on *how* the FWBL course and the daily work requirements of the participants' can be better integrated.

One way of integrating the processes is through different types of information technology allowing communication between participants and facilitator to be easier and faster. However, introducing different types of information technology is not an easy task and it creates challenges for the FWBL model. If a higher extent of information technology is introduced, it will be a challenge to keep PBL as the core educational perspective. In face-to-face situations the facilitator can in the present directly influence the communication and the learning processes of the participants. If PCs, mobile phones, ipads or other types of technology are introduced the distance between facilitator and participant increases.

In order to secure PBL as the educational paradigm, the structure and processes within the FWBL model must be further developed in order to prevent it from falling into a traditional understanding of learning and education. The main focus must continue to be the participants' learning processes through solving practical work-related problems, and not a question-answer relation between participants and facilitator. Hence, the introduction of information technology requires a strong frame for the collaboration. Furthermore, it is required that the participants possess a better understanding of FWBL and its theoretical foundation. An understanding of these elements highly influence the communication between participants and facilitator, hence the potential learning outcome of the FWBL course. An example of this is the participants' ability to ask relevant questions that support their learning processes, and do not 'only look' for an answer.

As mentioned, much responsibility is placed on the facilitator's shoulders in relation to the flexibility and ability to support the participants' learning processes. The need for flexibility increases when interaction goes from face-to-face to include communication via different technologies. In particular, it becomes more difficult to clearly define the specific challenges and problems of each single participant at a given point in time, and deliver the best possible facilitation. In the extreme, the facilitator will be expected to be online 24×7 in order to support a close link between work and continuing education, which is not realistic.

Integration of information technology into FWBL provides the possibility of overcoming some of the major challenges identified in this chapter. In particular information technology can support an increase in the level of communication between participants and facilitator: in particular, it can acquiesce the processes between work and FWBL. However, challenges occur too. It is of utmost importance that a common ground for the collaboration is developed including a common objective. Furthermore, it is important that the participants are clearly introduced to FWBL. Understanding FWBL strongly influences the actions of the participants' including how they use information technology when communicating with the facilitator.

The notion of 'the third context' is perceived as a valuable framework during the further development of FWBL. The reason being that 'the third context' contains some overall ideas and perspectives concerning how work and learning can be integrated by having a special focus on mutual orientation. Hence, 'the third context' does in relation to FWBL, as well as on a more general level, provide a context on how to overcome the gap between work and continuing education.

NOTE

1. All quotations are translated from Danish into English and slightly rephrased by the author in order to become reader-friendly.

REFERENCES

Berthelsen, J., Illeris, K., & Poulsen, S. C. (1977). *Projektarbejde – Erfaringer og praktisk vejledning.* Holstebro: Borgen.

Biesta, G. (2009). Pragmatism's contribution to understanding learning-in-context. In R. Edwards, G. Biesta & M. Thorpe (Eds.), *Rethinking contexts for learning and teaching. Communities, activities and networks* (pp. 61–73). New York, NY: Routledge.

Billett, S. (2001). *Learning in the workplace: Strategies for effective practice. Crows Nest, New South Wales.* Allen & Unwin.

Bottrup, P., & Clematide, B. (2005). *Workplace learning from the perspective of institutionalizes learning*, http://www.kubix.dk/pdf/174-m-workplace-learning.pdf

Boud, D., & Garrick, J. (1999). Understandings of workplace learning. In D. Boud & J. Garrick (Eds.), *Understanding learning at work* (pp. 1–11). New York, NY: Routledge.

Choy, S., & Delahaye, B. (2011). Partnerships between universities and workplaces: Some challenges for work-integrated learning. *Studies in Continuing Education, 33*(2), 157–172.

Dewey, J. (1933). *How we think. A restatement of the relation of reflective thinking to the educative process.* Boston, MA: D. C. Heath and Company.

Dewey, J. (1974[1936]). *Erfaring og opdragelse.* Copenhagen: Christian Ejlers' Forlag.

Dewey, J. (1988). Experience and education. In J. A. Boydston (Ed.), *John Dewey. The later works* (Vol. 13, pp. 1925–1953). Carbondale: Southern Illinois University Press.

Dewey, J., & Bentley, A. F. (1991[1949]). Knowing and the known. In J. A. Boydston (Ed.), *John Dewey. The later works* (Vol. 16, pp. 1–294). Carbondale: Southern Illinois University Press.

Elkjaer, B. (2003). Organizational learning with a pragmatic slant. *International Journal of Lifelong Education, 22*(5), 481–494.

Eraut, M. (2004). Transfer of knowledge between education and workplace settings. In H. Rainbird, A. Fuller & A. Munro (Eds.), *Workplace learning in context* (pp. 201–221). London: Routledge.

Fink, F. K., & Holifield, D. (2004). *Continuing engineering education as facilitated work based learning.* Paper presented at the IACEE 9th World Conference on Continuing Engineering Education, Tokyo, Japan.

Fink, F. K., Nørgaard, B. (2006). *The methodology of facilitated work based learning.* Paper presented at the IACEE 10th World Conference on Continuing Engineering Education, Vienna, Austria.

de Graff, E., & Kolmos, A. (2003). Characteristics of problem-based learning. *International Journal of Engineering Education, 19*(5), 657–662.

Gustavsson, B. (2003). *Vidensfilosofi.* Aarhus: Klim.

Illeris, K. (2004). *The three dimensions of learning. Contemporary learning theory in the tension field between the cognitive, the emotional and the social.* Frederiksberg, Denmark: Roskilde University Press.

Illeris, K. (2011). *The fundamentals of workplace learning. Understanding how people learn in working life.* New York, NY: Routledge.

Jørgensen, C. H. (2004). Connecting work and education: Should learning be useful, correct or meaningful? *Journal of Workplace Learning*, *16*(8), 455–465.

Jørgensen, K. M., Strand, A. M. C., & Thomassen, A. O. (2012). Conceptual bases of problem-based learning. In J. E. Groccia, M. A. T. Alsudairi & W. Buskist (Eds.), *Handbook of college and university teaching. A global perspective* (pp. 440–456). Thousand Oaks, CA: Sage.

Kolmos, A. (2008). PBL og Projektarbejde. In L. Krogh, J. B. Olsen & P. Rasmussen (Eds.), *Projektpædagogik. Perspektiver fra Aalborg Universitet* (pp. 13–26). Aalborg, Denmark: Aalborg Universitetsforlag.

Krogh, L., Olsen, J. B., & Rasmussen, P. (2008). *Projektpædagogik. Perspektiver fra Aalborg Universitet*. Aalborg, Denmark: Aalborg Universitetsforlag.

Mulcahy, D. (2011). Between work and learning: On pedagogic practice and interstitial space. *Studies in Continuing Education*, *33*(3), 203–217.

Nørgaard, B., & Fink, F. K. (2004). *Continuing engineering education as facilitated work based learning*. Paper presented at the 4th International Workshop on Active Learning in Engineering (ALE), Nantes, France.

Savin-Baden, M., & Major, C. H. (2004). *Foundations of problem-based learning*. Maidenhear, UK: The Society for Research into Higher Education and Open University Press.

Stegeager, N., Thomassen, A. O., & Laursen, E. (2012). PBL: Confronting the problems of transfer. *Symposium Proceedings of the 3rd International PBL Symposium: PBL and the Problematization of Teaching and Learning 7-9*. March 2012, Republic Polytechnic (pp. 99–106).

Svensson, L., & Randle, H. (2006). How to 'bridge the gap' – Experiences in connecting the educational and work system. In E. Antonacopoulou, P. Jarvis, V. Andersen, B. Elkjaer & S. Høyrup (Eds.), *Learning, working, living. Mapping the terrain of working life learning* (pp. 102–118). New York, NY: Palgrave.

Tennant, M. (1999). Is learning transferable? In D. Boud & J. Garrick (Eds.), *Understanding learning at work* (pp. 165–179). New York, NY: Routledge.

Thomassen, A. O. (2011). Den tredje kontekst: Integration af uddannelse og arbejde i virksomheder. In N. Stegager & E. Laursen (Eds.), *Organisationer i bevægelse. Læring – Udvikling – Intervention* (pp. 119–131). Frederiksberg, Denmark: Samfundslitteratur.

Thomassen, A. O. (2009). *Facilitated work based learning – Analyseret i et pragmatisk perspektiv*. Ph.D. thesis. Department of Learning and Philosophy, Aalborg University, Denmark.

Wahlgren, B. (2010). *Voksnes læreprocesser. Kompetenceudvikling i uddannelse og arbejde*. Copenhagen: Akademisk Forlag.

ABOUT THE AUTHORS

Lars Birch Andreasen is Associate Professor at the Department of Learning and Philosophy at Aalborg University, Denmark, where he is a member of the Research Lab: ICT and Designs for Learning. He holds a Ph.D. in Education from the Danish University of Education and an M.A. in Cultural Sociology from Copenhagen University. His research interests are dialogic communication, problem- and project-based learning, collaboration in virtual learning environments, information literacy, and lifelong learning.

Patrick Blessinger is the Founder and Executive Director of the International Higher Education Teaching and Learning Association and a Research Fellow at the School of Education at St. John's University in Queens, New York, USA. He has taught over 150 college and university courses and he has served as a program chair at colleges and universities in the United States and EU. He consults with HE institutions in the areas of technology innovation and internationalization and he serves as an academic and accreditation advisor for HE institutions. He is the co-founder and co-director of the Institute for Meaning-Centered Education. He is the founder and editor of the International HETL Review and co-editor of the *Journal of Applied Research in Higher Education*. He is co-editor of several volumes within the Cutting-edge Technologies in Higher Education book series (Emerald) and co-editor of the book, *Meaning-Centered Education: International Perspectives and Explorations in Higher Education* (Routledge). He attended Auburn University, Georgia Tech, and the University of Georgia. He is a peer-recognized expert and thought leader in the field of teaching and learning and he has received several academic awards including a Fulbright Scholarship from the US Department of State and a Governor's Teaching Fellowship from the State of Georgia, USA.

Paul Burt is the Learning Spaces Specialist at University College London, UK. His role is to provide a source of expertise at UCL in learning space design and use. He represents the needs and interests of teaching staff and students, advising on the design of spaces for enhancing and facilitating

297

teaching and learning. He previously worked at the University of Surrey as Senior Learning and Technology Adviser where he led the BoB project.

Wilma Clark, Ph.D., is a Researcher in Social Media and Digital Storytelling at Goldsmiths, University of London, UK. Prior to her appointment to this post in autumn 2011, she was a Researcher in Educational Technologies at the London Knowledge Lab, Institute of Education, University of London. There, her principal area of expertise was in the use and adoption of Web 2.0 and digital media in formal educational contexts. She has a Ph.D. in Cultural Semiotics (with Educational Technology). Her key interests lie in the field of systems thinking in education, with a particular focus on digital media.

Mary C. Embry is core teaching faculty in the Apparel Merchandising and Interior Design Department at Indiana University, instructing courses in international trade, social entrepreneurship, and sustainability. She is founder of Fair Trade Bloomington, a local Fair Trade nonprofit advocacy group and Board member of Global Gifts, a nonprofit Fair Trade organization with three stores, as well as a Board member of the Fair Trade Resource Network, an information hub for the US Fair Trade movement. Mary received a Master of Science degree with research focusing on Fair Trade and Service-Learning. She remains engaged in implementing strong pedagogical tools that immerse students in considerations of their role as global citizens. She also advises the Indiana University Students In Free Enterprise team, a nationally recognized student group for their efforts in using entrepreneurial approaches to impact the well-being and standard of living of people.

Jorge Brantes Ferreira holds a Ph.D. in Business Administration (Marketing), and is Assistant Professor at the Pontifical Catholic University of Rio de Janeiro. The author has previously published a book chapter about emerging technologies and breakthroughs in the book *La Comunicacion Humana en el Mundo Contemporaneo*, 3rd. ed. (McGraw-Hill: 2008). Currently Jorge is also leading a government-funded research group about mobile learning, working on several papers and research issues concerning the adoption and possible applications of mobile learning in higher-education environments.

Angilberto Freitas holds a Ph.D. in Business Administration at Pontifical University of Rio de Janeiro (PUC-Rio), Brazil, a Master in Management at Pontifical University of Rio de Janeiro (PUC-Rio), and a Bachelor in

Industrial Engineering at Fluminense Federal University (UFF). He is a professor and researcher at the Postgraduate Program in Business Administration at Unigranrio-Brazil in Rio de Janeiro. At the current time, the author is co-leading a government-funded research about the use of new technologies of information and communication to develop teachers' capability. Also the author has been publishing several papers concerning the use of technology for teaching.

Vicki Holmes is Deputy Head of the Centre for Quality, Support and Development at the University of Reading. She was previously Head of Learning and Technology at the University of Surrey, and also worked on a variety of institutional and national projects relating to learning technology and development of teaching practice. Vicki has an M.A. (Hons.) in English Literature and Language, an M.Sc. in Computer Science, and an M.A. in Education. She is also a Fellow of Higher Education Academy and Fellow of the Staff Educational Development Association. Her particular areas of interest are staff development, evaluation of practice, and organizational change.

Jennifer Little Kegler is a Reference Librarian and the Coordinator of Library Instruction at the College at Brockport (SUNY) where she has worked since 2005. Prior to working at the College she held similar positions at the University of South Carolina Aiken and Taylor University, Indiana. She earned her B.A., magna cum laude, from Houghton College and her MLS from the University at Albany. She works with all members of the college community to help them learn how to best search and use information resources for any type of project. She teaches a large number of classes for students in all disciplines regarding effective information literacy processes. She has published journal articles regarding information literacy instruction, faculty collaboration with librarians, and cognitive learning theory and online library research guides. She has presented at the state and national level on these topics as well as this current e-textbook research. In addition to the research interests above she is currently studying reading comprehension as it applies to the online environment, both for e-textbooks and all types of information.

Amarolinda Zanela Klein holds a Ph.D. in Business Administration from University of Sao Paulo (USP), Brazil, a Master in Management at the Federal University of Rio Grande do Sul (UFRGS), and a Bachelor in Management at Universidade Federal de Santa Maria (UFSM). She is a professor and researcher at the Postgraduate Program in Business Administration at Universidade do Vale do Rio dos Sinos (UNISINOS). She is also an ad hoc consultant in management and information systems. Since 1996 she has been working as a consultant and researcher on Information Technology for Organizational Competitiveness, and on IT and Organizational Change. She is a co-author of the Virtual Learning Environment for Mobile Learning COMTEXT®, and also a co-author of the *Book on M-learning and U-learning* (Pearson Education: 2010). M-learning and enterprise mobility are currently her key research areas.

Skyler Lauderdale is a doctoral student and University Graduate Fellowship recipient in the Department of Sociology at the University of South Florida. Inspired by his former career in mobile telecommunications, and in collaboration with Christina M. Partin, he has begun to research the inclusion of mobile devices and other innovative technologies in the classroom to facilitate learning. Several research papers are accepted for publication or currently in progress, and portions of his work have been presented at the Florida Association of Teacher Educators, the Association for Educational Communications and Technology International Convention, and the Southern Sociological Society. As a true academic nomad, his M.A. thesis, *It's a Support Club, Not a Sex Club: Narration Strategies and Discourse Coalitions in High School Gay-Straight Alliance Club Controversies*, reflects his interests in social movements, education, and narrative identity.

Audeliz Matias is Assistant Professor and mentor of science, math, and technology for the Center for Distance Learning at the SUNY-Empire State College, where she mentors and teaches a variety of courses in science and technology. She received her Ph.D. in geological sciences from Northwestern University. Prior to joining as a faculty member, Audeliz served as the coordinator of curriculum and instructional design for the science, math, and technology area for three years at the Center for Distance Learning. Dr. Matias is involved in innovation and emerging technology efforts for teaching and learning. She helped with the creation of several learning objects using multimedia maps as well as the Mobile Learning Task Force at her institution, which she chaired during 2010–2011. Her scholarly interests focus on geoscience education and effective practices in online learning including the use of virtual environments such as Second Life, social and media environments, mobile learning, multimedia maps, and the use of scientific datasets to promote active learning.

Patricia E. Maxwell, MLS, is a Systems Librarian for The College at Brockport, State University of New York, providing support for integrated library software and the College's institutional repository, Digital Commons @ Brockport. She is a project manager of the College's transition to a paperless campus through document imaging and systems analysis. Additional activities include facilitator of a Faculty Learning Community group exploring technology and learning, and contributing member of the State University of New York Faculty Advisory Council on Teaching & Learning (FACT2) e-Publishing Task Force. Patricia's research interests include human–computer interaction with a focus on e-textbooks. She has presented her e-textbook research to national and local audiences. A native of New Jersey, Patricia traveled for 25 years with her naval officer husband and raised three children, often on her own as frequent deployments caused temporary separations. In the course of her duties as a "temporary single parent," Patricia managed the household while also offering community service in cities across the United States as well as overseas in Seoul, South Korea, and London, UK. While in South Korea, Patricia was awarded the US Army's coveted (and only) medal for civilians, The Commanders Award for Public Service (2000), for her outstanding support and dedication to the Yongsan community. Later, in London (2001), Patricia began her MLS studies through Southern Connecticut State University's online program. That online learning experience inspired Patricia to conduct research in student satisfaction with digital reading and its effects on comprehension.

Andrew Middleton (M.Sc. in e-Learning, Multimedia, and Consultancy) is Head of Innovation and Professional Development, part of Quality Enhancement at Sheffield Hallam University, UK. He has taught Creativity in various disciplines, and researches academic innovation and literacy. He is Chair of the UK Media-Enhanced Learning Special Interest Group and runs workshops on how digital voice technologies are employed for learning techniques, including media-enhanced feedback, and how these can be used in post-compulsory education.

Jørgen Lerche Nielsen is Associate Professor at Department of Communication, Business and Information Technologies at Roskilde University, Denmark, where he is a member of the Centre for Designing Human Technologies and the Centre for Dialogic Communication Research. For more than 10 years he has been part of the web-based cross-institutional Master program in ICT & Learning. His research interests are learning processes in communities of practice, blended learning, challenges in problem oriented learning processes, networked learning, and change processes within higher education.

Anne Nortcliffe is a Senior Lecturer in the Faculty of Arts, Computing, Engineering and Science at Sheffield Hallam University, UK, with a Ph.D. in Control Engineering, and teaches in both Computing and Engineering departments. Anne applies a blended learning approach to her teaching and assessment and has successfully researched and developed a technological blended pedagogy using audio technology to support to her teaching and assessment feedback to enhance her student learning and experience, and uses problem-based learning to develop student learning and employability. More recently Anne's scholarly focus has been the development of students' learning through encouraging learning engagement through the student use of technology, audio, and smart devices.

Christina M. Partin, M.A., is a full-time sociology instructor at University of South Florida. She has taught large and small classes in both online and face-to-face for over six years. In this time, she has taught nearly 10,000 undergraduate students in her courses. She also trains and mentors the department's Master's Teaching Assistants who assist teaching her large classes. After completing her M.A. in Sociology, she has pursued her research interests and doctoral studies in Curriculum and Instruction, by focusing on interdisciplinary applications of instructional technology, higher education and adult learning, and social psychology. Together with Skyler Lauderdale, she embarked on an action research project that demonstrates the importance of using innovative teaching techniques, including mobile technologies, in the classroom. From this ongoing, iterative experience, Christina and Skyler have generated several publications, and portions of this work have been presented at the Florida Association of Teacher Educators, the Association for Educational Communications and Technology International Convention, and the Southern Sociological Society. Her publications and research in progress more broadly include the incorporation of technology into higher education, higher education and social, cultural, and economic capital, and ways to provide transformative experiences to students.

Bart Rienties, Ph.D., is Senior Lecturer at the Centre for Educational and Academic Development at the University of Surrey. As an economist and educational psychologist he conducts multi-disciplinary research on work-based and collaborative learning environments and focuses on the role of social interaction in learning. His primary research interests are focused on Computer-Supported Collaborative Learning (CSCL), the role of the teacher to design effective blended and online learning courses, and the role of social interaction in learning, which is published in leading academic journals and books.

Eliane Schlemmer holds a Ph.D. in Computers in Education, and a Master in Psychology from the Federal University of Rio Grande do Sul (UFRGS), Brazil, a Bachelor in Computer Science at the University of Vale do Rio dos Sinos (UNISINOS). She is a productivity researcher of CNPq, titular professor and researcher in Postgraduate Program in Education at UNISINOS, ad hoc consultant in the area of Digital Education and Online Education. Eliane is leading the Digital Education Research Group – GPe-dU UNISINOS/CNPq – and a member of the Managing Committee in the Catholic Network of Higher Education Institutions – RICESU – in Brazil. Since 1998 she has been working as a consultant in Information and Communication Technologies for educational and professional training. She has coordinated several research projects, aiming at creating technological products for companies and universities: Virtual Learning Environment (AVA-UNISINOS), Virtual Worlds (AWSINOS in Active Worlds, Ilha UNISINOS and Ilha RICESU in Second Life) Communicative Agent (MARIÁ), Virtual Learning Environment for Mobile Learning COMTEXT® (Skills in Context). Eliane is also the designer of technology-concept Digital Virtual Living Together Space – DVLTS (which is in the context of hybrid digital technology, integrating technology VLE, Meta-verse, conversational agents, and tools of Web 2.0).

Susan Stites-Doe has taught at the College at Brockport, State University of New York, for 23 years. Dr. Stites-Doe has a Ph.D. in organizational behavior from the University of Buffalo, and holds a full professorship in the Business Administration department at the College at Brockport, State University of New York. She was recognized with a Chancellor's Award for Excellence in Teaching in 2001. In 1999 she served as Faculty in Residence at Eastman Kodak and Company, where she worked with the Director of Diversity Management to conduct a benchmarking and best practice study on strategic diversity initiatives. Her journal publications feature topics such as leadership and CEO compensation. A current research interest involves students' satisfaction with the use of electronic textbooks. Dr. Stites-Doe is the Associate Dean of the School of Business at the College at Brockport,

State University of New York. She also serves on the Graduate Record Exam (GRE) Board of Directors, and the GRE Business Advisory Council, and has served on numerous boards of directors throughout her career. On campus, Dr. Stites-Doe serves as the chair of the Leadership Development Advisory Council, and as a member of the Brockport Auxiliary Service Board of Directors. In 2006 Dr. Stites-Doe was awarded a two-part Fulbright Senior Specialist Fellowship to visit Debrecen University, in Hungary. In fact, her favorite personal pastime is traveling to diverse corners of the world, and she regards her best trip as the next one. Dr. Stites-Doe is married and has two adult daughters.

Anja Overgaard Thomassen is Assistant Professor at the Department of Learning and Philosophy at Aalborg University, Denmark. She holds a Master of Science in International Business Economics (Cand.merc.) and a Ph.D. within Organizational Learning. In her Ph.D. thesis she investigated continuing education of highly educated employees through the method of Facilitated Work Based Learning (FWBL). The empirical investigation conducted as part of the Ph.D. thesis was based on two FWBL courses conducted in collaboration between Aalborg University, Denmark, and two software engineering development companies, using qualitative data. Anja's interest in organizational learning and development stems from her educational background within business economics. Especially she is interested in how collaboration between companies and educational institutions can be supported, which is an issue of high importance in a globalized and highly competitive world. Her research interests lie within the area of continuing education with special focus on Problem-Based Learning (PBL). Special attention is paid to how PBL can be a way of integrating education and work thereby overcoming the gap between education and work. Anja is actively involved in different research communities (see www.learning.aau.dk), she has been part of research projects focusing on organizational development. Besides being an experienced facilitator Anja is teaching within Organization Theory, Organisational Learning and Change Management at the Bachelor as well as Master levels.

Laura A. Wankel, Ed.D. is the Vice President for Student Affairs at Northeastern University in Boston, Massachusetts. Prior to Northeastern she was the Vice President for Student Affairs at Seton Hall University where she served since 1995. While at Seton Hall she also held titles of Vice Chancellor for Student Affairs and Vice President for Student Affairs & Enrollment Services. During her tenure she had been responsible for a variety of services and programs including Undergraduate Admissions, Student Financial Aid, Student Accounts, Registrar, Dean of Students and Community Development, Public Safety and Security, Student Health Services, The Career Center, Disability Support Services, Student Counseling Services, Housing and Residence Life and Athletics & Recreational Programs. Before Seton Hall University, Dr. Wankel served as Assistant Vice President for Student Affairs at the State University of New York at Purchase from 1987 to 1995. From 1983 to 1987, Dr. Wankel was Assistant Dean for Campus and Residence Operations at SUNY Purchase. Prior to that, she served in student affairs positions at the University of Pittsburgh.

Dr. Wankel has been an active NASPA: Student Affairs Administrators in Higher Education member at both the regional and national level. She has served as a program reviewer for several NASPA national conferences, member of the Region II Advisory Board, Pre-Conference Program Coordinator and member of the 1994 national conference committee. She has also been on the editorial boards for the NASPA Journal and the *Journal of Student Affairs Research and Practice* (JSARP). She has been the Regional Vice President for Region II of NASPA and serves on the NASPA Board of Directors.

Dr. Wankel holds a Bachelor's degree in American History from SUNY Oneonta where she graduated magna cum laude. She holds an M.Ed. from the University of South Carolina and an Ed.D. in higher education administration from Teachers College, Columbia University. Dr. Wankel also received a certificate from the Institute for Educational Management (IEM) from the Harvard Institute for Higher Education. Dr. Wankel has served in a consulting capacity to a number of education-related projects, including, Learn and Serve America and the Corporation for National and Community Service (AmeriCorps).

Dr. Wankel has a chapter on crisis management in *Understanding Student Affairs in Catholic Colleges and Universities* that is based on the tragic residence hall fire at Seton Hall University. She is co-editor of *Reading the Signs: Using Case Studies to Discuss Student Life Issues at Catholic Colleges and Universities in the United States*. She is co-editor of *Higher Education Administration with Social Media* and *Misbehavior Online in Higher Education* with Emerald Group Publishing Limited. She has also served on the Board of Directors of the Association of Student Affairs at Catholic

Colleges and Universities (ASACCU), and has presented on issues in higher education nationally as well as in Lithuania and Japan.

Therèsa M. Winge is Assistant Professor of Fashion Design at Michigan State University, where she teaches in the Apparel and Textile Design program within the Department of Art, Art History, and Design. Therèsa introduces students to emerging technologies and software with potential of improving the practice of fashion design. Her courses include the use of CAD (computer aided design) software, innovative pattern drafting strategies, and experiential learning opportunities for students.

David F. Wolf II is the coordinator of advanced learning design for the Center for Distance Learning at the SUNY-Empire State College. He oversees the coordination of complex learning objects under development for the online curriculum. David received Master's degree at Binghamton University in the multi-disciplinary program: Philosophy and Computer System Science. He has pioneered the development of interactive learning tools, simulations, thematic mapping, visual mashups, and mobile learning tools. His scholarly interests focus on: exploring multi-modal learning objects, interactive tools, presenting content to display temporal or geographic relationships, simulations, open learning, mobile learning, and developing effective complex problem solving techniques through multi-modal approaches that conform to universal design.

AUTHOR INDEX

307

SUBJECT INDEX

319